FIVE MASTERS

BOOKS BY JOSEPH WOOD KRUTCH

COMEDY AND CONSCIENCE AFTER THE RESTORATION
OUR CHANGING MORALS (A COLLABORATION)
EDGAR ALLEN POE : A STUDY IN GENIUS
THE MODERN TEMPER
FIVE MASTERS

JONATHAN CAPE AND HARRISON SMITH, INCORPORATED,
139 EAST 46TH STREET, NEW YORK, N. Y. AND 91 WELLINGTON
STREET, WEST, TORONTO, CANADA; JONATHAN CAPE, LTD.,
30 BEDFORD SQUARE, LONDON, W. C. 1, ENGLAND

FIVE MASTERS

A STUDY IN
THE MUTATIONS OF
THE NOVEL

By

JOSEPH WOOD KRUTCH

NEW YORK
JONATHAN CAPE & HARRISON SMITH

PRINTED IN THE UNITED STATES OF AMERICA

TO
MARK VAN DOREN

FOREWORD

T HIS book is long but not
pretentious. In the case of each of the writers discussed the
essay begins at the beginning and attempts to give some account of his life and character in so far as this will aid in the
understanding of the artistic significance of his work.

Obviously, the history of the novel cannot be treated
through the study of five novelists, but I have, nevertheless,
been careful to choose five who seemed to me figures of primary importance for the understanding of that history —
five whose work not only had a powerful influence in determining the direction taken by subsequent writers but which
also represented a break with tradition sufficiently brusque
to be called a " mutation." Doubtless the composition of the
list will seem fantastic to some who will ask why this name
was included and why that was left out. To such a question
I can only reply frankly that out of the list of possibilities
I chose the names of those who interested me most, those
whose works I promised myself the most pleasure in re-
reading and in writing about.

It will be observed that the proportion between the space
devoted to literary criticism and the space devoted to the
analysis of characters and deeds is not the same in all five of

the essays, there being, for example, relatively little about the life of Cervantes and relatively little about the works of Stendhal. As a matter of fact, very little is known concerning the life of the former and (thanks to the voluminousness of his journals and letters) a good deal about the life of the latter. Moreover, though I am aware that this is a heresy for which I shall probably be taken to task, I find Stendhal more interesting as a character than as an artist.

The novel seems to me a mixed form. No other literary *genre* contains so much taken directly out of the life of the writer or out of the civilization amidst which he lives. It was developed out of the need to get more of " life " into literature than was possible in more artificial forms and it is this fact which I offer as an excuse for the mingling of biography and criticism, psychology and aesthetics. A " pure " critical method is not required in treating a form of art which is not itself " pure," which is, as I consider the novel always to have been, merely *tending* to detach itself from autobiography and document and merely *tending* towards pure art.

Since bibliographies more extensive than I could find space to give already exist to aid the student of all five of my " masters," I shall not attempt to list the works consulted but shall content myself with mentioning the best general treatments of each — both in order to guide the reader who may be interested and in order to acknowledge my indebtedness (which in some cases is great) to all of them.

Hutton's " Boccaccio " and Huvette's *" Boccace "* have for some years been the best known biographies of their subject. Chubb's " Giovanni Boccaccio " appeared after my essay had been written. All that is known concerning the facts of the life of Cervantes is contained in Fitz-Maurice Kelley's " Cervantes: A Memoir." In the case of Richardson the chief original source is the six-volume selection from his letters edited with an extended memoir by Mrs. Barbauld about a hundred years ago. The best more recent lives are those by Austin Dobson and Miss Clara Thomson, the latter being especially valuable because of the use which it makes of the vast corpus of Richardson's unpublished correspondence. Stendhal's own writings furnish the biographer with almost inexhaustible materials, but next in importance come the various studies of Arbelet — especially his two very long books, " *Les Plagiats de Stendhal* " and " *La Jeunesse de Stendhal,*" together with his amusing " *Stendhal Epicier.*" Pierre-Quint's " *Marcel Proust; Sa Vie, Son Oeuvre* " was the first general study of his subject to appear as a volume and a revised edition was issued in 1928. " *Comment Travaillait Marcel Proust* " by the same writer gives a very extended bibliography of writings about Proust in various languages. Among those which I used most, besides Pierre-Quint's own book, may be mentioned the following volumes: The Duchesse de Clermont-Tonnerre: " *Robert de Montesquiou et Marcel Proust*"; the Princesse de Bibesco, " *Au Bal avec Marcel Proust*"; Lucien Daudet, " *Autour Soixante lettres de Marcel Proust*"; A group of friends, " *Hommage à Marcel Proust.*"

In quoting from the works of the authors whom I discuss I have always used an accepted translation when such exists. However, since much of Boccaccio, much of Stendhal, and all of the two last (and very important) volumes of Proust's novel have never been put into English, I was driven to the necessity of making a good many translations of my own. As I pretend to no great talent as a linguist I must apologize for whatever deficiencies may be discovered in them.

Owing to absence from the United States I was able to see none of the page proofs and only a portion of the galleys.

JOSEPH WOOD KRUTCH

CONTENTS

GIOVANNI BOCCACCIO

I

U PON the outskirts of the
city of Naples lies the tomb of Virgil. The body of the
great poet was laid there nineteen years before the beginning of the Christian era and during all the tumultuous
centuries which followed he was never entirely forgotten.

The Roman Emperors from Augustus to Augustulus
ruled or misruled the Empire whose glory he had celebrated. Successive hoards of barbarians danced amid the
ruins they had helped to create or strove to impose some
sort of order upon the chaos they had provoked. Then
Naples itself, falling under the victorious army of Belisarius
was detached from the Empire of the West and subjugated
to Constantinople. Later it set up a republic of its own which
endured for four centuries and finally it fell under the rule
of the conquering Normans. But during all those ages when
so much was destroyed or forgotten the fame of Virgil never
completely disappeared. The Italians, with the indestructible
monuments of Rome constantly under their eyes, could
never entirely forget that her greatness had been a physical
reality and in their minds no name was more closely asso-
ciated than his with the grandeur which he had celebrated.

His fame had, indeed, undergone strange transmogrifica-
tions. Few to whom his name was still vaguely familiar had

any idea of the character of his works and fewer still had read them. He must, they thought, have been a mighty magician . . . like Aristotle. He had, so legend asserted, created a marvellous brazen fly and from him Reynard the Fox had learned certain valuable secrets. Even as we approach the period with which we are concerned, a period during which he was again read as a poet, certain fantastic notions still prevailed for the Church had claimed him as her own. Had he not, it was asked, definitely revealed the divine character of his inspiration by clearly predicting in one of his Eclogues the coming of Christ and did not even students of profane literature agree that his deepest significance lay not in the vain fables which he recounted but in the allegorical meanings which lay hid within them?

Virgil was, in short, a symbol of intellectual greatness which each age had interpreted in terms it could understand and though the time had come again when certain newly refined ears caught his sweet melody they were frightened by the perception of delights which had no relation to that plan of salvation which the Church insisted should be the sole concern of man. Here undoubtedly was the voice of the world, hints of that human culture which had no relation to the only culture tolerated by a harsh God, and timidly men sought to deny that it contained any principle inimical to the philosophy which they accepted. But more and more his voice was heard. Ideas of fame and glory, aspirations toward tenderness and beauty, began to attach themselves to his name. He was the great poet in a sense unknown to the grim ages just past and his fame was a glimmer from some civilization which began to seem once more desirable.

This Virgil had lain some thirteen centuries in his tomb when a young Italian in his ardent twenties stood meditating at night beside it. His father was one of those merchants who were establishing the solid bourgeois prosperity upon which the culture of the Renaissance was to be founded, and he himself was, without exactly knowing it, a typical representative of the new man. Countless influences working upon him had served to set him apart from the medieval type. He had, for example, been accustomed from boyhood to cities more stately and more comfortable than any known in the western world outside of Italy; he had been at a court whose fashion and sophistication made it infinitely removed from the semi-barbarous state of society which still dominated the rest of Europe; and though he had applied himself somewhat to study, he was, by nature and experience, worldly. Learning did not seem to him as it had once seemed, to lead directly to the Church or the cloister; like the son of many a commercial father he had conceived no ambition to add to the family fortune; and he was full of vague aspirations.

As he stood in a ferment to which love added its perplexities his mind turned to that " sweet poesy " which since childhood had delighted him and the soul of Virgil spoke across the centuries:

"Contemplating that tomb and meditating for a long time with suspended soul both upon him whom the tomb enclosed and the fame of those bones, he began suddenly to accuse and to lament the fate which had violently constrained him to devote himself to trade which he hated. From this he was seized with a sudden love of the Pierian

Muses and returning to the house he broke with all merchants and gave himself ardently to the study of poetry; in
which, in a short space of time, his noble intelligence and
his ardent desires being joined, he became admirably pro-
ficient."

Such at least is the account of the conversion of Giovanni
Boccaccio given by his contemporary and earliest biographer Filippo Villani, who wrote it down in his *Liber de
Civitatis Florentiae Famosis Civibus* six or seven years after
Giovanni had died. One may, indeed, suspect a touch of
poetry in this account itself but if poetry is there it is poetry
of that sort which reveals the deepest truth, for if it is not
literal fact it is at least significant allegory. It was the world
of things human not the world of things divine which Boccaccio longed to feel and to sing; he was compelled to reach
back across many intervening centuries to touch hands with
men who had dropped the thread which he was to try
to pick up; and Rome was the centre of that light whose
beams reached him feebly. Virgil was the symbol of the
literature of the ancient world. Virgil was the guide chosen
by Dante whom Boccaccio adored. And it was at the ashes
of Virgil that he himself would light his torch.

Two other men, Dante Alighieri and Franchesca Petrarcha,
shared with him the literary fame of his century. Succeeding
ages have studied both more assiduously than they have
studied him but he was, nevertheless, more completely than
either of the others a representative of a new kind of culture.
Dante, who had died during Boccaccio's childhood, was still
essentially medieval. To him the world was still a school for

eternity, valueless in itself and valuable only in order that one might learn how utterly it ought to be despised. Petrarch, though far more sensitive than Dante to secular values, approached them only through the world of books. Scholar, recluse, and pedant, he was half a pagan — on paper — but the library claimed him and he both observed life and lived it through the eyes of the ancient authors whom he collected. For Boccaccio, on the other hand, " one world at a time " was the half-conscious motto. Though he might sharpen his wits upon the classics, the lust of life which ran strongly in his veins forbade him to become a mere scholar and he knew life and love through experience as well as through description. Hesitantly and with many reservations, Petrarch had defended the worth of human life in the world, implicitly he had indicated that it contained the elements from which a culture might be formed, but Boccaccio was the first modern writer who put that creed into practice. What Dante had fled from, what Petrarch had timidly contemplated, he passionately embraced and he produced as a result the first enduring work of a new kind of literature.

From whatever the other two wrote concerning life as their contemporaries lived it, certain lines went out to points of reference outside that life. In Dante they went out to great principles, fixed in eternity, by which all human events must be judged; in Petrarch they went out to the customs and the opinions of the ancient world; but in Boccaccio, the world of sense and experience was for the first time since the classical age complete in itself. Life as he and his fellows lived it needed nothing which it did not itself furnish to establish its values. Even if God had never existed and the Romans had never lived, Florence and Naples contained delight enough and meaning enough to form the subject of art. He was the first great writer to take part in the experiment, begun about that time and not yet complete, in which man has attempted to be all in all for himself, to take time, not eternity, for his province and experience as his only guide and judge. He was, in fine, the first *moyen homme sensuel* to attain greatness in modern letters.

Certain qualities negative as well as positive fitted him for his achievement. Dante, member of a great aristocracy, was trained in two great schools — theology and the tradition of courtly letters — from the first of which he inherited the closed and logical system of medieval asceticism and from the second of which he learned how love could be refined away until it became either merely a poetical convention, or a philosophical idea not incompatible with ascetic dogma. Petrarch, too, came from at least a middle class family but Boccaccio was a member of what Dante contemptuously called the " *populo grasso.*" At the time of life when the other two great poets were moulding their souls in accord with a polite and learned tradition at the University of Bologna, Boccaccio was cultivating the natural robustness of his temperament by contact with the world. Nature had given him and experience had cultivated that simple and vigorous good sense which we signalize in two of its other great examples — Montaigne and Molière — as the bourgeois spirit. Hearty in his appetites, he had no natural taste for sentiments drawn too fine or for reasonings too subtle. In him was always an irresistible tendency to return to earth after any attempted flight too high, for earth not heaven was his home. More exclusively than either of the others a man of the Renaissance, he was at once its beginning and its epitome.

II

It is not certain whether Paris, Florence, or the little town of Certaldo gave Boccaccio birth, but he was born in the year 1313 and born, significantly enough, from a temporary union between his father and a Parisian woman whom the latter had met in the course of a mercantile journey and whom he shortly after abandoned. Giovanni had, as a matter of course, received an elementary education and been as a matter of course also, apprenticed to another eminent merchant in order that he might learn the trade of his father; but before he had even learned what poetry was, he had made little rhymes of his own, and he spoke bitterly in later life of the six years which he had wasted in trade. His father, anxious to see him established in some lucrative profession, suggested the study of the canon law, but the affairs of the Church interested him as little as those of trade and the only result was the loss of another six years. He had, however, managed to make that study serve as an excuse for taking up his residence in the gay city of Naples and it is there that the real story of his life begins.

Naples under the rule of King Robert was not a city to which either a merchant or a scholar would intrust his son without misgivings, for the refinement and freedom of its manners might well be expected to corrupt both the prudent industry of the one and the moral gravity of the other. Though Robert, like so many of the petty rulers of the Renaissance, was suspected of having mounted his throne over the murdered body of a relative, he was a liberal and

capable ruler and his ideals were the new ideals of refinement and beauty which were rapidly undermining the
whole medieval world. Under his rule Naples had become
the centre of fashion in Italy at a time when Italy was leading the world in the achievement of that bodily comfort
which makes fashion possible. Poets and scholars were
honoured there, but the day was already passing when
poetry and scholarship were affairs of the cloister or inevitably connected with an austere piety. At Naples the days
were given to *fêtes champêtres,* the nights to splendid entertainment and amorous intrigue; there, in short, had already been founded that paradoxical society, nominally
Christian, but in all its acts completely pagan, which was
to rule Italy for two centuries and gradually reach the depths
of hypocritical corruption which made it possible for a
Borgia to sit on the papal throne and hold his orgies in the
Vatican itself.

We do not know at what age Boccaccio first saw the resplendent city but he seems to have been taken there as a
child and he has left us an account — how fanciful we do
not know — under the guise of an allegory which describes his first sight of the new streets and which tells how
his heart beat with delight when he met " a most beautiful
girl, in aspect gracious and fair, dressed all in garments
of green which befitted her age and recalled the ancient
dress of the city " and who welcomed him to it with a kiss.
In any event the memory of the city seems to have remained
in his mind as that of a sort of earthly paradise and he was
glad of any excuse — trade or the common law — which
would enable him to become one of its citizens. " Florence,"

he wrote of the grim town which had produced Dante and in which he himself had possibly been born, was " an unpleasant city, where people hold pompous discourses followed by commonplace deeds — a city full of pride, of cupidity, and of jealousy. Naples, on the contrary was joyous and peaceable, rich and magnificent."

The elder Boccaccio, in the position of a powerful merchant, had probably been able himself to present his son at the court, and the more the young man saw of it the less possible was it for him to devote himself to any career which the father would find acceptable. In Naples he instinctively recognized his own spiritual home and it in turn developed in him the joyous aspects of his nature. Hitherto he had been compelled to listen to merchants " skilful only in putting money into coffers " maintain that poetry was not lucrative when " they ought to have blushed to attack celestial things which they do not comprehend and should have confined themselves to crawling among things which the baseness of their spirits makes them barely able to understand." Here, on the other hand, poetry was valued at its true worth as the sole means by which a man's memory might be carried down to future ages and here too was a daily life which afforded a perpetual gratification to his wakened and eager senses.

Boccaccio's sensuality — of which more must later be said — was of a sweet and gentle sort. Nothing merely coarse or ugly delighted it and it was marked by none of the ferocity which so often accompanied the sensuality of the Italian; but young and fresh though it was it had seldom any admixture of anything not essentially sensual. He loved fields and flowers because he was exquisitely sensitive to the beauty of form and colour and not at all because he saw in them anything of a mystical meaning too deep for tears, and so also he loved women for the grace and beauty of their bodies and not at all because love was, as his master Dante thought, the lowest rung in the ladder which leads up to God. For such a nature, Naples with its sunny days spent with beautiful women in the field and its soft nights spent with these same ladies in brilliant assemblage was a very paradise.

An atmosphere to which poetry and fashion both contributed served to give sensuality its last touch of refinement and to produce in Boccaccio an intoxication of delight. Whenever in later years he had occasion to describe this life his page was lit up with the bright memory, and whenever he describes anything which he intended to be replete with charm it seems to be of Naples that he is writing. One thought only, he says, "how to amuse oneself, dancing to the sound of music, discussing affairs of love, and losing ones heart over sweet words." Sometimes the youths and maidens went in gay companies to the forest where tables, filled with all manner of delectable dainties, were spread before them. Some would glide along the shores in boats, others would divest themselves of their shoes and stockings to wade for shells and others would fish from lines. Courts of love, for the dissection of the amorous passion, were held in Spring-time and the concern was not always exclusively with theory. More than one woman, he confesses, came to Naples a Lucrece and left it a Cleopatra but that was not, for the young Boccaccio, too deplorable a transformation. Let him describe in his own words the city as it appeared to his charmed imagination:

I do not think that to behold the Daughters of King Priam, with many other of the Phrygian Ladies when, attired and beautified in the bravest sort, they presented themselves, and came before their father-in-law and sovereign, to dance, to feast and make merry, was either a more rich or goodly sight than for to see in many places of our City the Majestical meeting and brave assemblies of celestial demi-goddesses in the same, which, after that in fair troops they came to the public Theaters (every one to the utmost of her power showing herself most brave, and making herself most beautiful) I doubt not but that any Gentleman stranger, but indifferently conceited and judicious, had arrived there (having considered their haughty countenances, their noble behavior, and viewed their costly apparel and rich ornaments, rather princelike than convenient for many nay, most; Gentlewomen there) would not have judged them women of this later age, but would have thought that some of those ancient and magnificent Ladies had been returned again to the world, saying with himself:

She for her stateliness doth resemble Semiramis. This other (gazing on her sumptuous apparel and Jewels) would rather be deemed Cleopatra. Another (considering her courtly and lovely graces) he would have compared to fair Helen. And another (viewing well her gesture and sweet actions in his mind) he would affirm to be not unlike queen Dido. . . .

And after that the Sun hath once begun to send forth his beams cooler than before, then do the honorable Princes of our Ausonian kingdom meet together in that habit as their high estate doth require. Who, after that they have beheld the divine graces of every lady, and fed their greedy eyes with every

Gentlewoman's beauty, and marked well their dancing, commending some more some less, but all generally, going away with almost all the Knights and Gentlewomen (as well married as unmarried men) after a little while, in great and most brave companies, with rich and new fashioned apparel, and clean contrary to the rest, with Masks, and other goodly shows, they return back again.

What tongue is there, be it never so famous for golden eloquence and choice of words, or wit, never so much commended for excellent sentences and exquisite invention, that could perfectly or particularly set down the Noble and gorgeous Habits, and the sundry brave suits of apparel (as pleasant for variety as wonderful for magnificence), which was seen there. Not Homer, certes, so worthy among the Grecians, nor Virgil, so highly praised of the latins, which with stately verse did write the infinite adventures and accidents, which both those noble men, and which the Grecians, Trojans and Italians, had of yore in their open wars, private peace and stratagems.[1]

It is hardly necessary to say that in such an atmosphere Boccaccio fell in love. Indeed he did so more than once and he has left us the literary names of two ladies, Pampinea the "white dove" and Abrotonia "the blackbird," who played the Rosaline to his Romeo; but the lady who remained for him throughout his youth the symbol of love was she who has come down to us under the name of Fiammetta, or the little flame. The first of his books was written, he tells us, at her command and in all but one of the other works of imagination which he wrote in the vulgar tongue she plays the role of a sensual Beatrice.

[1] This translation is the Elizabethan English one made by Bartholomew Young.

Doubtless the element of literary convention plays a part in all this. Petrarch with his Laura as well as Dante with his Beatrice had made it obligatory upon any poet to exalt a queen of his heart and if Boccaccio had experienced no enduring passion it would have behooved him to invent one. But though he was incapable of remaining content with either the intellectual adoration of Dante or the formal homage of Petrarch (who showed surprisingly little inclination to render the object of his love less inaccessible than he lamented her to be), Fiammetta was a woman of flesh and blood whom Boccaccio had, in the flesh, embraced. Try as he would in describing it to refine his love away into that pale and decorous shadow which the convention of courtly poetry demanded, it remains substantial and real. In the person of Fiammetta one may recognize, not the inspirer of an ideal passion, but the woman who first called out and satisfied the most ardent desires of which he was capable and who therefore remained in his mind as the symbol of that substantial sort of love which it was his particular function to celebrate.

This Fiammetta has been almost certainly identified with one Maria, the illegitimate daughter of King Robert, but practically all that we know of her comes from Boccaccio himself who wove some version of their love affair into more than one of his works. His stories are not in all respects consistent with one another and all are embroidered with fancy. It is easy to see him forming a legend on the model afforded by the story of Dante and Beatrice and far less aware than later readers have been of how different the meanings of the two stories were; but all that he tells us of her is significant both of the literary conventions of his day and of the way in which he was preparing himself for his greatest achievement by discovering how inappropriate they were for the expression of what was most important and valid in himself.

On a beautiful Spring morning, Saturday the Vigil of Easter, he had gone with a fashionable company to the ten o'clock mass in the Franciscan Church of San Lorenzo. Gay as the court of Naples was, intellectual skepticism was no important part of the life there, and Boccaccio was no more inclined than his companions to question the authority of the Church or to neglect its ceremonies. On this particular occasion he noted in himself the sweetness of the melody which the choir was singing and he listened to the Holy Mass being celebrated by a priest " successor to him who first girt himself humbly with a cord, exalting poverty and adopting it." For the moment at least he was living spiritually in that medieval world of which Francis was the finest flower and he felt himself touched by its sober poetry. Yet at that very instant the Renaissance entered. Suddenly he became aware of the presence of a beautiful young woman and in an instant there rushed in upon him the whole complex of ideas and desires of which a beautiful woman is the symbol. At the vision he forgot both the humble Francis and the pale God whom Francis served. The prayers which he had addressed to them had been half the result of habit — the voice of his forefathers not of himself — but now a prayer gushed forth to the God who was really his. " O Love," he cried, " most noble lord whose strength not even the gods were able to resist, I thank thee for setting happiness before my eyes:

already my cold heart feeling the softness of thy rays begins to warm itself: Therefore I, who for a long time have fled frightened from thy mother, now pray thee to enter with thy deity into my heart. No longer is it possible for me either to fly from you or to desire to fly, but humbly and devotedly I surrender myself to thy will."

Of this lady who now made him the worshipper he had doubtless long wished to be, he has left no description which will differentiate her from the subject of countless poems in the tradition of courtly love. She was, he says, tall and slender. Her hair, " so blond that the world holds nothing like it," shaded a white forehead of noble width, beneath which were the curves of two black and most slender eyebrows and two roguish eyes and cheeks of no other color than milk." Yet this very absence of particularity is significant in the history of one who was already in love with love and when he saw her, Boccacio felt all the emotions which the lover was supposed to feel. " No sooner had I seen her than my heart began to tremble so violently that I felt it through every pulse, and not knowing why nor perceiving what had happened, I began to say ' Alas, what is this? ' " But when he saw that she, aware of his gaze, hid her face with a veil, he moved from his place to another from which he could still see her and, probably not wholly aware of the irony, he feasted his eyes upon her beauty while the priest sang the office " full of sweet melody." Once she looked at him and when the service was over he joined his companions at the Church door and saw her pass out.

Next day — it was Easter — he went again to the Church, this time to see her only, and was rewarded by a sight more beautiful than before. She was shining with gold, made beautiful, he says, "by both nature and art," and when he saw her he remembered the little girl, dressed like her in green, who had welcomed him to the city of Naples and who had later appeared to him in a dream. "This," he said to himself, "is she who was ordained to rule my mind, and who was promised me for lady in my dreams."

Now when Dante, whose story of the beginning of his "New Life" here doubtless coloured strongly Boccaccio's experience, had first seen Beatrice he went away and meditated. He made no effort to cultivate in the flesh even a friendship with her who is the symbol of his desire and his salvation. The theologized love which he celebrated was detached wholly from love in the earthly sense and he had no idea of compromising the value of Beatrice as a symbol by any knowledge of Beatrice as a woman. Boccaccio, on the other hand, however much he might admire Dante and however much he might fancy their experiences similar, was by no means capable of understanding such odd behaviour in a lover. Love was to him too a God, but a pagan one. The experience which he had just received was no mere unadorned lust of the flesh, for it was the inspiration of a thousand beautiful fancies and poetic ideas, but neither was it an affair of the mind alone. His function was to beautify the senses, not to escape from them, and there was in him no fastidious repugnance either toward profane love or the intrigues by which it is accomplished. He could meditate beside the tomb of Virgil but he could be a practical gallant as well — doubtless, even, had been one before — and so it was toward practical steps that he turned his attention.

Fiammetta was married. Some youth nearer her own sta-

tion in life than the humble student who had glimpsed her at
her devotions had already taken her from the convent where
she had been bred and established her as one of the reigning
beauties of Naples. Well might Boccaccio lament, as he tells
us that he did, the social gulf which separated them and not
without excuse were the moments of despair which alternated
with youthful hope. But if this difficulty was great it was,
fortunately for him, the greatest which he had to face, since
the technical virtue of Fiammetta was more easily assailable
than the pride of her position. She was known to have had
lovers before now and she would be committing no very
startling infraction of the code of Naples if she should have
them again.

In those days love, springing into a new luxurious growth,
had not yet been assimilated by society and it was essentially
a lawless thing. The medieval Church, with its utter distrust
of the flesh, had looked with suspicion upon ardent passion
even in marriage and the new sense of its worth had grown
up as a thing apart, an affair of poets and courtiers not of
moralists or theologians. It had its code — both Boccaccio
and Fiammetta had heard it expounded during the sessions
of that Court of Love which constituted one of the amusements of Naples — but that code had no relation to the code
of the Church. Ovid's " Art of Love " was an important part
of its canonical scriptures and Ovid was no great respector of
the matrimonial institution. " All those who take wives,"
Fiammetta remarks in the book devoted entirely to her, " are
enamored of other women; for the abundance which wives
give their husbands makes that which was before so delightful
soon cloying " and she was but naïvely repeating an observa-

tion which the casuists of love accepted as a commonplace. Decorum required that love should be secret but the ladies of Italy had accepted the Spartan conception of Virtue — it was necessary only that one should not be found out.

It was, then, no difficult matter for Boccaccio to make the acquaintance of his lady. He encountered her at a fashionable gathering — in the parlor of a convent! — and the talk turning upon the romances of love which ladies read in their hours of idleness, Boccaccio spoke of the ancient tale of Florio and Blanchefleur, of how the two young lovers had been faithful to their love through the surprising vicissitudes of fate, and Fiammetta, turning to him, bade him write down for her such a romance as that, " a little book in which the beginning of love, courtship, and the fortune of the two lovers, even to their death, shall be told." " Hearing," he says, " the sweetness of the words which came from that gracious mouth and remembering that never once till this day had that noble lady asked anything of me, I took her prayer for a command and saw therein hope for my desires." For us the result was some seven hundred pages of youthfully elaborate prose in which the story is retold with what seems to us an intolerable prolixity and burdened with all the irrelevant scraps of learning which its author could summon; for him it was the first step in his serious literary career and a new claim upon the attention of his lady.

Here, as everywhere, the story of Boccaccio is confused, but from now on the love affair which was to remain for him the most emotionally significant event of his life and which was to furnish the centre of the experience out of which he formed his art developed with great rapidity. At first Fiam-

metta would have none of him and he was cast into despair,
but soon he became an accepted member of her band and in
the ambiguous, half-formal, role of *cavalier servente* he spent
his days and nights either in gay society or in indicting amorous verse. Whatever pretense he may have kept up before this
to a study of the canon law was now abandoned and his father
became, as a result, more anxious than ever. All the Floren-
tines who happened at that time to be living in Naples, so
Boccaccio tells us with characteristic contempt, seemed to
speak with his father's voice and one and all they told him
that while it was bad enough to waste time with literature it
was worse to ruin oneself for love. But to Boccaccio, now in
the full tide of his romantic awakening, the sage reproofs of
those who reproved him with wasting his time did no more
than to reveal their grovelling souls and, speaking of Love,
he could triumphantly reply:

Oh how many are the good things that proceed from Him!
Who moved Virgil? Who Ovid? Who else but He inspired
both them and the other poets who have established their eternal
fame in sacred verses which would never have come to our ears
had it not been for Him. What shall we say of His virtue? What
indeed if not that He had power to give such sweetness to the
harp of Orpheus that he called with that sound the surrounding
forest, that he made the running streams pause, and the fierce
lions and all the other animals come with the timid deer into
his presence; that likewise he quieted the infernal furies and gave
sweet repose to sorrowing shades; and besides all that, that it
availed to recover his lost wife. Therefore Love is not the slayer
of honor, as you say, nor the cause of indecent perplexity, nor
the provoker of vices, nor the donner of empty anxiety, nor the

unworthy occupier of other people's freedom; therefore with all skill and all effort ought everyone who is not his servant strive and endeavor to win the grace of so gracious a lord, and to become his servant quickly, because it is through him that we become virtuous. That which is pleasing to the gods and to the strongest men should be pleasing to you also; follow him, love him, serve him, and may such a lord live always in our souls.

One day when a company had repaired to a wood he found himself alone with Fiammetta and she gave him such proof of her favour that he knew the time had come when he might hope for more than a mere tolerance of his love. But he knew also the depths of her coquetry and he knew that he must appear to seize what he would have. Bribing her maid in the absence of the husband, he made his way to her chamber and there, while she accepted his presence but seemed to reject his further advances, he poured out the eloquence of his love, and when that was not enough he, not unwillingly, played out the comedy to its last extravagance. Drawing a dagger from his belt he exclaimed, " I come not, O lady, to defile the chastity of thy bed, but as an ardent lover to obtain relief for my burning desires; thou alone can assuage them, or tell me to die; surely I will only leave thee satisfied or dead, not that I seek to gratify my passion by violence or to compel any to raise cruel hands against me; but if thou art deaf to my entreaties, with my dagger I shall pierce my heart." Not even Fiammetta could demand gallant rhetoric more extreme or more accomplished than that and now for the first time she yielded to her enraptured lover.

Even though space allowed, the modesty of English would scarcely permit to be translated here the passages in which

Boccaccio describes this meeting, and yet only by reading them can one quite grasp the state of his soul. For him, if not for Fiammetta, the gallant game had grown earnest and he reached the height of sensual experience. Untouched by mystical solemnity, it was nevertheless enriched and intensified by the whole complex of ideas with which his love of poetry connected it. It was the great secular sacrament, and in it he was experiencing for himself that which was the subject of the great poets whom he had studied. All the fresh, full ardour of his nature found itself here for the first time satisfied and he had not yet learned the meaning of satiety. He could conceive of no felicity beyond this and he could not perceive in it any lack. As long as even the memory of it remained vivid it was bound to seem the most significant of human experiences, something beside which all creeds and doctrines were pale.

But if Boccaccio was thus essentially naïve, Fiammetta was an experienced coquette. Love was no new thing to her and she gave herself with no illusions like his. For some months, for a year perhaps, their felicity endured, but at the end of that time Boccaccio could hide from himself no longer the fact their union was not what he had supposed. In his mind he, too, had doubtless known that the two of them were playing a comedy. Eternity is a lover's word and passions as pagan as his were doubtless the occasion of other wandering desires. But he was at least moved more deeply than she because, if for no other reason, he was moved for the first time, and the thought that she, with vulgar excuses and little deceits, should bring the greatest experience of his life to a close, plunged him into the depths of despair. Through a whole series of poems written at the time, we can trace the growing doubts and finally the cry of certain anguish. Fiammetta had passed on to other delights and he was expelled from the only paradise which it is given for a nature like his to know.

Doubtless he had thought little of the future but the future was now before him. The time had come for him to digest his experience and fate decided for him that the close of this epoch should be appropriately marked by external events. Some sort of calamity overtook his father, with whom he had quarrelled but upon whom he had nevertheless depended. Sometime after the close of the affair with Fiammetta, Boccaccio was called upon to leave even the scene of his happiness and betake himself once more to the grim city of Florence which always seemed to him so cold and so ignoble. In Naples he had lived poetry, here at best he could only write it.

III

Such was the *donné* of experience with which Boccaccio began his literary labours, and commonplace as it may seem in its superficial aspect it was sufficient to furnish him with as many problems as his genius could, in its whole lifetime, solve. The whole of his passionate youth had been thrown into that experience and the thoughts and feelings which it generated were the realest things which he was ever to know. No art and no philosophy which did not recognize and interpret what he had there lived through could ever, until the coming of middle age had quieted his passions, have any validity for him. He had given himself to an experience in the course of which his consciousness had reached the intensest level of which it was capable and it was the quality of that experience which he must somehow communicate.

He had come to Naples ardent and naïve. In its gay and pagan atmosphere he had been made forever incapable of seeing the world through medieval eyes and though he had no philosophy with which to replace it, that conception of man's place and function which had but recently been summed up for all time in the Summa Theologica of Saint Thomas was as unreal to him, as little capable of being instinctively accepted, as it is to us. Innocently sensual as a faun and quite as ignorant of the fact that the tortures of the flesh are no less real than its ecstasies, he had surrendered himself to love only to awake and find how bitter an awakening can be. And his tragedy was not one which could resolve itself in any traditional way.

What he felt was not the sense of sin which Theology would

have taught him to expect and for which it could offer its remedies. His suffering led him toward no renunciation of the flesh, for the flesh was still for him, potentially at least, the source of all beauty. A natural man in a natural world, he had been deprived of the thing which made that world most delightful and though his tragedy was purely secular it was immeasurably poignant for all that. He knew that love, considered merely as a natural phenomenon, was great and powerful, but he had no fit vehicle for the expression of the intensity of emotion which he had felt. The passion which Petrarch could never have undersood, Dante had reserved for God and for Ambition, and if any other poet of his time had given himself so utterly to a purely human passion that poet had never been able to communicate his experience. There were ways in which what passed for the love of God could be expressed and there was a courtly convention by which, under the guise of allegory or of classical mythology, one might elaborate gallant conceits, but there was no modern literature of passion as intense and yet as unadorned as his had been.

Naturalist that he was in every fibre of his being, Boccaccio had not been lifted to a mystic level. Though he had been playing no merely gallant game — the earnestness of his ecstasy and his despair told him that — neither was his experience one which could be transmuted into any purely spiritual thing. It was not the Platonized love of Dante which had been visited upon him, any more than it was the mere literary convention of Petrarch, but instead the implacable Aphrodite whose might the pagans had felt and whose power he was constrained to admit. He was thus the first modern, not doubtless to feel, but to strive to describe a great and yet wholly secular passion and he was compelled to find his own means of expression. One was not, according to the medieval ideas which Boccaccio was compelled, in a measure, to accept, supposed to feel as he had felt. Love was either trivial or divine, a game or a sacrament, and he had found it neither. He could not accept his experience without revolutionizing the accepted hierarchy of values and he could not express it without inventing a new tradition of literature.

Little as he was gifted with the power of self-analysis, he must have perceived, instinctively at least, that this world of his experience had no connection with that of Dante. He must have known that while the latter's mystical ecstasy was something which he had never attained, his own delighted absorption in the world of the senses made possible a kind of experience from which Dante's ascetic preoccupation with the spirit shut him out. But he had no models at once serious, realistic and purely sensual. He had to confess and to consolidate a worldliness, passionate and yet wholly naturalistic, which had grown up in the Italian courts without ever having found literary expression, and he was not yet capable of creating a new literary style which should imply as it must a new sort of acceptance of the natural universe.

The generations which immediately followed his and which looked back upon his achievement, saw in him the first man cast in their own mould while, to them, Dante was already remotely alien. But Boccaccio, acutely aware of the defects of his formal education and looking with awe not only upon the haughty self-confidence of Dante but upon the learned and frigid eloquence of Petrarch, had no sure sense of the worth of his own perceptions. He strove long to identify them with accepted modes of feeling before he ever achieved a clear statement of himself or immortalized his own attitude, and how heavily the tradition represented by the literary models of his time was against him may be seen even in the scattered quotations which have been used in recounting the story of his love, for they are replete with an artifice which, charming as it is, is far from appropriate to his essentially realistic spirit.

He was no mystic, but for the present he knew no way to dignify his experience except the mystic way, and so, speaking of a vision, he attempts to make a mystical identification between Fiammetta and the little girl in green who had greeted him upon his first entrance to Naples. Because no great tradition of secular love lay behind him, he could only suggest the essentially serious character of his passion by uttering an apostrophe to Venus and, in general, by borrowing both his language and his images from the classical poets. Absorbed though he was in contemporary life, he had no body of contemporary *belles lettres* which would serve as a model of realistic description.

Nor did Boccaccio, in any of his youthful works, succeed in approaching his subject matter except through devious ways. Though the contemporary world as he knew it was what really concerned him and though it was to be his achievement as an artist to show how that contemporary world could be made the subject of art, he was the first literary artist to attempt the task and he illustrates in his development how difficult are any of those mutations which seem to succeeding ages so natural and so inevitable. To his contemporaries, aware of the fact that their secular culture was something new and undisciplined, it seemed significant only in so far as it could be translated into the terms of the ancient culture of Rome, and so through the whole series of his early works Boccaccio, circling continually about his central experience, can never give it direct expression. Sometimes he imitates the allegory of Dante. Sometimes he and Fiammetta are transmogrified into Huntsmen and Nymphs inhabiting not Naples of the Fourteenth Century but some vague classic Arcadia and speaking not the language of their passion but a poetic jargon pieced together out of showy scraps of a rhetoric, tawdry and faded. Boccaccio was feeling with intensity and vigour but he was interpreting his emotion in terms not genuinely appropriate to the quality of his experience.

Neither the " Filocolo " which he undertook, it will be remembered, at Fiammetta's bidding and which he was years in completing nor either of the other two works — the heroic " Filostrato " and the epic " Tesiade " — which he wrote while still at Naples, carried him far upon his way. Concerned as each of them is with an old story and, as far as he could make them, conventional in feeling, neither represents a real struggle with his problem, and not until, returned sadly to Florence, he embarks upon his " Ameto " does he come to grips with it. No modern has ever read this grotesque composition without amazement and no one could consider it as other than essentially ridiculous, but in it Boccaccio exposes completely for the first time the hopeless confusion into which he had fallen both as a man and as an artist and from which he was compelled to extricate himself before he could become capable of any clear or steady vision of the world.

The form of this piece, written partly in prose and partly in verse, is that of the pastoral and its theme is love. Ameto, a semi-savage youth who subsists upon the spoils of the chase and who may be taken, perhaps, as a symbol of the animal in man, happens one day to come suddenly upon Lia, a divinely beautiful nymph, and he is seized with the to him unknown passion of love. Through its miraculous influence he becomes aware of his own rudeness and, inspired by a new vision of human refinement and feeling, he persuades Lia to accompany him in the hunt. Winter, however, separates them and it is not until spring has come again that he finds her with a company of nymphs and shepherds in the neighbourhood of a temple. Each of the nymphs in turn now tells the story of her life and love, and by each the soul of Ameto is ravished still further. While he listens with his ears, his eyes devour the charms of each nymph in turn and, picturing to himself in no very delicate terms the delight of possessing one of them, he is all but lost in a sensual ecstasy when suddenly the Goddess of true love descends in her own person and reveals herself, no less to the surprise of the reader than to the surprise of Ameto, as the queen of a quite Christian heaven. Briefly she rebukes his sensual misconceptions, she bids him accept all that he has seen as symbolical, and the pastoral comes to an abrupt close with a hymn to the Trinity. Looking back we perceive that the company of nymphs, in spite of the wholly gallant character of their adventures, really represent a collection of the chief abstract virtues and that the whole composition is a grotesquely unsuccessful allegory.

In this preposterous *mélange* one may easily discover certain significant features both in the feeling and the expression,

but more significant yet is the theme upon which the
" Ameto " begins. Later, in one of the most famous and perfect
tales of the " Decameron," that which tells how the doltish
Cymon was made human by love, Boccaccio returned to it
with perfected art, yet even here instinct leads him to the
meaning of that Renaissance of which he was a significant
part, for love was at once the beginning and the symbol of
the secular culture whose value it was his function to affirm,
and in spite of the inappropriate tag with which the
" Ameto " is concluded, it is this fact that he is inarticulately
struggling to assert.

Dante had refused to regard the human passion of love as
other than a symbol. In his Platonized theology it was only an
imperfect earthly shadow leading man on to divine love, and
thus he made it, like all human things, valuable only in so
far as it contributed to conduct the human mind from the
visible to the invisible world. But historically at least, Dante
was wrong in his interpretation of that " New Life " which
was beginning for him and for the world. The strange sweetness which filled him when he gazed upon Beatrice and
which he recognized as something undreamed of by those
medieval teachers who had described love as a coarse and de-
grading lust, was not, as he thought, only a new and sweeter
way by which men were to be led to God. Rather it was a
sign of that softening of the soul which was to make life too
fair a thing merely to be fled from. Those who felt it were
capable also of feeling the multifarious delights which art and
literature were preparing for them and which constituted a
world valuable in itself and not leading of necessity to any
non-sensuous realm. The love which Dante so magisterially

celebrated and to which Boccaccio was here paying his falter-
ing tribute, was the mother not of Religion but of Culture.
Christianity had turned the barbarian animal into one kind
of man, romantic love was equally capable of turning him
into another, and it was a perception of this fact which Boccaccio was expressing in his allegory of love, the civilizer of the
new man.

Yet though when he had come to compose the "Ameto"
instinct had led him this far, he had neither the boldness of
imagination nor the clarity of intellect to develop his conception. What he later developed as a perfect tale here served only
as an impotent beginning from which he quickly passed into
the confused allegory which transformed his nymphs into
moral virtues and which led him to his grotesque conclusion.
From a poetic conception he slips into mere lubricity and
then, flying to the other extreme, sets up his hymn to the
Trinity, very much as though he had found himself trapped
into heresy and wished to recant as expeditiously and as un-
mistakably as possible.

We have no documents except those which his works themselves afford for the study of Boccaccio's spiritual history, but
it is not unreasonable to suppose that he himself was aware of
the utter disharmony of the "Ameto" and of the fact that
that disharmony must somehow be resolved, for in his next
work, "L'Amorose Visione" he strives to effect some sort
of compromise with the theology of Dante which would leave
him free to celebrate that earthly love which he was by no
means ready to abandon for the love of God. Here the form
is once more that of an allegory and the allegory is again
borrowed from Dante. Like the master whom he had so in-

appropriately chosen, Boccaccio too finds himself lost somewhere near the midway of this mortal life and with an artistic soul to save. Thinking of Fiammetta and his love for her he falls into a sweet sleep and to him, as to Dante, there appears in his vision a guide, though appropriately enough the guide for him is not Virgil but a woman. Offering to lead him to his eternal salvation she points to an imposing but forbidding castle and though at first there seems no entrance she indicates at last a tiny door, narrow and low, which leads to a difficult stair. Over this door is written " Entrance to Eternal Life," but Boccaccio turns to the right where another door, wide and high, bears the following inscription, " Riches, honor, treasures, earthly glory, these are that which I give to those who enter me, promising them happiness and the joys of love," and to the horror of his guide it is this door which Boccaccio enters. "That," she cries, " is the road to perdition " and " Quite so," he answers, but with that air at once sly and naïve which is so characteristic of him he adds the doubtful assurance, " Presently we shall return to the narrow gate; meanwhile I should like to see for myself."

Thus Boccaccio, breaking with Dante and the whole ascetic tradition, takes for the first time his own road in the full realization that he is taking it. In the vast secular world to which the broad and pleasant gate leads him he sees all the glories of the world which his soul, rebelling against the medieval doctrine, refuses to consider mere vanity and filth. Gazing upon huge allegorical pictures which symbolize respectively Science, Glory, Love and Wealth he recognizes the likeness of many resplendent figures — among them, Virgil for Science, the heroes of King Arthur's Table for Glory,

Helen and Guenevere and Lancelot for Love — and at last he comes into the bodily presence of Fiammetta herself. The guide gives them one to another and then at last they enjoy in their perfect union the highest felicity of the soul. It is true that after a time the guide returns and promises them that now they shall enter together the narrow door, but Boccaccio, bringing his poem to a close, does not trouble to describe that event. No atheist and no heretic, he does not reject the Church's plan of salvation, but for the moment he is in no hurry to escape from this very pleasant world which may be only an inn in which travellers repose upon their journey to eternity but which is, nevertheless, a very delightful caravansary.

Childish as the allegory may seem to an age which no longer expresses itself in such terms, the poem represents for Boccaccio an immense advance toward clarity and self-knowledge. Entirely unphilosophic in mind and quite incapable of dealing with general ideas, he had, by the aid of the concrete images of allegory, thought his way through to a compromise which made possible the development of his genius. Incapable of combating the medieval philosophy upon its own terms and not bold enough frankly to reject its conclusions, he turns away with a smile to his own concerns. Doubtless Dante and the doctors are right. Some day, he hopes, their austere way will seem attractive to him too and he does not wish to send his soul to the perdition they have so eloquently described. But trusting to the mercy of God and some ultimate repentance, he will make the world for the present his concern. In it, taken by itself, there are joys enough to make man happy, beauty enough to ravish the soul, and problems enough to keep busy an artist who should undertake to paint it.

This turn to the right which Boccaccio took was the one which the generations immediately following took after him and the compromise of Boccaccio was the compromise of the Renaissance. He showed how it might secularize itself without ceasing to be nominally Catholic, and how, by according a nominal assent to religious and moral dogmas, it could free itself from the necessity of any concern with them in the worldly life which it had completely detached.

Our immediate business is, however, with the art of Boccaccio, and the effect of the clarification which "L'Amorose Visione" accomplished was immediately apparent. He is done now with that struggle to spiritualize himself which could result only in grotesque if unintentional parodies like the "Ameto" and, for the time being, done with allegory too which had served its purpose and led him to self-knowledge. Recognizing the world as his province he need no longer disguise or allegorize it; he can describe it exactly as he sees it without attributing to it mystical meanings which could never be for him other than conventions and without disguising it under the form of pastoral or heroic romance. Henceforward human experience is his theme and he will describe it in human terms.

But one thing now remained to be accomplished in the long unconscious preparation for the startling mutation which produced his and his generation's masterpiece, "The Decameron." Self-knowledge, laboriously and torturously won, had made realism possible and had brought him to the place where he could deal with his own experience in terms genuinely appropriate to its quality; but though he could now be realistic he was not yet objective. Fiammetta was still the centre of his universe and it was still his personal experience which alone could furnish him the materials for his art. Hard upon " L'Amorosa Visione " came, however, the prose work which he called by her name and which not only constitutes an achievement in itself but also marks the end of his apprenticeship. The " Fiammetta," from which the quotations used at the beginning of this essay to describe life at the court of Naples were taken, may still be read with pleasure for itself alone, but it served also to free Boccaccio from the obsession of an experience which had taught him to know himself and which needed only to be mastered in order that, through it, he might learn to know the world also.

In this tale he represents Fiammetta as herself recounting the story of their love. The moment which he has chosen is that in which she, whom he represents deserted, not deserting, is at the full tide of her grief over a loss, and the method, in which there is no touch of allegory, is a method obviously no longer inspired by Dante, but borrowed from Ovid, in whose " Heroides " may be found the earliest example of the psychological analysis of the effects of secular love. Certain affectations still remain. The style is still rather precious and there are many classical allusions, ostentatiously paraded, but the background and the manners described are those of that real Naples upon whose sunny days and warm amorous nights he is looking back, and the voice one hears is the voice of passion real and undisguised. Not since Ovid wrote had anyone so vividly portrayed the effects of a love which is neither the mere lust of the medieval comic tale, the mysticism of Dante, nor the extravagant emotional posturings of the troubadours, but something at once full-blooded, powerful, and yet never coarse. Nothing approaching it in subtle yet realistic psychological portraiture had been written in the modern world, nothing which so skilfully anatomized a real passion.

Most of the works, either in literature or in pictorial art, which survive to us from an age as remote, not merely in time but in mind, as the Fourteenth Century, take most of the charm which they still have for us from a certain quaintness, but though the " Fiammetta " has its passages of quaint charm it has something more substantial as well — there is still warmth in the love and still poignancy in the sorrow which it describes. Such is the strength of the emotion which gave it birth and such the art with which that emotion was described that one is still moved by a keen compassion for the sorrows of a fictitious woman upon whom was projected the anguish of a man dead these six centuries.

Those who have written about Boccaccio have devoted much thought and indulged in much speculation in the effort to explain the fact that in this, his first realistic work, he chose to represent himself as having abandoned Fiammetta when, in all the veiled versions of the affair which had appeared in his earlier writings, and almost certainly in fact also, it was she who betrayed him. Certain scholars have attemped to see in it something in the nature of a revenge. Boccaccio, they imagine, had already sufficiently recovered from his passion to be humiliated by the part he had played and to wish to strike back at his faithless mistress. Accordingly, so they say, he wrote this work in order to put himself in a different light and to place Fiammetta in the humiliating position of a woman abandoned by the man she had loved too well. Nothing, however, could less suggest malice or revenge than the tone of the "Fiammetta." Tenderness and sympathy dominate its mood, and if we seek for an artistic explanation we will find one which is not only more easily reconcilable with the book itself, but which will serve as well to illustrate the workings of that instinct which was slowly leading him to develop his powers. Once he had decided that the central character in this sympathetic study of the pains of love betrayed was to be not himself but Fiammetta, it is obvious that he must transfer the burden of infidelity to the other party and it is not difficult to see why instinct led him to choose to project his emotions upon her rather than to recount them of himself.

As an artist Boccaccio was passing from the autobiographical to the objective stage. He was still too absorbed in his personal experiences to write about anything except them, but he was already moving toward the creation of character, and the plan of the "Fiammetta" afforded a compromise. The emotion which gives to the character its living warmth is his own but it is projected upon a character not himself. Using his own feelings, he transfers them to Fiammetta, and still having himself to draw upon, he adapts his own emotions to the changed circumstances afforded by the change of sex, thus using his own soul in order to understand another.

Thus "Fiammetta" serves to complete the education and training of Boccaccio as an artist. When he began it he had already learned to accept himself, and when he finished it he had learned also how to see not only himself but other people as well from the standpoint of his own view of the world. Fiammetta, whom his own passion had enabled him to study and to understand, served as the bridge over which he passed from himself to the world, because in describing her he was at once describing himself and another. Moreover, he had for the first time actually succeeded in what he had many times unsuccessfully attempted — he had, that is to say, given adequate expression to his love and his pain — and as a result he was freed from its obsessive weight. Naturalism no longer affrighted him as it had done when he had struggled so hard to translate his experiences into mystical terms, and he had mastered the emotions which had disrupted while they matured his consciousness. He could now look at the world around him with a penetration which he had learned in studying himself, and describe it with a detachment to which he had earned the right by a final acceptance of his own tragedy. He was living now in his own naturalistic world and seeing others as well as himself in its terms.

IV

For a century at least before Boccaccio began the "Decameron," popular story-tellers had delighted their non-literary audiences with anecdotes and tales. Some were merely brief records of practical jokes or popular witticisms; some revealed the memory of tragedies or comedies acted by real Italian people; and some embodied the *dejecta membra* of Greek or Oriental stories which had survived in fragments from an earlier civilization. Neither Dante nor Petrarch would have deigned to notice them, but Boccaccio, when he had come to know himself, recognized the materials of a native art and he made them body forth a view of the world which seemed to his contemporaries and successors the most adequate and the most sensible that had ever been given.

A hundred stories ranging in plot from rude farce to romantic tragedy and ranging in mood from Rabelaisian brutality to tender sentiment compose the collection, and though it is not likely that he invented a single one of them he did make each his own by realizing it completely and recognizing the unity which lay behind an apparently endless diversity. He saw in the rough boisterous comedy and the bloody tragedy, as well as in the romance which the popular tales embodied, a crude expression of the Italian temperament, something quite different from the classical modes of feeling which the learned were attempting to revive but something more completely comprehensible to him, and so, ceasing for the time being to aspire, he devoted himself to the task of making them art by giving them perfect form.

Everyone is familiar with the famous setting. A plague, the worst of the many that devastated the people of the middle age, has descended upon Florence. In a few brief paragraphs whose vivid, unadorned force is both extraordinary in itself and doubly surprising when compared with the diffuseness which marks all Boccaccio's previous writing, he describes the terror and despair which the visitation brought with it and then, like a man whose concern is with the bright things of life and who is completely devoid of any impulse to seek its meaning in its agonies, he turns his attention to a group of young men whose sole concern is to escape from a threatened danger. Doubtless their fathers would have prepared for death. Terror would have driven them to repentance and they would have thought of nothing except the life to come; but to these young men, gay with a new sense of the pleasantness of life, the possibility of leaving the world suggests nothing except the duty of using whatever days may be left to them, and with a common sense indifference to the ills of others whom they cannot succor, they plan with their ladies a retreat to a villa among the hills.

Servants go with them, the regulations of a little community are quickly ordered, and they soon are ready to devote themselves to the chief business of their life, which is, of course, diversion. Upon each day of their sojourn, it is arranged, each member of the company shall entertain the others with a story and each day a newly appointed queen shall set the general subject with which these stories shall deal.

And so with a sense of well-being which the realization of a danger escaped serves only to heighten, they seat themselves upon one of the sunny upland meadows below which the pest is raging in the grim stone town, and there they unlock their minds, pouring forth the tales which in idle moments they have heard and embellishing them with sly wit or tender sentiment. One perceives at once that a certain decorum which the homogeneous character of the company makes it unnecessary to define shall prevail. No grossness of language shall be used, nothing merely shocking shall be told, for the tellers are all cultivated even though they are not squeamish. But they are, on the other hand, constrained by no external forces. All members of the same social group, all friends together, they have withdrawn from the world for a time and there are no restraints except those which they would impose upon themselves. Their intellects are free and they do not fear gossips. The shadow of no doctrine and of no philosophy falls across them. They may consider what phenomena they please and conclude from them whatever they like.

Unorthodox in morality and philosophy most of the tales turn out to be, but such is the company's sense of safety and freedom that there are few signs of the bitterness which so generally marks a protestant literature. As though with one accord the first three story-tellers, who have been left free to choose their topic, choose tales reflecting a scant respect for dogmatic theology and for the clergy, and various members of the company return from time to time to similar themes as if to indicate how little they are influenced by the weight of that great authority against which they have not so much revolted as by which they have suddenly found themselves no longer impressed. But even here the tone is rather of tolerant satire than of anything approaching invective, and, throughout, the stories reveal all the suppleness and variety of a mind keenly receptive but little concerned with any conscious doctrine to be proved or illustrated.

No incident is too vulgar, none too romantic to concern these young people who are interested in all the varieties of character and experience which can be brought within their comprehension and who are willing to consider with an equal and almost childlike delight both the witty trick played by one peasant upon another and the high adventures of noble Dukes in war and love. No mystics — save perhaps those who have been made such by love — appear. For these people nothing ineffable, nothing transcendental exists. They know no character more exalted than that of the *honnête homme*. But within the limits of the purely human their interest and their sympathy is all inclusive. For them only the sensual world exists but that world is present in all its variety.

Before this profusion one stands for a time bewildered. It seems hopeless to attempt to characterize anything whose parts are so diverse and one is tempted to say that the absence of an informing view of the world is the only thing which will serve to explain such catholicity in the choice of subject-matter. But such is not indeed the case. Various as the individual stories are the greatness of the whole consists in the fact that a unity of mood pervades it and that that mood is the one which the experience of Boccaccio with his world had generated.

If one searches the apparently boundless diversity for some story which may be taken as typical and which will illuminate the rest, one cannot perhaps do better than to light upon that tale of Cymon and Iphegenia, which was foreshadowed in the cumbersome allegory of the " Ameto." It has never so far as I know been previously singled out by commentators, but the fact that it is given a position (first story of the fifth day) in the middle of the collection and that it is told on the day when Fiammetta is queen might lead us to suspect that to Boccaccio himself it was the key to his work, and its symbolism is transparent.

Cymon, we are told, was the dull and oafish son of a man of great wealth and distinction in the island of Cyprus. His brutish nature had resisted every effort to instruct it and he remained so completely without manners or learning that the citizens of the island had bestowed upon him the name of Beast. But, wandering one day in the woods, he came upon a beautiful woman sleeping there, and then he who had been insensible to all else felt the power of love. Suddenly, in the rude, uncivilized breast which had hitherto been incapable of receiving the least impression of politeness, a thought arose which seemed to intimate to his gross and shallow understanding that this was the most agreeable sight that was ever seen.

Love having thus pierced his heart, when no other lesson of any kind could find admittance, in a little time his way of thinking and behaviour were so far changed, that his father and his friends were strangely surprised at it, as well as everybody that knew him. First of all, then, he asked his father to let him have clothes like his brethren: to which his father very willingly consented. Conversing too with young gentlemen of character, and observing their ways and manner of behaviour, in a very short time he not only got over the rudiments of learning, but attained some knowledge of philosophy. Afterwards, his love for Iphigenia being the sole cause of it, his rude and rustic speech was changed into a tone more agreeable and civilized: he grew also a master of music; and with regard to the military art, as well by sea as by land, he became as expert and gallant as the best. . . . What, then, most gracious ladies, shall we say of Cymon? Surely nothing less than this: that all the noble qualities that had been infused by Heaven into his generous soul were shut up as it were by invidious fortune, and bound fast with the strongest fetters in a small corner of his heart, till Love broke the enchantment, and drove with all its might these virtues out of that cruel obscurity, to which they had been long doomed, to a clear and open day; plainly showing from whence it draws those spirits that are its votaries, and whither its mighty influence conducts them.

The meaning of this story is explicit enough and it illuminates the whole collection. Not only are most of the tales concerned with secular love, but love is regarded once more as the mother of all things. Not only does it flower in brave and gallant deeds, but it is the beginning of all civilization. It makes possible art and learning and courtesy. Without it man is a beast, but when it descends upon him he is reborn with the power to become human. Moreover, this love is not something esoteric or aristocratic, but something which works in every man, moving the peasant in peasant-like ways and the courtier in ways which befit the refinement of his nature. It inspires the rude trick of the country gallant bent upon cuckolding his stupid neighbor as well as the romantic passion which sends the hero overseas in pursuit of the mistress whom pirates have ravished. Because of it the tricky priest deludes the rustic maid with his story of how the Devil must be put in Hell, and because of it Isabella dies of grief. But such variety is only a proof of the universality of the power. Working everywhere, in high and low, it moves the world and gives it its significance.

And if, then, a love which remains essentially sensuous even at its most romantic is the most nearly intangible value which the " Decameron " anywhere recognizes, the fact is of enormous significance both in its positive and its negative aspects. On the one hand Boccaccio enthrones a purely *natural* force as the supreme power in the universe and on the other he dispenses with all considerations which are not founded upon experience with nature. A certain lip service is, to be sure, paid to God and to religion; the characters sometimes refer in purely conventional terms to a life beyond this life or to powers which are outside of nature; but they do not really believe in either and if their deification of love enables them sometimes to conceive of life in poetic terms they see love as merely a refinement upon animality. It is not for them as it was for Dante an imperfection through which they are made aware of a Perfection existing above Nature, and so, by a sort of anticipation of the more scientific naturalism which was to follow, they regard man much as a modern rationalist would regard him since, for them, too, he is already a risen animal not a fallen angel and one must look not at the sky but at the earth if one would explain him. Thus the spiritual centre of the universe is shifted, Nature replaces God, and romantic naturalism has begun. The secret of the soul is to be found not in theology but in romance and Venus not Jehovah is the ruler of the universe. The divine spark

planted in man is his power to love; it is under love's influence that the soul develops; and in the enjoyment of love
is the supreme felicity.

Such naturalism involves as its corollary an interest in common things and in vulgar men which had hitherto been regarded as unworthy the attention of the philosopher or the
artist. To Dante, man at his greatest was the most imperfect
thing worth considering, because if one began with him one
had as a subject of contemplation all the realities which lie
between him and God. But to Boccaccio, man at his greatest
was the end not the beginning. In surveying the world one
must go down, not up, from the point which he represents.
Love working among the humblest makes them too significant, and so the " Decameron " is concerned with all the vulgar manifestations of human life which Dante would have
scorned, while it leaves out nearly everything which would
have seemed to him significant.

Both its subject matter and the manner of its treatment was
novel not merely for Boccaccio but for any writer who was,
like him, a self-conscious artist. In refusing for the moment
to concern himself with either learning or spirituality he was
turning his back upon the whole tradition of polite literature
and in deigning to treat the manners, appetites, and actions
of vulgar life he was yielding himself to a spirit which had
never before been considered worthy of a voice save in stories
or poems which made no pretense to artistic finish.

Nor was Boccaccio himself unaware of the apparent sole-
cism, for he was no abstract thinker capable of offering any
explanation like that which has just been given and the " Decameron " is the result of the triumph of his bourgeois in-

stincts over the artistic creed which he had naïvely inherited. Whenever in the course of the book he speaks in his own person, he is careful to dismiss the work as a mere trifle intended for the amusement of ladies and as such both he and his learned friends were bound to regard it. He apparently did not dare to send it to Petrarch and the light in which the latter regarded it is clearly shown in a letter which he wrote to Boccaccio some twenty years after the book was complete and in which he tells how he had accidentally come across the book " published I presume during your early years " and how, since it was obviously intended " for the multitude," he had merely skimmed through it. But though Boccaccio made no protest against this cavalier dismissal and though, indeed, he would doubtless have approved of it, yet the book was nevertheless his one enduring work for the very reason that it was conceived in a spirit which Petrarch despised and of which Boccaccio himself was distrustful. It was the harmony, existing only for the few brief years between his instincts and his conscious effort, which made the accomplishment possible and which explains the perfection which the " Decameron " alone among all Boccaccio's works can be said to possess.

Ceasing in it to concern himself with moral or philosophical abstractions, allowing free play to the sceptical common sense which was natural to him and indulging without restraint his quick sympathy for human things, he seems suddenly to have cast off all spiritual affectations and with them have disappeared also all affectations of style. All the tawdry ornament, all the inappropriate learning, and all the childish ingenuity which seem in his earlier works the signs of a mind conscious of a weakness for which it is desperately endeavouring to compensate, have here been discarded. Boccaccio, who had seemed before so confused, so torn, and so uncertain, is here completely integrated and completely at his ease. Before, he had perpetually lacked confidence in his education, his knowledge, his capacities, and his temperament. Here he is dealing and permitting himself to deal with material which nowhere escapes his grasp because it nowhere transcends his knowledge or his understanding, and he is aware of that fact. He feels completely at home in the world with which he is dealing. Here are no characters he does not know, no emotions he cannot feel, no aspirations too exalted for him to share and no thoughts too fine for his plain mind. Knowing what he has to say and knowing that he can say it, his simple, dignified prose marches forward with confident ease.

Here, in brief, his spirit has ceased its efforts to be something which it is not. He no longer gasps grotesquely while he tries to breathe an air too rarefied for his lungs. He has given up trying to be learned and spiritual. These people — merchants, citizens, lovers and peasants — are his own people. Like himself they are all in spirit members of that *populo grasso* — whose crassness Dante despised — and they are not ashamed to find the human more interesting than the divine. Their robust appetites, their low laughter, their homely habits, are those of his own people. He knows them and they know him. They may range from peasant to courtier and their adventures may include the high adventure as well as the practical joke, but even in love they are still human and with bodies no less than minds and souls.

The " Decameron," so often called the Human Comedy

of Boccaccio in contrast with the Divine Comedy of Dante, constitutes, it has been said, not an evolution but a revolution in literature. Perhaps the attempt which has here been made to trace the process by which Boccaccio, driven on by the intensity of his own secular experience, first broke through the medieval tradition of other-worldliness in order to express his own emotions and then interpreted the society of his times from a similar point of view, will make more easily understandable the spirit of his *magnum opus,* but its perfection must still seem the result of something not less than a mutation. And if Boccaccio hesitated to recognize the work as the true expression of his temper, the generations which followed embraced it with an enthusiasm which revealed how clearly they recognized themselves in its unadulterated naturalism. In the hands of Bandello, Cincio and Sachetti the novella became one of the most popular of literary forms and was passed on to other races where its appearance was always a sign that the Renaissance had arrived, but the spirit was even more important than the form. Dante might become a revered classic and Petrarch be remembered as the perfect type of the literary man, but the liberated animality of Boccaccio continued to be the most perfect type of the norm of Renaissance character.

And never, be it added, was that character more amiably embodied. Materialism, scepticism, and sensuality are doubtless socially dangerous qualities. It may be that the road from the " Decameron " leads inevitably down to the abyss of Aretino unless it be quickly abandoned. But Boccaccio himself reveals only the sunny side of his qualities. In him the senses are not jaded but still fresh and young. Their delights are newly discovered and, as though escaped from the gloomy confines of a monastery, he looks with innocent eagerness upon the " fair new world that hath such creatures in it." Debauchery is possible only to those for whom pleasure has lost its freshness and the Renaissance was to grow debauched, but Boccaccio never passed beyond the youth of his senses. Above all he was never touched, even for a moment, by that lust of cruelty which grew as his successors debilitated themselves with indulgence. "Giovanne della Tranquilitate," his contemporaries called him, and though the epithet may seem, in some respects, hardly appropriate to one who had been so torn by a passion as he had been, it does, nevertheless, serve in some measure to suggest the joy with which he regarded all natural beauty. For centuries human life had been regarded as of no account in itself and now he was among the first to embark upon it with fresh delight. He came into Nature as to an inheritance and his heritage seemed all that any heart could desire.

V

If only we might take our farewell of Boccaccio at the moment when the " Decameron " was achieved, we might think of him as one of the happiest of mortals. It would be pleasant to imagine that its harmony was for him an enduring one and to suppose that he passed his life in a serenity so complete. Such, however, was not the case. As the book was, artistically, his one perfect work, so too the serenity of mind which it represents was for him but a moment in the midst of a life singularly confused by moral problems with which he had not the strength of mind to deal. The timidity which had bewildered his youth returned as his vitality waned and he fell once more into a perplexity, this time sorer yet than that which had beset him in the days when he had struggled to interpret his passions in terms of Dantesque mysticism.

We have already seen with what difficulty his instincts won their victory over the formulated philosophy of the Church and we have remarked that the reason played no part in the winning of that victory. We must remember that the rational defence of sceptical materialism was yet to be formulated and we must realize that the naturalism of the " Decameron " was a truancy not a rebellion. Boccaccio had never denied the authority of the Church and never questioned the ultimate validity of its doctrine. In him the lust of life had asserted itself and for the moment he had cast off without ever conquering the mystic asceticism which was the orthodox doctrine, not only of the Church, but of art and scholarship as well. When he told the guide who conducted him in " L'Amorose Visione " that he would return in time to enter the narrow gate he was not speaking in jest for he had never dared to deny to himself that only through that gate could he be saved. He was free only so long as his vitality should endure, and once the eager tumult of his sensibilities should subside sufficiently to allow him to hear once more the dictates of his conscious mind it was inevitable that he should, with a sigh, resign the delights of this world in order to gain the next. And that moment had already arrived. An incident reminded him with cruel force that his youth was past and with it there passed also the confidence which had enabled him to dismiss with youthful insouciance all the considerations whose absence makes the " Decameron " possible.

Boccaccio was forty-one years old when he had the misfortune to fall once more in love. Taken by the charms of a widow of Florence, he addressed to her an amorous declaration and she not only refused but mocked him as well. His indiscretion was whispered about the town and, humiliated in the depths of his soul, he took his revenge in the ferocious satire known as " Il Corbaccio." This incident will serve better perhaps than any other, to mark the turning-point of his career. It shattered the glad confidence in life which had sustained him, and from that moment he began the descent which led him at last to a troubled old age.

If Boccaccio had possessed one ounce of what is commonly called spirituality, the new orientation of his thoughts would not have been for him so utter a calamity. He might, having accepted the flesh and celebrated its beauty as frankly and as fully as any man has ever done, have come at last to transcend it, but he was, however much his conscience might trouble him, forever incapable of becoming more than the natural man. His idea of felicity was purely pagan; he loved the life of the senses and there was nothing in the Christian philosophy which was capable of either joying or fructifying his spirit. Sin and salvation were terrifying words whose meaning he sought in vain to comprehend while he succeeded in doing no more than perplexing himself. Asceticism was for him no more than a denial without compensations, and religion no more than the shadow of fear. It froze the genial current of his soul and reduced him to a querulous frustration. For a nature such as his there is no choice but that between paganism and the obscene, inverted fleshiness which is its obverse. The animality of Boccaccio could be corrupted but it could not be refined, and he was one of those for whom the sense of sin is merely a degradation.

Nothing could be more surprising as coming from the author of the " Decameron " than " Il Corbaccio " proves to be. He who had described so often the beauty and charm of women turns to denounce them in unmeasured terms and he who had just completed the work which celebrates Love as the *summum bonum* of life pronounces an anathema upon it. " Woman," he says, " is an imperfect animal " and after heaping upon the whole sex all the abuse which the ingenuity of thirteen centuries of asceticism had devised, he turns to denounce the monstrous illusion which leads men to suppose that good can come from the love of such creatures. Turning to the angelic visitor who has come to show him the error of his ways he demands to know what he shall do in order to redeem himself from his errors and the guide replies: " You have loved these creatures because they have seemed beautiful to you and because they appeared libidinously delightful. I want you to hate all such beauty which has been or may be for you the occasion of so much sin; I want you to take revenge for the offenses you have committed and in that will be salvation both for you and for them."

Nothing in all the book is original with Boccaccio. In it he merely repeats the commonplaces of monkish satire and it might quite as well have been written in a tenth-century cloister. Smarting under a personal humiliation he not only completely loses his equilibrium but relapses at once into the darkest abyss of the middle ages. The flesh in which he had trusted so much had betrayed him and *naïf* that he was, he had no philosophy of his own which would enable him to digest that betrayal, no motive for denying any longer that man and the world are vile.

During the years which immediately followed he grew steadily more grave. He devoted himself to the scholarly pursuits which to his now troubled soul seemed relatively innocent and at last, some eight years later, the final blow fell. He was living in the still hated Florence when he received a mysterious visit from a man who represented himself as a messenger from a certain Pietro Petroni who had recently died in the odour of sanctity after having been the recipient of certain visions. Boccaccio, he reported, had but a few years to live and it was time, if he valued the safety of his soul, to abandon the study of secular poetry. Oppressed as he had been with hardships and worry, Boccaccio was stricken with terror. Gone was the light-hearted scepticism which had led him in the " Decameron " to mock at priestly tricks, and in a panic he wrote to Petrarch his intention to burn his manuscripts.

Fortunately the calm Petrarch, incapable alike of the full-blooded paganism which had once been Boccaccio's and of the superstitious terror which now overcame his naïve soul, wrote him a long letter full of humanistic commonplaces. The mysterious visitor was, he said, not improbably an impostor, and even if he were not, his assurance that Boccaccio had but a few years more to live implied no more than he himself already knew. As for secular learning, much could be said for it. Perhaps it was not the most suitable occupation for a man whose life was already dragging to a close, but some little indulgence was permitted to a man who had loved it all his life as Boccaccio had done. It would be best to take no extreme and sudden steps. Let Boccaccio prepare himself gradually to meet his maker and let him console himself with the thought that the piety of a learned man is more valuable than that of one who is ignorant.

Evidently Boccaccio resolved to follow the advice of his less impetuous friend for he did not burn his papers, but the last vestige of rebellion was gone from his spirit and from now on he conformed to the learned conventions of his time. Shortly before he had composed in Latin the gloomy "*De Casibus Illustrium Virorum*" in which, with a spirit completely medieval, he catalogues the sad fates of once fortunate men, and now, under the press of poverty, he undertook to give some public lectures upon the subject of the Divine Comedy. But even this he regretted for he had turned his back upon everything which the Renaissance represented, and he who had once delighted to write for the pleasure of fair ladies now held it a profanation to expose the secrets of the learned to vulgar understanding. In this as in everything he revealed how utterly he had reversed himself and when he wrote at an uncertain date his defence of poetry which occurs in a compilation called " *Genealogia deorum gentilium,*" he had come to the point where he could say no more than the timid clerk could say. In his youth poetry had seemed to him the most glorious of human achievements because it celebrated and made immortal the deeds of men; because, in a word, it gave dignity to human life; but now he could only say: " I confess it would be far better to study the sacred writings than these, even although they are good. I think such studies are more acceptable to God, to the Pope and to the Church. But we are not all nor always led by the rare passion and so sometimes are drawn to Poetry."

Sadder still is the letter which he wrote a year or two before his death to a friend who had remarked that he possessed Boccaccio's works. The man of sixty looked back upon his maturest achievement without favour. Not only had he lost, with his ebbing vitality, the joyous acceptance of nature which had made him the first of modern times to find her all sufficient, but his soul, shrunk to a prudish timidity, could no longer understand the man he had been. He would not, he said, accuse his friend of wrong-doing if he should follow out his intention of reading these works when he had nothing better to do, but he begged him above all not to read the tales to the ladies of his household. He knew how likely they were to corrupt an honest heart and he had no desire that respectable ladies should think of him as a licentious old man. He had written them in his youth and he blushed for his sin.

Two years later Boccaccio was dead and as one surveys his career in retrospect one cannot but be struck with the fact that it is, in certain aspects, strangely simple and in others strangely complex. Nothing, for example, could exceed the naïveté with which he permitted the mere accidents of his own existence to determine the premises of what served him as a philosophy of life. He believed in love because love had made him happy and because, even when Fiammetta had betrayed him, he had sweet and dignified memories. But when the widow of Florence mocked as well as refused him, he behaved as though he had never dreamed before that such a thing could happen and he revised the universe in order to denounce the woman who had caused him this bitter humiliation. Yet naïve as his organization was, the vivacity of his nature was sufficient to make it possible for him to do as much as one man can do towards the creation of a new literature. A certain mere insouciance served him in an effort to throw off a philosophy which no mind had successfully combated, and in a moment of gaiety he revealed the Fourteenth Century Italian to himself.

Moreover, one cannot fail to note how the curve of his life anticipated that of the Renaissance as a whole. The latter plumbed depths to which he would never have descended but like him it was still haunted by supernatural fears which it strove to forget but could not reason away, and its naturalism was debauched for the very reason that it was uneasy. The conceptions which had nourished the genius of Dante were wholly alien to its nature and it could make no use of them, but religion, reduced to fear, hung the shadow of superstition over the whole epoch. A gloomy apprehension, ready at any moment to express itself in an outburst of fanatical penitence like that which broke over Florence under the influence of Savonarola, haunted its choicest spirits and they had no philosophy capable of defending their instinctive naturalism.

Two centuries after Boccaccio's death all Italy, stricken by fear, allowed its new culture to decline into the gloomy formalism which supervened after the Council of Trent and Boccaccio, who was, in a sense, the epitome of the age, anticipated its end when he prophetically relapsed into a cheerless acquiescence in a dead tradition. The equilibrium of the " Decameron," like that of the age which produced it, was unstable. Its premises had never been either reasoned out nor completely comprehended by the man who assumed them and they were lost to him as soon as the gay mood in which they had been generated passed away. At his best and most original, Boccaccio never advanced in thought beyond a charming, childish naïveté and he could never, save for a few happy moments, believe in himself. Never robust enough to sustain the role of pioneer, he was frightened by his own temerity, and fears which belonged by rights only to others clouded in the end a spirit which was, in its own nature, as sunny as Naples itself.

MIGUEL DE CERVANTES

I

BOCCACCIO had solved in his own summary fashion the problem of the Renaissance as that problem had revealed itself to him in the earliest dawn. Yet his solution did not, as we have already seen, last out a lifetime even for him, for he died in despair and the generations which followed must have smiled at his simplicity even while they admired the perfection of his literary skill.

Waking to find in himself impulses unrecognized in the medieval view of human nature, he had seen the world under the form of a simple dualism — the promises and threats of a dogmatic church versus the insistent demands of rebellious flesh. The problem as it presented itself to him was largely a pragmatic one — a question of choice between the vivid pleasures of love and the shadowy satisfaction said to be found by others in the peace of God, between the bright court on the one hand and the cold monastery on the other. Seeing it almost exclusively in these simplest, most practical, and crudest terms, he was too little intellectual, too little capable of being interested in abstractions, to be concerned with even its next simplest aspect (that of faith versus reason) and he certainly never dreamed under how many forms — various as are the temperaments of men and subtle as the mind is capable of being — it would present itself.

But the Renaissance was too eager and too keen of mind to discover in itself no more than a renewed longing for those delights which Ovid had celebrated and the Church bid men forget. As soon as the medieval synthesis began to dissolve, questions analogous to that with which Boccaccio had struggled presented themselves in every department of both active and speculative life. As a *moyen homme sensuel* he had had to choose between the pleasures of this world and those of the next but as a result of the same general movement the philosopher had to choose between reason and faith; the physicist between experiment and metaphysics; and the artist between realism and idealization. Wherever men turned or to whatever department of thought they devoted themselves, they came into the presence of some form or other of the fundamental conflict between that truth of the senses and that dream of the ideal which had revealed itself to Boccaccio so crudely, and all that is most vital in their thought resolves itself into the effort to discover the relationship between the two. Not only was Boccaccio's solution too summary to be satisfactory but even his perception of the problem was too elementary a one to seem long important except as the basis of a certain isolated work of art. To the philosophers and the critics of the Sixteenth and Seventeenth Centuries he was already almost as much of a *naïf* as he is to us.

Miguel de Cervantes was the next supreme genius who expressed himself by the creation of a new form of prose fiction and to move forward through time to him is to find

oneself in a world far more aware of the intellectual implications of Renaissance thought than Boccaccio's had been,
and in a society shaken to its foundations by the political
results of this thought. Secure in its pride and power, the
Church had smiled tolerantly at the pranks of Boccaccio
and at those who followed him; it had yielded to pagan
tendencies and adopted for itself the same loose compromise which had satisfied for a time the author of the " Decameron." But though it could endure a Borgia upon the
papal throne it could not endure the stubborn argumentative
rebellion of the north which had too little genius for imaginative literature and too little taste for pageants or balls to be
satisfied by a merely careless permission to enjoy itself.
Satire could be tolerated and even debauchery could be tolerated but rationalistic dissent could not and in 1562, when
Cervantes was fifteen years old, there was opened the great
third session of the Council of Trent whose purpose was to
consider, not merely what steps should be taken to combat
Protestantism, but more especially how the still Catholic
countries could be set in order, and its shadow lay over the
whole period of Cervantes' effective life.

With the opening of the council the epoch of the Church's
compromise with paganism was over; it set itself fiercely
against rationalism in any form and it enforced its discipline in the torture chamber of the Inquisition. But it set itself hardly less earnestly against the practical paganism
which it had formerly condoned. The " Decameron," against
which no one had effectively protested for two centuries,
had been placed upon the Index of Prohibited Books a
short time before and, slight as that fact is, it is highly sig-

nificant. It reveals the temper of the new times and it will serve to suggest how different was the atmosphere in which the mind of Cervantes developed from that in which Boccaccio had lived.

Spain, indeed, had never had a joyous adolescence like that of Italy. No generation there had ever waked as Boccaccio's did to find a bright new day fit to be enjoyed with pagan fulness by fresh senses. Spanish blood flowed in the veins of the Borgias and in those of some others who embodied the cruelest and darkest tendencies of the Italian Renaissance, but that very fact is enough to suggest that the race had no talent for the more innocent, faunlike sensuality of Boccaccio and his fellows and certainly Spain itself never embraced nature with any such joyous, untroubled delight. Through the earlier Renaissance she lay sombre and almost sullen, but she roused herself to leap with passion into the Catholic reaction. The blood of the heretics pleased the worst of her citizens and the most liberal, like Cervantes, were essentially sober men. She could be fanatical or she could be subtle, but she could not play as Italy had played nor see the world in the gay colours of the " Decameron."

And so, just as we could not understand Boccaccio except against the background of his race and time, we cannot understand Cervantes without picturing him, not against the sunny sky of Naples, but against one of those threatening, storm-tossed cloudscapes which El Greco loved to paint. Cervantes was no inquisitor, no theologian even. He had known the world and loved the world. But he saw life in sombrer colours than Boccaccio had seen it and his problem was one far more complicated than that presented to Boccaccio, whose warm blood directed him in the making of a simple pragmatic choice. He too had to write a romance in the course of which the central problem of the Renaissance — the conflict between the ideal and the real — should be solved; but he could neither see it in such simple terms nor solve it in so summary a fashion by merely objectifying the one element and disregarding the other.

Perhaps "Don Quixote" is an achievement no more startling than the "Decameron" and in one sense the two are equal, for if the earlier created the novella as a literary form the other represents its author's discovery of the essential method and spirit of the modern novel. But "Don Quixote" is a far more complicated and subtle thing. We miss in it Boccaccio's simple perfection and we get in exchange a maturity which his age had not reached and perceptions of which his spirit was never capable. In one book is the free laughter of youth, untroubled and a little cruel; in the other the smile which does not bubble up from the heart but which plays around the lips of the thinker and which implies no triumph. Life to Cervantes was no ten days' entertainment and ultimate wisdom was not to be discoursed while one sat above a plague-stricken city, with a pleasant company of youths and maidens in the midst of a flower-besprinkled meadow.

II

Almost nothing is known of Cervantes' early youth but he was born in 1547 the son of an apothecary-surgeon and there was little in his subsequent experience likely to develop in him any pure ebullition of animal spirits for he lived always in close contact with the sternest realities. His father was, apparently, an improvident man and he himself entered as a youth into the service of the Cardinal Aquiviva. In 1569 he was in Rome, possibly on some business of the Cardinal's, but at least as early as 1570 he had enlisted in the Spanish army. Two years before he had contributed some poems to a volume commemorating the death of King Philip's third wife, but it was as a soldier that he first sought the glory which he was all his life to pursue.

Concerning his earliest campaigns we are left in ignorance but on October 7, 1570 he was on board the *Marquesa* when that ship took part in the battle of Lepanto. Some years later a companion had occasion to describe in an affidavit the conduct of Cervantes on that memorable day and the incident, one of the few of his life concerning which we have any detailed record, happens by good fortune to be one very far from impertinent to the interpretation of his literary work.

The young soldier, we learn, lay below deck ill of fever. His companions urged him to remain where he was, but he, indignantly rejecting their advice and declaring that he would rather die for his God and his King than lie in this ignoble retirement, begged to be placed in the most dangerous position. Accordingly he was told off by the captain of a galley to command a party of twelve in a long boat put off to the left of the Spanish fleet, and in that exposed position he received three bullets from the infidel guns. Two penetrated his chest. The third maimed his left hand for life but maimed it, as he himself said, " for the greater glory of the right."

Some two centuries after his death it was to be said of him (foolishly enough) that he " laughed the chivalry of Spain away " and there have always been unimaginative people to see in his great romance only the mockery of a sturdy common sense holding up the romantic folly of the idealist to merciless ridicule; but he had, nevertheless, spent the major part of his existence in beating the wings of his spirit against the bars of the commonplace and the little story of Lepanto furnishes the first of many proofs that a worldly prudence was not the most distinguishing feature of his character. In his youth at least he participated to the fullest possible extent in the spirit of Spanish gallantry at the time when that gallantry was at its height, and the one adjective which will perfectly describe his action in rising from a sick bed (where he might have decently remained) in order to expose himself to the dangers of battle is an adjective which was not then known, for it is none other than that " quixotic " now to be found in the dictionary of every European language. Cervantes honoured — as some passages of his great romance will show — the profession of the soldier, and he honoured it, not because he thirsted after conquests, but because in war might be found some flitting earthly shadows of the Chivalry which existed in its ideal form only in the land of romance.

After his convalescence Cervantes took part in several other campaigns including that which resulted in the capture of Tunis by Don John of Austria, but five years after Lepanto the ship on which he was returning to Spain fell into the hands of three Turkish galleys. Cervantes and his companions were carried off to Algiers to be sold into captivity and there, despite four gallant but ineffectual attempts to escape, he spent five years more of cruel slavery. Finally, after great difficulty, his family succeeded in raising the necessary ransom and by the end of 1580 he was back in Madrid.

He was now thirty-three years old and an experienced soldier, but he was soon to discover how little the certificates of distinguished military service which he presented to the government availed him in seeking a livelihood. Apparently he was employed as some sort of official messenger but poverty oppressed the whole of his family and we find him in 1583 pawning, in behalf of his sister, five rolls of taffeta which she had received as a gift. The first flush of his youth had already been passed in gallant services but he was exactly where he started so far as any assured position in the world was concerned, and yet neither now nor at any time did his writings reveal any trace of disillusionment or bitterness. He had received, to be sure, none of the rewards of the knight, but he was already too deeply penetrated with the spirit of that Renaissance Platonism which insisted upon and accepted the inevitable imperfection of all actuality, to be surprised at that. He never repented his own quixoticism for it had been, no doubt, its own reward.

Turning now from the sword to the pen he produced

some twenty or thirty plays (of which only two survive) without, apparently, deriving any very great profit from them, and in 1584 he sold to a townsman all his rights in his first romance, "Galatea." Few people will care to read this work today but one turns to it for some clue as to the development of Cervantes' mind. What was the inner life of the man who had passed fourteen toilsome years since the quixoticism of Lepanto?

Two traditions of prose fiction — the one poetic, the other realistic — lay ready to his hand. The second was particularly rich, for not only had Boccaccio showed how the novella might be made the vehicle of a satiric common sense, but in Spain itself there already existed in addition the so-called picaresque tale of realistic adventure — a prose form which could be made to contain as much observation of contemporary life as an author had the talent to make. Since it is the nearest, though still distant, relative of "Don Quixote," one would naturally expect it to be the form which Cervantes would choose in view of the fact that his own life had assuredly been adventurous enough and of a sort sufficiently well calculated to develop in him a sense of the importance of the meaner realities. Had he "learned his lesson" in youth, had there been in him any capitulation to prudence and common sense, he would assuredly have done so; but one will search the "Galatea" in vain for any evidence of interest in matters of every day.

An artificial story of shepherd and shepherdess, it stems, not from either experience or any tradition of realistic fiction, but instead from those idealized pastorals of which Boccaccio's "Ameto" is an example. To us it is tawdry, and faded, and dull, but it was precious to Cervantes because it was something purely "ideal." As a soldier he had sought to pluck honour from the cannon's mouth, and when he turned to letters he turned, not to the satiric form which the Renaissance had invented to express its perception of things as they are, but rather to the one which embodied its dream of the Golden Age; and there is good reason for believing that it remained, faded though it now is, his favourite work because it best embodied one of those ideals which seemed to him the soul of literature.

All the money he was ever to receive for the "Galatea" had been paid into his hand — and probably spent — before the work was published. Desperately fighting to keep his head above water, he wrote two more plays (both now lost) but it was soon evident that he could not hope to support himself by his pen and with every sign of reluctance he admitted his practical failure as an author. In 1587 he obtained a position as commissary with the Spanish forces and was soon plunged into the complicated business of victualling the great expedition which was to meet with disaster off the coast of England. In 1590, after the *débâcle* had taken place, he drew up a petition to the king, recalling his past services and asking to be nominated to a post in America. The refusal of the request with a note which recommended him to "seek something nearer home" may have saved a genius to the world but it cannot have brought much comfort to a hardly pressed man.

The familiarity which Cervantes' writings exhibit with the thought of his time would seem to imply that he never gave up his intellectual interests and he doubtless solaced himself with books during even his darkest years, but his practical difficulties must have absorbed him more and more. Some years before, he had married a girl eighteen years his junior who brought him only a modest dowry and now as he was passing through middle age into physical decline he had a household which he could barely support. His pay was reduced and it was besides chronically in arrears. So desperate were his straits that in 1590 he had to find a friend to stand security for him when he received on credit some cloth for his clothing and he was soon to be involved in a tangle destined to harass him for years. When the official accountants examined his bills and vouchers they discovered a deficit, not particularly large but larger than any sum he could raise, and though there is not the slightest reason for suspecting anything worse than bad bookkeeping he was sentenced to jail in 1592. After a short time he was released, but it was years before he was actually free of all the complications in which he had become entangled, and his poverty was more desperate than ever.

Nor was there as the time approached for the writing of his masterpiece any lightening in his life. The prologue to "Don Quixote," published when he was in his fifty-eighth year, speaks of the work as being " just what might be begotten in a jail " and whether or not we take this literally and assume that the work was conceived or begun during another brief period which he spent in confinement, the fact remains that for him all life had been in some sense a prison. In spite of his persistent idealism he was, at fifty-eight, a failure both outwardly and inwardly. Not only had he failed as a soldier, a public servant, and an author, but these failures were the signs of an inward incapacity to adjust himself to the world.

III

Though documents to prove the fact are lacking, it is probable that Cervantes was again committed to prison at Seville in 1602. Not since his days as an Algerian captive had he been so beset with troubles but it was about this time, whether he was at the moment in jail or out of it, that the whimsy which was to grow into a masterpiece first flickered across his troubled mind. Perhaps he had been even then attempting to divert himself with some of those debased romances of chivalry, all full of indomitable knights and marvellous adventures, which furnished the library of Don Quixote. Certainly he had at one time or another read widely and, one may judge, with considerable delight in that branch of literature. But circumstances were hardly favourable for the appreciation of such fantastic imaginings. The world in which he found himself was all too different from the world of enchanted forests and wandering maidens in which Amadis de Gaul found himself. No amiable enchanter and no invincible knight was likely to deliver *him* from prison. He had never suffered wrong at the hands of any giant or sorcerer but he had, on the other hand, been sorely oppressed by just those humble difficulties involved in getting food or clothing which were never mentioned in the romances of chivalry.

Thousands had read these books with avidity. Suppose that one, with slightly disordered wit, should lose the capacity to distinguish between imagination and reality and suppose that he, equipping himself as best he could, should sally forth into the humdrum world. How unlikely would he be to encounter any of those ogres whom he was prepared to meet but how certainly would he find himself involved in difficulties not to be solved by gallantry or honour! Helmet and lance would not avail him against the flock of swine which he would meet upon the road and a profession of chivalric principles would not satisfy an innkeeper.

Out of a fancy no deeper than this may well have been written the first few chapters in the course of which the Don, intoxicated with his reading, first sets out in search of adventures and succeeds in encountering nothing more dignified than a few mishaps. The witless old gentleman who charges a windmill and who allows himself to be the victim of a few practical jokes played upon him by the inmates of an inn to whom he applies for reception into the order of knighthood is no more than the two-dimensional hero of a simple burlesque. He is scarcely more than merely mad and he seemed funny chiefly because the Spaniards of that time, like the Englishmen of a later date, who used to make visits of pleasure to Bedlam, thought insanity comic.

But though Cervantes himself may not have been at first aware of the fact, the whimsy which seized him floated up from the depths of his being. It was, in fact, one of those fragments which, emerging like dreams into our consciousness, mean much more to us than we at first perceive, and his own soul was far more bound up with that of Don Quixote than he imagined when he made him so unequivocally a butt. Perhaps, as we have said, the Don was born at the moment when Cervantes had most reason to scorn all except practical wisdom; but he had not always been so hardheaded. We have only to notice how intimate is the familiarity which the Don exhibits with the details of the chivalric romances to realize how assiduously his creator had read them and we need only remember the history of his life and his previous literary efforts in order to realize how far his temperament had been from that of any mere exponent of common sense. How then could he ridicule Don Quixote without ridiculing himself, or how could he fail to sympathize with this man whose only fault was to find himself in a world which provided no opportunities for the exercise of the high and selfless principles which he wished to profess?

And so the figure which he had created in derision began to grow under his understanding and affection. Various inconsistencies in the narrative of "Don Quixote" testify to the haste with which Cervantes wrote it and reveal how impossible it would have been for him to go back over what he had already written, but he discovered possibilities as he went along and realized how deeply he was concerned in what may have at first appeared to him as merely burlesque.

Most readers first become aware of the change as the result of a certain resentment. They wince rather than laugh when some new drubbing is inflicted upon the harmless hero. Pity grows into respect and emotions change sides. Perhaps Cervantes, even as he wrote, became aware of a similar phenomenon, and certainly he began to endow his fool with more and more wisdom. Despite the insanity which makes him persist in interpreting every commonplace event in terms of romance, the Don speaks nobly, and as he grows in stature his page, Sancho Panza, grows with him. Conceived at first as no more than a simple-minded foil to his extravagant master, the latter grows wiser in one kind of wisdom as the Don grows wiser in another until, though the one is mad and the other a clown, they have come to represent the two types of human wisdom — that which knows how things really are and that which knows how they ought to be.

When faced with any given situation Sancho's wisdom teaches him immediately the most practical way in which it can be met. If promising, he knows just how it may be made to yield the greatest reward in food or money; if threatening, how it can be eluded with the minimum number of thwacks and the minimum amount of labour. But the Don is so athirst for glory that his imagination triumphs over his perceptions and he accepts whatever interpretation will enable him to exhibit the greatest virtue.

Thus upon one occasion when the pair were journeying in search of adventure, they heard a noise in the wood. The Don advanced, spear in readiness, toward the giants whom he hoped to find and when he discovered instead only a fulling mill whose alternately falling hammers were the occasion of the awful din, then Sancho mocked him. But Don Quixote unperturbed replied: "Look here, my lively gentleman, if these, instead of being fulling hammers, had been some perilous adventure, have I not, think you, shown the courage required for the attempt and the achievement? Am I, perchance, being, as I am, a gentleman, bound to know and distinguish sounds and tell whether they come from fulling mills or not; and that, when perhaps, as is the case, I have never in my life seen any, as you have, low boor as you are, that have been born and bred among them?

But turn me these six hammers into six giants, and bring them to beard me, one by one or all together, and if I do not knock them head over heels, then make what mockery of me you like."

And who can say at just what point in his reasoning the madness of the Don begins? Who doubts that the courage to face giants is both more admirable and more rare than the ability to recognize a fulling mill when one hears it and what moralist will deny that virtue consists rather in the inward readiness than in the chance presence of circumstances which call it forth? Who, in a word, will not laugh with Sancho and yet wish that it were possible to put the laughter on the other side?

The fertility of Cervantes' invention has been many times praised but the real marvel is not so much that he could devise endless adventures for his Knight and Squire but that in every one of them each character should be, as in the brief adventure just referred to, both right and wrong. Never by any chance does the knight win; and yet never, in another sense does he lose. At the beginning of each new incident we see why he is going to fail but we never feel that he ought to do so. In derision he is dubbed " The Knight of the Rueful Countenance " but, like many who have adopted proudly an epithet first hurled at them in mockery, he wears it with pride instead of shame. It is not his business to be successful or to be gay — the Sanchos can be that — but rather to be consistent. Chivalry is the noblest ideal which he knows and he will not ask if it pays.

In the delightful twenty-fifth chapter of the first part the mere extravagance of the Don reaches its highest point.

He has proceeded to the most rugged spot to be found in a certain mountainous district and when Sancho demands of him what he proposes to do in such an out-of-the-way place he replies:

Have I not told thee that I mean to imitate Amadis here, playing the victim of despair, the madman, the maniac, so at the same time to imitate valiant Rolland, when at the fountain he had evidence of the fair Angellica having disgraced herself with Medoro and through grief thereat went mad, and plucked up trees, troubled the water of clear springs, slew shepherds, destroyed flocks, burned huts, leveled houses, dragged mares after him, and perpetrated a hundred thousand other outrages worthy of everlasting renown and record. And though I have no intention of imitating Rolland, or Orlando, or Rotolando (for he went by all these names) step by step in all the mad things he did, said and thought, I will make a rough copy to the best of my power of all that seems to me most essential.

And when Sancho protests " that the knights who behaved in this way had provocation and cause for these follies and penances " and when he demands " What lady has rejected you, or what evidence have you found that the Lady Dulcinea del Tobosco has been trifling with Moor or Christian? " the Don replies in a very ecstasy of gratuitous and uncalled-for virtue:

There lies the point and that is the beauty of this business of mine; no thanks to a knight-errant for going mad when he has cause; the thing is to turn crazy without any provocation, and to let my lady know, if I do this in the dry, what I would do in the moist; moreover I have abundant cause in the long separation

I have endured from my lady till death, Dulcinea del Tobosco; for as thou didst hear that Shepherd Ambrosio say the other day, in absence all ills are felt and feared; and so, friend Sancho waste no time in advising me against so rare, so happy, and so unheard-of an imitation; mad I am, and mad I must be until thou returnest with the answer to a letter that I mean to send by thee to my Lady Dulcinea; and if it be such as my constancy deserves, my insanity and penance will come to an end; and if it be to the opposite effect, I shall become mad in earnest, and, being so, I shall suffer no more.

The whole scene is presented as far as possible from Sancho's own angle of vision but, though the Don is never allowed in the whole course of the romance to be more wholly absurd than here, yet even in this passage Cervantes has a sort of respect for his madness.

At the moment he wrote it he had not forgotten that he himself had produced the first half of a romantic pastoral and some pages back he had given the half promise that it should some day be completed. He did not know just how the extravagances of romantic love could be fitted into everyday life but he did know that there was a world of art in which they had a place and he knew that here as everywhere the madness of the Don consisted in nothing except the refusal to make a distinction between what was possible to the imagination and what was possible in the pursuits of everyday life. The peerless Dulcinea was in reality only a country wench but even had she been more she would still be less than her lover would imagine her and he puts into the mouth of the Don a real defense: " Thinkest thou that the Amarillises, the Phillises, the Sylvias, the Dianas, the Galateas, the Filidas, and all the rest of them that the books, the ballads, the barbers' shops, the theatres are full of, were really and truly ladies of flesh and blood?" Imagination has created all the most perfect ladies. Without it there could be no poetry and he who sees his lady just as she is is no lover worthy of the name. Just where does imagination end and madness begin? Cervantes, in short, never doubted that his Don was mad but he perceived a noble method in that madness. He who believes nothing more than his eyes can see or his hands can touch must remain like Sancho with a peasant soul, but he who cuts himself loose from those same eyes and hands will, on the other hand, be carried like Don Quixote God only knows where.

Such was Cervantes' own predicament, lost, as he was, in the problems of the Renaissance. Uncertain how to adjust his own conduct to the conflicting claims of the idealistic impulses native to his temperament and of the humble worldly wisdom which increasing financial difficulties made more and more necessary, he was uncertain also how to find his intellectual way through the wilderness of incompatible ideas of which he, though no professional scholar, was well aware. As a man he had inclined, now toward that common-sense Aristotelianism which accepts the world revealed through the senses as the ultimate reality and now toward that Platonism (grown more common since the Renaissance) which insists that these material realities are but vain, insubstantial shadows of ideal realities; as an artist he had vacillated equally between those impulses toward poetry and romance which are the natural result of the second view and that tendency toward literal realism which is the logical accompaniment of the other. Moreover, the further he went with his comic romance the more completely did it seem to involve all these things and the more subtle were the problems which it presented. How real is the ideal world which experience never reveals but the existence of which aspiration and desire affirm? Is it wiser to surrender as Sancho does to the senses and successfully achieve the few gross satisfactions which they promise or to pledge one's allegiance to higher things and to compensate with inward success for outward failure?

Following thus his fancy wherever it would lead him, discovering always new Quixoticisms for his hero and new examples of naïve shrewdness for his Sancho, Cervantes wrote on and on without coming, apparently, any nearer to an answer to the questions which teased him. The book had already grown to very substantial proportions and it was necessary to call a halt even if no conclusion had been reached. Books, however delightful they may be to their authors, must restrain themselves within reasonable dimensions if they expect to find readers, and Cervantes was, besides, very badly in need of the money which this one might possibly bring him.

With a wife and an illegitimate daughter (offspring of a vague amour which had taken place long long ago) to care for, he had not for some years had any regular means of support. As far back as 1598 we find him reduced to a state where he was compelled to find security that he would pay for two hundredweight of biscuit within three months, and though by the time the first part of " Don Quixote " was completed he had doubtless managed to get his release from prison he was still in desperate straits. At least the narrative could be brought to some sort of temporary conclusion and so he sends the curate and the barber of the Don's own village out to meet him. They succeed in persuading the redoubtable knight that a temporary rest from his adventuring would be wise and they convey him, full of high thoughts though he is, back to the village in a cart filled with straw. But though the curate launches out again into a denunciation of all chivalric literature, the result of the Don's adventures, far from curing him, has been merely to infect even Sancho with some faint tincture of the chivalric spirit, for to his wife who demands: "Now tell me, my friend, what have you made by your squirings? What gown have you brought me back? What shoes for your children?" Sancho replies with evasions: "But I may tell you this much by the way, that there is nothing in the world more delightful than to be a person of consideration, squire to a knight errant, and a seeker of adventures. To be sure most of those one finds do not end as pleasantly as one could wish, for out of a hundred that one meets with, ninety-nine will turn out cross and contrary. I know by experience, for out of some I came blanketed, and out of others belaboured. Still, for all that, it is a fine thing to be on the lookout for what may happen, crossing mountains, searching woods, climbing rocks, visiting castles, putting up at inns, all at free quarters, and devil take the maravedi to pay." And thus, after a few references to further but unrecounted adventures of the indomitable Don, the First Part ends with a modest line slightly misquoted from Ariosto:

"Perhaps another will sing [them] with a better pick."

After that nothing remained to be done except to write an introduction which should explain to the reader what Cervantes could not quite explain to himself — the purpose and the meaning of his book. Therein he calls it "a dry, shrivelled, whimsical offspring, full of thoughts of all sorts such as never came into any other imagination"; just what " this sterile ill-timed wit of mine might beget"; "just what might be begotten in a prison, where every misery is lodged and ever doleful sound makes its dwelling." And in order to escape from the difficulty of explaining what he cannot explain he represents that a friend broke in upon his perplexity to tell him that the book needed no introduction — especially none of the learned sort then in fashion. "As this piece of yours," said the friend, "aims at nothing more than to destroy the authority and influence which books of chivalry have in the world and with the public, there is no need for you to go abegging for aphorisms from philosophers, precepts from Holy Scripture, fables from poets, speeches from orators, or miracles from saints. Strive that in reading your story the melancholy may be moved to laughter and the merry made merrier still; that the simple shall not be wearied, that the judicious shall admire the invention, that the grave shall not despise it, nor the wise fail to praise it. Finally, keep your aim fixed on the destruction of that ill-founded edifice of books of chivalry, hated by some and praised by many more; for if you succeed in this you will have achieved no small success."

Now this passage has often been cited by those who would argue that "Don Quixote " is no more than a burlesque of chivalric romance, that Cervantes never dreamed of giving the book an esoteric significance and that the whole praise which is due him is summed up in Byron's statement that "he laughed the chivalry of Spain away." We have, they argue, Cervantes' own word that he aimed "at nothing more than to destroy the authority and influence which books of chivalry have in the world," but surely it is not impertinent to point out that, here at least, we have nothing of the kind and that he has, on the contrary, invented a friend to relieve him of the necessity of defining his purpose. That friend assumes that this intention is mere burlesque and Cervantes, at loss how to explain his subtler conception, lets the statement pass. The book must please all classes and there is no need to puzzle those who will not see below the surface. "The simple shall not be wearied" but "the grave shall not despise it." "Don Quixote" is a universal book not because all can appreciate it equally or in the same way but because, like all "universal books," it can be all things to all men.

Thus accompanied by a letter of introduction no less ambiguous than himself and interlined with invisible messages for those who could read them, Don Quixote went forth into the world to conquer it.

IV

This First Part of "The Ingenious Gentleman Don Quixote de la Mancha" was issued at the beginning of the year 1605. Cervantes sold the manuscript to a bookseller and the fact that the latter secured his rights only so far as a part of Spain (Castile) was concerned has been taken to mean that he set no great store by the prospects of its popularity. But if such were indeed the case, then the bookseller was wrong and another publisher hastened to profit by his fellow's mistake. In a very short time "Don Quixote" had covered all Spain and even, though in those days fame was slow to cross national boundaries, overflowed into other countries. In 1607 an edition read eagerly over northern Europe was printed in Brussels and there are various references in English books of about the same time to show that the countrymen of Shakespeare had also become thoroughly familiar with the adventures of the Knight of the Rueful Countenance. Cervantes received but little financial profit from his success but for the first time in his life he was a famous man.

Under the circumstances one would naturally expect the speedy appearance of the Second Part. When a poverty-stricken author captures the imagination of the public as completely as Cervantes had done, when his next work seems mapped out for him and the way is prepared, not only for greater fame but for greater profit as well, one expects him to seize his opportunity. Yet Cervantes did nothing of the sort. First months and then years passed. He presented to the public his "Exemplary Novels"—a collection of short stories — and he even renewed with less success than before his effort to write plays; but while everyone else was talking about Don Quixote he had nothing more to say concerning the adventures of the man whom he had abandoned in mid-career.

Authors are sometimes hurt almost as much as they are pleased by the success of some one of their works and find themselves famous for reasons not entirely welcome. Thus Boccaccio had been led away from his own genius by the pressure of his age and it is difficult not to believe that Cervantes was all but diverted in similar fashion. He was essentially a grave and thoughtful man. He loved beautiful letters — poetry perhaps above all — and if he had created something very beautiful its beauty was of a sort too new for even him to understand. What he had done was certainly not what he had once planned. Perhaps the raucous laughter of the populace which found his hero merely funny hurt him in some half-understood way and certainly he had not intended to crown his difficult and arduous life with a farce.

This sense of failure was, moreover, fostered by the critical canons of his time. He was a man of the Renaissance and to say that is to say that he was the inheritor of a long literary tradition with which " Don Quixote " broke. The revival of interest in literature as a conscious art, accompanied as it was by a renewed study of classical models, had led to the establishment of certain recognized forms of literary expression and " Don Quixote " belonged to none of them. Men had recognized the two faces which life presents and they had evolved a class of literature appropriate to the presentation of each, but, holding as they did that a certain purity of tone was the distinguishing characteristic of true art, they were inclined to regard any mingling of forms or spirits as essentially vulgar. One might, for example, write (in either prose or verse) an epic as Homer and Virgil had done; but the epic had its laws: it scorned vulgar things and vulgar people, it recounted none but great deeds, and it was marked by an unfailing grandeur of style. And if, on the other hand, one wished to describe the adventures of common people one had not only the tale in the Italian style which Boccaccio had brought to perfection but one had besides the picaresque romance which recounted in an amusing and realistic way the rough-and-tumble adventures of a rogue living by his wits at the bottom of society. But the epic must never sink and the picaresque romance must never soar. Each was what we should call highly artificial and yet each could be brought to a certain perfection by virtue of the very fact that neither sought to comprehend any emotions not immediately consonant with the general tone of the work.

Now in the "Galatea" Cervantes had written a respectably "pure" work of art since he had adopted for it that pastoral form which was recognized in respectable literature. Toward the end of his life he was to set great store by another "pure" work — this time a heroic romance — which to us is duller if possible than the "Galatea" itself. But he could not, on the other hand, be other than aware that "Don Quixote" violated the literary canons of his age. Outwardly it was nearer to the picaresque romance than to anything else — it was strung upon a thread of comic misadventures and it not only dealt realistically with common people but carried such realism further than it had ever been carried before — yet it touched upon high things which had no place among the vulgarities of the picaresque romance and it seemed to strive for that synthesis of the comedy and the tragedy of life, which we recognize as the distinguishing mark of the modern novel but which, to the contemporaries of Cervantes, must have seemed to constitute something dangerously like a mere defiance of the ideal of stylistic purity which was thought of as distinguishing serious literature from the formlessness of mere vulgar story-telling.

And so Cervantes, much as he must have loved " Don Quixote " and clearly as he must, at moments, have perceived its greatness, hesitated to finish what he had begun. Like Boccaccio he refused to recognize the nature of his genius and like Boccaccio he turned his back upon it even after he had written his masterpiece. Though he, more than any one else, created the modern novel he continued to dream of the pure pastoral or the pure drama or the pure heroic romance and he let ten long years slip by between the publication of the first and second parts of his great work while filling the time with unsuccessful efforts to do far lesser things.

At last, however, he did send the Don forth upon new adventures. The untimely appearance of a spurious " Second Part " seems to have speeded his pen for he spoke of the bogus continuation with great bitterness and it is possible that it taught him to realize more fully how great his own work was. In any event " Don Quixote, Part Two," was concluded in time to be issued from the press in the latter part of 1615, when its author was already in his sixty-ninth year.

Hardly have we begun to read this Second Part when we

realize that important developments have taken place in the method of the work and that it is everywhere more ambitious and more rich than before, as though Cervantes, having resigned himself to the necessity of expressing himself in the form which the world had approved, was determined to make it afford a scope for every power which he possessed and every idea which he held.

On the one side the book becomes, even more completely than it was before, a realistic novel marked by a vivid fidelity never approached before and never surpassed since. Certain scenes — that for example which occurs in the fifth chapter of the Second Part where Sancho discusses his plans with his wife — might have been signed by any of those writers from Fielding to George Eliot to whom we sometimes give credit for the invention of the method by which humble character is realistically represented with humorous fidelity. And yet, while the realistic background is drawn with more consummate skill than before, the change which has taken place in the two chief characters is one which lifts them still further above the merely human level, and the greatest of the miracles wrought by Cervantes is that by which a unity is achieved under conditions which might seem to make such unity impossible.

Though these characters move through a world which is essentially a literal reflection of the one in which the readers of the book lived — though the characters themselves seem to have part of their existence in that same plane — they also transcend it. Sancho becomes, even more than he was before, an empirical philosopher and the Don, even more than he was before, his Platonistic opponent. The latter is still mad,

still incapable that is to say of interpreting the evidence of
his senses in the same way as his fellows, but his delusions
(if such they be) are systematized into a philosophy and he
comes even nearer than before to the point where he himself is able to recognize them, not as delusions, but as forms
of thought. Thus the transformation which had begun to
take place in the " First Part " was completed during the
interval which elapsed between its publication and the beginning of the " Second Part." Far from remaining a mere
object of ridicule, Don Quixote has gradually assumed qualities which make him first loved and then respected until at
last Cervantes has come so near to identifying himself with
his creation that he can permit the latter to speak for him.
That which he had created out of a whim, sent forth into the
world as a character, and received back from it as a symbol
had become eventually himself.

Those readers who have enjoyed " Don Quixote " chiefly
because of those elements which relate it to the picaresque romance have sometimes maintained that the " Second Part "
is inferior to the first. They have pointed out that the far-
cical adventures follow one another in less rapid succession
and they seem sometimes unable to appreciate the fact that
the enormously increased richness of the background and the
substitution of the comedy of character for mere burlesque
would in itself much more than compensate for any diminished emphasis upon those rough-and-tumble adventures
which, indeed, tend rather to weary than amuse most modern readers. But the truth of the matter is that by the time the
beginning of the " Second Part " was reached " Don
Quixote " had almost completely outgrown the form in

which it was originally cast and ceased to have any essential relation to the picaresque romance. Cervantes had begun it as such, intending, perhaps, no more than a diversion and almost certainly unaware that it was to be the major work of his lifetime, but as he began to put more and more into it he was compelled to create a form which would serve a purpose entirely outside the scope of the simple *genre* to which he had first thought of it as belonging.

Doubtless it would be impossible to put one's finger upon any one paragraph and say: " At this point Cervantes was for the first time aware of the implications of his story. From here on it is evident that he was, to some degree at least, aware that if he followed the adventures of his hero far enough he would be brought face to face with all the problems of his life." But once he had divined the nature of the hold which the Don had upon his affection, once he had perceived that the madness of the latter was the result, not of a mere perversity, but of a determination to see the world in a fashion more acceptable to his spirit than that adopted by those who took the senses as the sole arbiter of truth, it was inevitable that all the cruxes of Renaissance thought should be involved.

In the first place the presence of a hero who sees giants where others see windmills and who is called " mad " for no other reason than that he cannot agree with his fellows as to the interpretations to be put upon the sensations which he receives through his eyes and ears, raises at once the fundamental and much canvassed question of the dependability of these same senses. Every effort to penetrate the nature of reality must begin with some definition, tacit or explicit, of the attitude toward the validity of the evidence which they offer and Cervantes was consciously aware of this fact. Orthodox medieval philosophy had accepted their evidence as far as it went but Renaissance Platonism had sometimes questioned it. And Cervantes himself had been driven, by the very unsatisfactoriness of his own relations with the physical world, to wish, at least, that he too might dismiss the universe in which his body had its being as mere delusion.

Nor do we, indeed, have anything except the weight of vulgar opinion — surely no very satisfactory criterion of truth — to convince us that the things which the eye sees are more real than those which the imagination conceives. If the " madness " of Don Quixote were common and the " sanity " of Sancho Panza were rare then their roles would be reversed. It would be the Sanchos whom we should believe deprived of their wits, since it is only by a sort of popular vote that we can decide whether a thing " really is " a windmill or a giant and since, for all we know, the world may bear no direct relation to what anybody sees there, " sanity " may be, after all, only that species of madness which happens to be most prevalent.

But this is only the crude and obvious aspect of the problem, for even if we grant that the world as Sancho sees it corresponds more closely than does the world as Don Quixote sees it to certain realities, the question still remains whether or not those realities are the only or even the most important ones. Not even the Aristotelianism of the Middle Ages, firmly as it accepted common sense as its starting point, ever conceived the possibility that the senses revealed all or that demonstrations such as those which Sancho gave were conclusive so far as the ultimate reality and importance of things was concerned, while to Plato, whose influence had grown enormously with the Renaissance, the world of senses was only a world of distorted shadows and the realest reality could only be reached by reason when reason refused to be misled by vain appearance.

And even if, to grant still another concession, the world of Sancho's is the only world existing outside of man, are there not worlds which he has created for himself which may be no less important for him than those which he shares with the beasts? By acting as though love were more than lust and life less important than honour he has succeeded to a certain degree in making them so. If he has not actually transformed windmills into giants he has performed other miracles of the imagination and of the will no less striking by creating chivalry out of free-booting and the mystical devotion of Dante out of the animal instinct for generation.

Now the task of Cervantes was in part, as has already been hinted, one which had to do with the creation of a literary form capable of expressing a sense of the complex nature of human experience more adequately than was possible by either the satiric or the romantic *genre* which the current canons of taste recognized as legitimate. But the need for such a form grew out of the fact that his vision of life was complicated by the extent to which he had assimilated the perplexities of Renaissance thought and to which its problems — the dependability of the senses, the reality of the supersensual world, and the power of persistent idealism to create values not originally existing in the world of nature — were present to him in a form not to be solved as simply as they had been solved by either the dogmatic faith of the medieval Christian or the naïve materialism of the Renaissance sceptics.

To such a one as Boccaccio and his hard-headed fellows who may stand for this materialism in its simplest form, the medieval world of Dante had seemed a world of the merest quixoticism. Opposing the senses to the imagination, they had called upon eyes and ears to bear witness to their contention that this was a world not of giants but of windmills and that it should be treated as such. But the effect of their protest was not so much to establish their point of view as to raise a problem by making it necessary for every man either to choose between the two or to find for himself some satisfactory conception of the relations between them.

The authority of the Church finally succumbed to critical attacks and in certain departments of thought the materialists won unequivocal victories as when, for example, experience (i.e. experiment) replaced metaphysics as the method of natural science. But they did not succeed in making humanity at large content with the world of pure nature nor convince it that this world of nature was *all*. They merely drove their opponents to subtler defences of supersensual values and raised up in Cervantes the first great modern champion of that realism which finds in natural fact a challenge to discover hidden realities. Humanism, the name which we give to the most characteristic philosophy of the Renaissance during its period of highest development was not, essentially, either that revival of classical learning or that materialistic scepticism with both of which it has sometimes been identified, but rather an attempt to realize the implications of the fact that life is led upon two planes — the human and the natural — which intersect but do not coincide. It attempted to determine where the assumption that man is merely a shrewder sort of animal was fruitful and where it was not, and " Don Quixote " is a statement of this problem in comic terms.

When Cervantes wrote, it had already been discussed for at least two hundred and fifty years and he had acquired (as recent and thorough study of his work has demonstrated) a wide if not systematic familiarity with the most important expressions of Renaissance thought. Not only were his own experiences as hero calculated to provoke in him meditations upon the relative worth of such principles as led to the chivalric actions of his own youth and such as might have resulted in a more comfortable old age, but his reading had been of a kind which made it inevitable that the figures of Sancho and Don Quixote should become, as soon as he created them, symbols of the realistic and the idealistic currents of Renaissance thought. Sancho becomes essentially the representative of that realistic and critical spirit of which Boccaccio is the first great exponent and the Don rises to the point where he is able to comprehend the real reason behind his unwillingness to let the senses set the limits of his world. Thus the quixoticism of Don Quixote is more than mere chivalry and more than a generous folly in dealing with persons or events. It is the expression of a faith in the power of the human being to create values by virtue of his faith in them and to generate a world above the world of nature in which his human as opposed to his natural life may be led. His, in a word, is that philosophy more recently called the philosophy of "As If" and that philosophy achieves its defence by making the "mad" hero of the story more admirable than any of his sane adversaries.

In the second part of the work a kindly duchess is entertaining the Don and, hoping to plumb his madness, she turns the conversation upon the Lady Dulcinea — the country wench whom he has chosen as his mistress and whom he insists upon endowing with all beauty and all virtue. "If," she says, "we are to believe the history of Don Quixote which has come out here lately with general applause, it is to be inferred from it, if I mistake not, that you never saw the Lady Dulcinea, and that the said lady is nothing in the world but an imaginary lady, one that you yourself begot and gave birth to in your brain, and adorned with whatever charms and perfections you chose." To this charge the Don replies, not as a mad man defending his delusions, but merely as one who has chosen to see the world through poetic imagination, for it is thus (the italics are mine) that he retorts: "There is a good deal to be said on that point. God knows whether there be any Dulcinea or not in the world, or whether she is imaginary or not imaginary; these are things the proof of which must not be pushed to extreme lengths. I have not begotten nor given birth to my lady *though I behold her as she needs must be.*" And in saying that he committed himself to the world of poetry rather than to the world of fact, to that world which critics had defined when they said that it is not the business of the poet to recount things as they are but as they ought to be.

Thus Cervantes, speaking now through the mouth of Don Quixote, now through that of Sancho Panza, drew a picture of *the world as it is* traversed by *man as he ought to be;* and giving his credence to the hard-headed materialists of Italy, he reserved his affections for those who are willing to act *as though* the mind and the imagination were the supreme realities. No mere slave of fact could have drawn a more meticulously real or living picture of the society of his day and he never (with one exception to be noted later) failed to distinguish between the two planes upon which the action of his story moves, so that his background never loses the sharpness of its realistic outline, never wavers between fact and fancy. But in one heroic figure he embodies everything which that background is not and the effects of this glaring contrast between the realism of the setting and the fantastic poetry of the central character constitutes a harmonious whole for the simple reason that its existence in the form of the ever present contrast between fact and aspiration is the thing of which our experience in living makes us most persistently aware.

Even this fact does not, however, comprise all the greatness of the author for the form which he created to express what was for him the most important duality of the moral universe was one which was ready to be used in a thousand ways. Not for another century and a quarter, not, that is to say, until the rise of the great English novel, did another man appear who could handle it, but Cervantes had discovered for himself how to give to fiction a quality which it had never had before. Doubtless he was not the first to perceive that some kind of emotional complexity differentiates the experience of living from the one which we undergo when we read a *conte* of Boccaccio. Others must have recognized before him that when one lives through an experience one does not feel it to belong to any pure literary *genre* or to be, that is to say, as Boccaccio would have made it, indubitably comic or indubitably sad and nothing else. But he was the first successfully to attempt a piece of prose fiction in which the simplification of the tale was discarded in favour of a more complicated form capable of suggesting this emotional ambiguity of life.

Critics who discuss the modern novel sometimes describe this peculiar excellence which Cervantes introduced as a "three-dimensional quality" and the metaphor implied is more appropriate than it might seem at first blush to be. The plastic appearance of a natural object, the sense of depth which we experience when we regard it, arises as a result of the fact that each of our two eyes sees it from an angle of its own. In some mysterious fashion the brain fuses the two flat but slightly disparate images which the two retinas receive and from that fusion is generated the sense that the object exists, not on a plane, but in space. Now what Cervantes and what, after him, all the masters of Eighteenth and Nineteenth Century fiction accomplished, was something exactly analogous. Instead of accepting a sort of monocular vision as inevitable in fiction, instead of adopting, as all previous authors of the prose tale had done, some one point of view — satiric, or romantic, or heroic or what not — he was able to see his material from the two different angles which are necessary for a stereoscopic picture. Sancho Panza and Don Quixote are the names of the two eyes through which he looked forth and in some fashion or other the account which describes what the two of them see is made to do the work of the brain. Thanks to it the two do not contradict but rather supplement each other — they are fused. And out of that fusion comes a sense of solidity in the moral realm which is utterly new in Cervantes.

Doubtless he himself did not know just what it was that he had accomplished and it was perfectly possible for him to write in the older, simpler style. Thus in " The Exemplary Novels," already referred to, there is no suggestion of his supreme excellence and if one will turn either to them or to the various tales interspersed between the chapters of " Don Quixote " one will perceive very clearly what that excellence is. So strong were his own romantic predilections that even in the midst of his masterpiece he was compelled to take occasional refuge in pure romance, to compose the interludes which he called " The Story of the Shepherdess Marcela," " The Ill-Advised Curiosity " etc., and in them he slipped back into the manner of the primitive novella. They seem flat and, in comparison with the richness of the main story, almost silly, but no sooner has he finished one than he seems without effort to re-enter the far more substantial world of his two heroes. It would be fantastic to suppose that he wrote these minor tales deliberately to call attention by contrast to the virtues of his great work, but certainly they can be made to serve that purpose.

No other man whose name is remembered in the history of story-telling ever did so much to advance the art which he practised. It is no little thing to have stated, as he did, the chief intellectual problem of his age in a novel and if, to the realization of this achievement be added a realization of the fact that he painted the realistic details of everyday life with a hitherto unapproached fidelity, one can hardly hesitate to award him a place in the front rank of the fiction writers of all time. And yet neither of these things is so important as that subtler creation which we must still call "three-dimensional fiction." Every writer who achieves it in narrative is modern; whoever cannot may possibly write memoirs or be content with one or another of the styles of tale-writing which have survived, but he cannot be what we call a novelist because the power to suggest the emotional and intellectual complexity of any series of events is the very essence of the art of the modern novel.

V

Cervantes was in his sixty-ninth year when the Second Part of "Don Quixote" was published. About a year before he had given us in the Prologue of "The Exemplary Novels" a pen portrait of himself with his "aquiline visage," his "smooth unruffled brow," his "silver beard" and the teeth which were "not important" because he had "but six of them and those in an ill condition and worse placed because they do not correspond the one with the other." No information seems available concerning the amount of financial profit which he received from his new publication but it was not great and there were not many years left him through which he might endure poverty.

Yet he had no intention of resigning the pen before death should snatch it from him. Instead of resting upon his laurels he was startlingly — perhaps febrilly — fertile of projects. One of them, the "heroic" and unreadable romance of "Persiles and Sigismunda," was actually executed but of the others, including the long-promised continuation of the "Galatea," not a trace has been found. Apparently he still hesitated to rest his whole claim for fame upon anything as "irregular" as "Don Quixote" but failing strength cut short the expressions of his allegiance to older standards.

In the Prologue to the "Persiles" (published after his death) he tells us of a ride along the road from Esquivivia to Madrid and recounts with obvious pleasure a chance meeting with a bespectacled student who, upon learning his name, saluted him as the " joy of the muses " and then proceeded to diagnose his ailment as dropsy. This ride (if not imaginary) was probably the last which the joy of the muses was permitted to take. About the same time in a letter to a patron he had remarked that his malady increased " so greatly that I think it will make an end of me, though not of my gratitude " and on April 18, 1616 he received supreme unction. Next day he rallied sufficiently to compose the dedication to the " Persiles " and four days after he died. He was buried in the habit of a Franciscan, for Cervantes, like a good Spaniard and a good Catholic, had punctiliously arranged for a decent termination to his life by becoming a tertiary of the order some two weeks before. If he felt that his country had wronged him he never revealed the feeling and if his speculations were sometimes bold he had never permitted himself an expression of which the Church could disapprove.

All the supreme creations of character — Pantagruel, Falstaff, Hamlet and Crusoe — have an existence independent of the work in which they first appear. We know more about them than Rabelais, Shakespeare, and Defoe have told us because these characters, refusing to be confined within the pages of a book, have walked out into the world to take a place there as real as that occupied by any man who ever left a memory behind him. Every critic who has discussed them, every reader upon whose imagination they have taken hold, has added something; their symbolic significance has been enriched by every thought to which they have given rise and men have been glad to father their own fancies upon characters already so substantial.

Legends have grown up around them as they have grown up around the most appealing of historical characters, and the Falstaff who now belongs to the universal imagination is almost as much greater than the Falstaff of Shakespeare's plays as the Cleopatra of the universal imagination is greater than she of history. When one of these magic names is mentioned our minds are flooded with light, not all of which comes from the author who created the character, and filled with a harmony to which countless overtones are added from the countless imaginations which have responded with sympathetic vibrations to the original chord.

Each, moreover, has been enriched by what the Greeks called " pathos " — each, that is to say, is surrounded by an aura composed in part of the memory of those who have cherished it. When a character has passed through many inferior hands it becomes hackneyed and cheap but when many noble minds have concerned themselves with it it is not worn but enriched. Like an heirloom it becomes more precious because of those who have possessed it, and something of those who have touched it adheres. What many men have wept over is the sadder for their tears and what many men have laughed over is made not merrier, to be sure, but more precious by the echoes of that dead laughter. Thus the great figures of legend and literature grow more meaningful as they endure. When we touch them we touch not only them, but also and at the same time all those who have felt for them, making ourselves part of a great continuous tradition of human sensibility.

And though Don Quixote shares with these other great figures the distinction of being greater than anything which even the imagination of Cervantes or of any other one man could compass, he is nevertheless unique in one respect. His creator, having sent him forth into the world, took him up again after he had become a legend and himself completed what he had begun.

No other author ever quite did just this with any conception before. Perhaps Shakespeare came nearest to it when he carried Falstaff through three plays, but it is generally admitted that the Falstaff of the "Merry Wives" is less rather than more than the Falstaff of the other plays and it can hardly be said that Shakespeare fully utilized the legend he had created. But Cervantes took full advantage of his opportunity. He gave Don Quixote to the world in the first part of his romance and then took him back again to be completed after the world had already made more of him than an author unaided could have done.

Thus Don Quixote is the genius of Cervantes, plus the genius of his Spain, plus the eager imagination of all Europe during the three hundred years which have elapsed since he first went gloriously mad. Some laugh when his adventures are read and some weep; but no one has yet definitely answered the riddle which he propounds. Nor will it ever be answered until we know for sure whether madness be not, after all, the highest wisdom.

SAMUEL RICHARDSON

I

DURING the course of the hundred and fifty years immediately following the publication of "Don Quixote" an enormous number of persons learned to read. One result of this fact was the creation of a book-buying public larger than any known before and the consequent rise of authorship as a possibly profitable profession. Another was the establishment of middle class taste as a major factor in determining the form and spirit of fiction.

Hitherto, though the author had often belonged to the lowest class of society he had written primarily for the highest — unless of course his words had been intended, like those of Shakespeare, to be heard rather than read. Henceforward he was very likely to feel in some manner or other the influence of the solid, respectable and money-making element of the community.

In the English literature written by the contemporaries of Cervantes (and Shakespeare) there had been little evidence of any concern with this element. The citizen or " cit " had begun to appear as a usually contemptible character in the Jacobean drama and more frequently in that which succeeded the restoration of Charles the Second. But since, broadly speaking, he neither read nor wrote, his point of view had been unrepresented in literature, and from the books of *belles lettres* current even a century after the death of Shakespeare one might almost suppose that society had maintained the old pattern. The ideals which dominate them are still the ideals of the scholar, the *littérateur,* the man of fashion, or the martial aristocrat, and things are still seen from the point of view of the one or the other. Yet it was during the hundred and fifty years just referred to that England became a nation of shop-keepers and it would be a vast mistake to suppose that the small part played by the middle class in drama or fiction was any measure of its importance in the national life.

Though this class had not as yet established any contact with literature it was growing rapidly in wealth, in power, and in self-confidence. In hundreds of counting-houses merchants and tradesmen were building up a substantial order entirely outside the old aristocracy and without physical or spiritual contact with it. The power of the new order was founded upon wealth instead of position; its manners were regulated by respectabilities instead of fashions. And in the great commercial houses of the city it had a source of tradition entirely independent of the court. Something of puritanism lingered in its prejudices but it was a puritanism so vulgarized by·prosperity that the extravagances of any enthusiastic piety were hardly less foreign to the spirit of the cit than were the gaieties of the Restoration gallant. His was a narrow, practical, thrifty, cautious, hardworking, and inflexible order, totally new.

Humble at first and content to regulate his household in his own way, he began gradually to extend his influence into government and then to raise his voice in protest against the manners and ideals of classes with which he would not previously have dared to meddle. It was primarily through him that the movement for the "reform" of the English stage took place at the end of the Seventeenth Century and it is his influence also which is to be seen indirectly at work in the writing of Addison and Steele who might, as a matter of fact, very reasonably be considered as the apologists to their own class for the ideals of another. But so great was his suspicion of art — so profound was his instinctive distrust, not only of its "immoralities," but of its incautiously adventurous idealisms as well — that it was long before he realized the possibility of making it a vehicle for the expression of his own spirit. He feared that his daughter might be prepared by *belles lettres* for seduction at the hands of some fashionable gallant whose tongue had been oiled by poetry and romance, but he dreaded such a calamity hardly more than the possibility of finding himself cursed with a son who had imbibed from literature a distaste for the profitable routine of the counting-house. Art at best was a waste of time and the citizen had managed to rise because he did not like to see anything wasted.

Chivalric idealism, romantic love, and the ecstasies of mystical religion are, no less than martial or gallant adventures, essentially luxuries. They may be cultivated by the vagabonds who do not particularly care about getting on in the world and by those whose position places them above the necessity for doing so, but they are likely to be looked upon with an understandable suspicion by the members of a class which thrives upon prudence, thrift, and common sense.

The merchant goes to church on Sunday, makes a suitable match, and tends to his affairs. He has no more time for metaphysics or mysticism than he has for romance and hence the rise of the middle class means inevitably the rise of a tepid sort of literature adjusted to his sympathies and his comprehension.

Defoe, the first great bourgeois writer, did not succeed in taking the curse off fiction just as George Lillo, the author of that dramatic homily for apprentices called " The London Merchant," did not succeed in making the theatre entirely respectable. Defoe was as moral as he was prosy but he had had more actual experience with politicians and hacks than with respectable citizens and his tales were either of adventure or of crime. Time was necessary for the process by which literature was infused with bourgeois ideas and it remained for Samuel Richardson to discover how domestic life could be made the subject of improving fiction. Richardson happened to be — if the word has any meaning — a genius; but every detail of his experience was calculated to mould him into the exact image of substantial respectability. Only a happy accident made a novelist of him but it was obvious that if he should ever take his pen in hand it would be in the interests of virtue — as virtue is conceived by the tradesman.

II

Richardson was born, somewhere in Derbyshire, in 1689. He was a quiet boy and his father, a joiner practising his trade in London, soon began to observe in his hopeful son traits which suggested a career in the Church. In the first place the young Samuel was known to his school-fellows by the cumbersome nickname of "Serious and Gravity." In the second place he had already, when not yet eleven years old, written to a widow of fifty a hortatory letter full of quotations from scripture directed against her alleged hypocrisy.

Nor were these facts the only ones which seemed to fore-shadow success in the ministry, for the youth also ex-hibited at an early age that capacity for lending a sympa-thetic ear to female confidences which was later to stand him in good stead in a secular profession but which has been the making of many a popular clergyman. Though a bashful boy, he was not, he says, more than thirteen years old when he used to frequent the sewing circles of the neighbourhood and when three young ladies who had "a high opinion of my taciturnity" came independently to him for aid in com-posing answers to their lovers' letters. He served them gladly and so much to their satisfaction that he had evidently already developed a capacity (later conspicuously exhibited) for writing feigned letters which seem authentically female by virtue of a certain modest ardour.

But in spite of these talents so early exhibited, financial difficulties made it necessary for the father to give up the plans he had already formed and to bind out the budding moralist to a printer. To the printshop he accordingly went and with a characteristic determination to " do the duty nearest him " he became, if we may believe his own improving account, the very model of the industrious apprentice. Though he had had only the most elementary of formal educations his scrupulosity forbade him to use either the time or the candles of his master for any efforts at self-improvement and thus the ideas which he imbibed in the establishment where he worked were uncorrupted by any thoughts or feelings unsuitable to the place. In due time he appears, as was eminently proper, to have married his master's daughter, and by easy stages he rose to be owner of his own publishing business. After bearing him six children, none of which survived beyond the age of four years, this wife died but the loss was promptly made good by a marriage in the following year to the sister of a bookseller.

Richardson was now leading what is called a useful life and it must be confessed hastily that he was not in any ordinary sense literary. He cared little for reading and at the age of fifty he had written nothing for publication except a few prefaces and dedications composed as so many articles of trade. What he had done, as financial competence and a certain amount of leisure were achieved, was simply to move into a comfortable house just outside of London proper and there to exhibit with considerable satisfaction the virtues of his class.

Nor was he by any means lacking in class consciousness for despite his eminent success in the city he believed that he " knew his place." As innumerable passages in his writings show, he looked upon those whom it had pleased God to make his betters with a suitable respect and he knew how to value, not only a lord, but a lord's second cousin as well. Yet he was far from displeased with himself because he did not see how anybody could deny the exemplary character of his career. He had never, he said, been in a "bad house" in all his life, nor ever, so far as he was aware, even in the company of a loose woman. He was honest, industrious, kindly, Christian and prosperous. That members of his circle respected him was a matter for satisfaction but hardly for surprise. He was obviously worthy of respect and since he had never set any example except a good one he saw no reason for trying to seem unaware of the fact that his company and his conversation were of a highly improving sort.

Up to 1739 he had revealed no tendencies or talents not easily predictable by anyone familiar with his boyhood character. He still wrote letters with a fluency and a delight positively abnormal and it seems that at one time he kept up a voluminous correspondence with a gentleman distinguished by nothing except his willingness to receive and reply to the epistles which it evidently gave Richardson some peculiar pleasure to compose. But beside these harmless epistolary indulgences he was remarkable for nothing except his delight in mild conversations ranging over the narrow field which lies between moral discourse on the one hand and gossip on the other.

Naturally his preference for female society rather increased than diminished. Women gave him the deference which he liked, they were more inclined than men to receive with complacency the instruction which he loved to give in matters touching either manners or morals, and in other less tangible ways they were more congenial company for a man whose habits of persistent industry had sheltered him from the boisterous world of masculine London. From women he had learned pretty much all he knew or was ever to know about " life," and even after he had become an international figure it was still women who made up the most numerous company of those who came to form a kind of court around him. They helped him to formulate that essentially domestic view of things which was the distinguishing character of his novels and they repaid his unusual respect for " women's notions " with a tender veneration which was in part filial and in part, no doubt, mildly erotic.

Thus at the age of fifty Richardson was the good man appropriately rewarded. He was also, to all appearances at least, both happy and content and it is not likely that his beneficent influence would ever have extended beyond a narrow circle had it not been for the fact that a publishing firm happened to ask him to compile a sort of " Complete Letter Writer " for the benefit of semi-literate persons.

Now the Devil himself could not have conceived a trap more appropriately baited since the proposal was one which invited Mr. Richardson to do the two things which pleased him above all others — namely to write letters and to give good advice to inferiors. Accordingly, after making the characteristic proposal that the scope of the book be enlarged so that it might instruct the humble readers " how they should think and act in common cases as well as indite," he threw himself into the task with enthusiasm and produced a collection of one hundred and seventy-three let-

ters, advertised as the work of a man who had given particular attention to the problems of courtship and marriage,
and published with the following title: " Letters written to
and for particular friends, on the most important Occasions. Directing not only the requisite style and forms to be
observed in writing Familiar Letters; but how to think and
act justly and prudently, in the common concerns of human
life."

The subjects of the letters are various and their moral
tone as high as is consistent with their compiler's inveterate
inability to dissociate righteousness from prudence. Most
of the correspondents, whatever their sex or position, have
the editor's penchant for the hortatory and the feigned
recipients are accordingly advised upon all sorts of subjects
— the impropriety of following immodest fashions in clothing, the dangers to which a too ardent courtship exposes the
young girl, and the inevitable vexations of all processes at
law. There are, besides, letters of condolence which " with
small variations may be used to a husband on the death of
his wife, and on other melancholy occasions of the like
nature "; letters from " a young lady in town to her aunt in
the country "; and letters written back and forth between
humble but modest lovers. All the correspondents are assumed to be very much alike in their fondness for commonplaces of all sorts and hence all are likely at any moment
either to launch into a sermon or to indulge themselves in
the pleasure of making long observations not particularly
original in character. " Let who will speak against Sailors;
they are the Glory and Safeguard of the Land. And what
would have become of Old England long ago but for them."

Yet the book is almost fiction and marked everywhere by a copious though completely undistinguished imagination.

Richardson did not profess to take much pride in the compilation. It was intended, so he said on a later occasion, "for the lower class of people" and he advised a friend that it was not worth his perusal. But it gave him an idea. In composing it he had discovered a perhaps unsuspected capacity to imagine incidents and a certain talent for writing in character. These were the gifts of the writer of romance and though Richardson had a very low opinion of novels in general it occurred to him that he might turn the foolish and reprehensible taste of the generality of mankind to good account by preaching to them under the guise of fiction. One or two of the letters already written had been concerned with the conduct of a servant girl improperly importuned by her master, and when Richardson wrote them he began to remember an incident of the same kind which had been related to him many years ago and which had remained in his mind because of the instructive conclusion to which the events had led.

"I thought the story, if written in an easy and natural manner, suitable to the simplicity of it, might possibly introduce a new species of writing, that might possibly turn young people into a course of reading different from the pomp and the parade of romance writing, and dismissing the improbable and marvellous with which novels generally abound, might tend to promote the cause of religion and virtue." No purpose less tangible or less important than the promotion of "the cause of religion and virtue" would have seemed to him sufficient to justify the expense of time necessary to read, much less to write, a story; but the case of the serving maid Pamela seemed to him so remarkably edifying that he began to write it in the form which the Familiar Letters suggested.

Certain difficulties were involved since the unfortunate girl had to be endowed with an almost superhuman capacity for epistolary composition if she was to be supposed, as is actually the case, to recount all her adventures as they occurred, and Richardson was sometimes put to such straits to explain how she obtained time and paper for her letters at certain crucial moments that Pamela is made to guard her pen and ink almost as carefully as she does her virtue and to plan means for dispatching her letters with more ingenuity than she used in her efforts to escape the violent attentions of her master. But Richardson had never written anything but letters and throughout his whole career as novelist he was accordingly compelled to make each of his characters a victim of his own epistolomania.

In this species of composition his fluency was, however, amazing. He began " Pamela " on the tenth of November, 1739 and finished the second volume (692 printed pages in all) exactly two months later. But from the beginning he had what he could never do without — female approval. "While I was writing the two volumes my worthy hearted wife and the young lady who is with us, when I had read them some part of the story, which I had begun without their knowing it, used to come into my little closet every night with: Have you any more of Pamela, Mr. Richardson? We are come to hear a little more of Pamela, etc."

Thus encouraged he proceeded with enthusiasm and the

book was published anonymously in November, 1740 under the following characteristically explicit title: "PAMELA: or, Virtue Rewarded. In a series of Familiar Letters from a beautiful Young Damsel, to her Parents. Now first published in order to cultivate the Principles of Virtue and Religion in the Minds of the Youth of both Sexes. A Narrative which has its Foundation in Truth and Nature; and at the same time that it agreeably entertains, by a Variety of *curious* and *affecting* Incidents, is entirely divested of all those Images, which, in too many Pieces calculated for Amusement only, tend to *inflame* the Minds they should *instruct.*"

"Pamela" was not intended for "the lower class of people" exclusively but it was aimed straight at the great bourgeois public which cared more for respectability than for art and its success was never for a moment in doubt. Only the existence of a great hunger never before fed can explain the amazed delight with which it was received, and almost from the day of its publication to the day of its author's death Mr. Richardson, that great and good man, was immersed (though never overwhelmed) in a flood of flattery more deep and soothing than any ever enjoyed before or since by fortunate penman.

Perhaps Rousseau and Voltaire made more *noise* in the world. Perhaps their renown was greater. But by the generality of mankind they were suspect. One admired their genius while one depreciated their tendency and even as one applauded one entered caveats unnecessary in the case of the great champion of indubitably *virtuous* ideas. Here at last was a literary genius as understandable and as sound as he was brilliant — someone who could be taken to the bosom without reserve. He drew tears, not for Hecuba, but for his own readers and that was much; but it was not all. In principles he agreed with the great public against the wits. He was as right-minded as he was great. And here, for once, was a man who had not been compelled to make the choice generally considered inevitable: he was both clever *and* good.

Hence the trickle of praise which had begun with the "worthy hearted wife" gradually swelled into a torrent of admiration as persons further and further removed from the domestic circle of the author added their tributes. Shortly after publication Richardson sent a copy to Aaron Hill — a minor *littérateur* who deserves to be remembered less for any of his writing than for the fact that he named his three daughters Urania, Astrea, and Minerva — and to Hill's credit it must be said that he struck the right tone at once. On December 17, 1740 he begins coyly (while still pretending to have no suspicion as to the identity of the author) with an expression of pleased amazement. Who, he asks, would have dreamed to find under the "modest disguise of a novel all the soul of religion, good breeding, discretion, good-nature, wit, fancy, fine thoughts and morality." But who pray is the author and "how has he been able to hide hitherto, such an encircling and all-mastering spirit?" "If it is not a secret, oblige me so far as to tell me the author's name" for the book will live and "twenty ages to come may be the better and wiser for its influence."

By December 29, all pretense of ignorance concerning the author has been dropped but there is not therefore any need

to moderate the fulsomeness of the flattery. Mr. Richardson will be pleased to know that not even the youngest
hearts are untouched by the beauty of his work. A few
evenings ago when it was being read aloud in the blameless
family circle of the Hills a six year old child had crept under
a chair and been there forgotten until " a succession of
heart-heaving sobs " revealed his presence. " I turned his
innocent look towards me, but his eyes were quite lost in his
tears; which running down his cheek in free currents, had
formed two sincere little fountains on that part of the carpet
he hung over."

But even this was not for Richardson quite enough. He
asked Hill for critical suggestions and Hill knew exactly
what was wanted. He goes over " Pamela " twice — once
" with the eye of a cynic " and once with that of " vigilant
friendship "; but with neither the one eye nor the other can
he " pick out anything that might not suffer by altering."
" Upon the world of a friend and a gentleman, I find it not
possible to go further, without defacing and unpardonably
injuring beauties which neither I, nor any man in the world,
but their author, could supply with others as sweet and as
natural! " " Where," as he not unnaturally asks a little
later, " will your wonders end or how could I be able to
express the joy it gives me to discover your generous rising,
not like a pyramid, still lessening as it labours upward, but
enlarging its proportions with the grace and boldness of a
pillar, that, however high its shaft is lifted, still looks larger
at its capital."

It is true that Hill expected and received from Richardson
some slight return in the form of very moderate praise of his

own work. It is also true that Hill was financially obligated to the author of " Pamela." But his laudations were hardly less hyperbolical than those of persons who owed the fortunate author nothing whatever. Mr. Pope, to be sure, contented himself with saying rather ambiguously that the book " would do more good than many volumes of sermons " and indeed it was not as yet from the literary that the author received the highest praise. But ladies of fashion were said to carry the volumes about with them just to show that they too were reading what everybody talked about and at least one preacher promptly recommended the book from the pulpit.

The further down one went in the intellectual scale the more touching were the evidences of its power to stir hearts and moisten eyes. At the village of Slough the inhabitants gathered around the blacksmith while he read the incomparable romance aloud and when he came to the place where the heroine triumphs his hearers set up an involuntary shout. Moreover, other children besides the precocious infant at the Hills' were touched, and one little girl, " not twelve years old," was inspired to compose a poem which began

> " O Pamela, thy virtuous mind
> Riches and honour has resigned;
> Riches were but dross to thee,
> Compared with thy mod-est-y."

Without doubt the " new species of writing " had caught on, but the most remarkable feature of its vogue was the fact that the emotions which it aroused were not apparently

aesthetic in character but somehow warmer and more intimate. Richardson was at once overwhelmed with personal
letters. Was the story true or false? Who was the original
of the incomparable Pamela? Everybody was delighted but
everybody was also disposed to weep tears which seemed to
be, in part at least, tears of relief. Something long awaited
had been let loose upon the world. A new pattern of feeling
had been created.

III

If the book which thus became, not so much a literary event, as the occasion of a crisis in the history of human sensibility, had subsequently got itself lost; if it, together with its author's succeeding works, had passed out of the range of our possible knowledge like most of the odes of Sappho and some of the books of Livy, then we might well have been excused if we had lamented our loss as one of the saddest in literary annals. But the marvellous romance — which many good judges believed unequalled by anything of its kind until the appearance of Mr. Richardson's second work — was not lost, and it remains, on the contrary, to be read by any reader curious enough to peruse the pages marked by a certain fatuity effectively concealing whatever merits they may possess.

Pamela is a lady's maid left by the death of her mistress at the mercy of the latter's rakish son, Mr. B. Mr. B. loses no time in proposing to set her up as a sort of *maîtresse en titre* and when she retreats under a barrage of virtuous sentiments the young man is so impressed that he redoubles his efforts to obtain a prize made triply valuable by a resistance founded upon such honourable sentiments. An attempted rape is somewhat mysteriously frustrated by the indignation of the intended victim and the villain (drawn in lurid colours) plans a stratagem. Promising Pamela that she shall be conducted in safety to her poor but virtuous parents he has her carried instead to a farm house managed for him by a sinister female and, soon putting in his appearance, he resumes his threatening importunity.

Poor Pamela is now in the most desperate straits. Her citadel is assaulted alternately by cajolery, by abuse, and by another attempt at violence so nearly successful that the monster is at one time fairly between her sheets. Moreover her writing materials are almost exhausted when Mrs. Jewkes (the traitor's housekeeper) gives her "a bottle of ink, eight sheets of paper and six pens, with a piece of sealing wax." "This," says Pamela, "looks mighty well" and she can now continue to scribble at a desperate rate an epistolary account of her trials and a full exposition of her sentiments. Beset though she is, she will never, she assures her parents, forget either the humbleness of her position or that virtue which is her only glory. With great complacency she describes the admiration which her conduct has aroused among the better sort of people and she recounts at length the frenzy to which her exemplary inflexibility had driven Mr. B. How great are her trials but how great is her glory!

Mr. B. continues alternately to flatter, to threaten, and to rail. He calls her by every abusive name he can think of. He loads her with obloquies. But this madness is merely the sign of a defeat not quite acknowledged for suddenly, almost in the midst of his most venomous insult, he surrenders to an impregnable propriety. Will Pamela, who can be neither seduced nor violated, consent to marry him?

The reader is surprised but Pamela is not. She is immediately mistress of the sentiments which she believes appropriate to the circumstances. She remembers her place and the gulf between her and her master which nothing can really bridge. She is overwhelmed and she is grateful. Can

Mr. B., rich and elegant as he is, stoop to her? It seems that he can and the remaining third of the book, devoted to Pamela's triumph, includes a full account of both her sentiments and her wedding dress. "Mr. Colbrand being returned, my master came up to my closet, and brought me the license. O how my heart fluttered at the sight of it. . . . I made bold to kiss his hand: and, though unable to look up, said, 'I know not what to say, Sir, to all your goodness: I would not, for any consideration, that you should believe me capable of receiving negligently an honour, that all the duty of a long life, were it to be lent me, would not suffice me to be grateful for.' "

Such a synopsis — and indeed any possible synopsis — can reveal only the absurdity of the story. Nor is the novel itself — redeemed though it is by Richardson's remarkable talent for creating a convincing character — likely to produce upon the reader any impression except one of amazed incredulity at the humourless obtuseness of its feeling. Mr. B. is so devoid of any reality as to make it impossible to discuss his motives or his character. Richardson knew nothing whatever of "worldly" life and his own tepid imagination was so incapable of conceiving either the nature or the effects of an unruly passion that his villain is merely a monstrous lay figure suggestive of nothing except the bugaboo which haunts the dreams of spinsters warned too often against the villainy of mankind. And if Pamela is real enough, her complacent vulgarity is so completely beyond all description that even promiscuity would seem, beside her calm determination to resist all importunities until the monster consents to buy her off, at least commendably generous.

One hardly knows where to begin to state the objections both moral and psychological which immediately rise in the mind of any modern reader and it is indeed hardly necessary to do so. One may surely venture to leave unparticularized those which have to do with the heroine's perfect willingness to accept as a compliment the proposals of a man who has just shown himself incapable of the most elementary decency and one may also safely omit speculations concerning the character of this hero who, even after his capitulation, condescends with an insufferable complacency to the girl whom he has just " raised to his level." But since the virtue of the heroine and the admirable moral to be drawn from her story were the points upon which contemporary admirers most strongly insisted they may both be given a cursory glance.

"How happy am I," upon one occasion Pamela exclaimed, "to be turned out of door with that sweet companion, my innocence" but innocence is, of all the virtues, the one in which subsequent commentators have found her most conspicuously lacking. It is true that she set a prodigious value upon what she was accustomed to call "her jewel," but innocence is surely not the word best suited to describe the quality of a mind which spent most of its waking hours in a feverish contemplation of the possibility that the body which contained it might conceivably be seduced or violated. Though the ways of the world were not known to her through experience, the defect was made good by the activity of an imagination very ready to conceive and perhaps exaggerate all the dangers which an innocent spirit would discover with surprise. Pamela anticipated every move made against her, and her "purity" was maintained at the cost of a perpetual preoccupation with fears for its safety.

Nor is it possible, as one follows with amazement the proud exposition of her principles, to discover in them anything except the logical development of a shrewd determination to get as much as possible out of the world, for if we judge her by the evidence of her own letters she is a prig at best and a designing minx besides. Richardson had set out to describe his ideal of feminine character but he had created instead a coarse-minded opportunist because he had himself achieved a cynicism more complete than is possible to any except those unaware of the nature of their own principles. The virtue of Pamela is no more than a realization of the fact that her virginity is by far the most valuable of her possessions and a wise determination not to lose what has a perfectly tangible value. The society in which she lives has agreed that a continence, broken only upon those occasions and under those circumstances sanctioned by civil and ecclesiastical law, is the *sine qua non* of that decency without which a woman has no claim to any consideration whatsoever, and while prudence thus directs her to maintain it, her creator encourages her to believe that in so doing she is rising to the greatest possible height of moral excellence.

Yet it is possible to account for every detail of her behaviour without any reference whatsoever to any principle belonging in the realm of morals. Like all maidens she had a jewel and the precious possession was one to be safeguarded with all the watchfulness of a traveller who passes through some bandit-infested waste. The thing — though to all appearances no more than a pretty trifle — has a value, thanks to which it can be bartered or sold, and therefore it must not be lost. He who allows it to be taken from him is criminally careless; he who gives it away is a fool. But in the end it must be sold. Thus, in the spirit of a dealer in precious stones Pamela goes about her business. It is not the man but his terms which she objects to and when he meets hers she accepts them. She and her parents rail against the wickedness of those who cannot hold out as she has done but by wickedness they mean folly. Skill in trade is a citizen's virtue. Pamela held out for a good price and in the end she got it. Thus is virtue rewarded.

This word Virtue slipped as easily from Richardson's pen as it did from the tongue of Pamela but there is no evidence that it had for him any awful or mysterious meaning. Usually it is merely a synonym for a technical continence mechanically maintained and it never implied anything not definable in common sense terms. Honesty, industry, amiability and even generosity find a place in his creatures as they found a place in his own character, but these qualities are always useful to those who possess them and no man was ever less capable than he of understanding anything which approached the quixotic. Perhaps he would have refused to equate virtue and prudence — to admit that honesty and benevolence and continence were virtuous *because* they brought ease and security and competence — but the fact that they did so was the outward sign of their character and the way in which God revealed his love for those who practised them.

Unable to distinguish between an inward state of soul and the conduct to which such a state was conventionally sup-

posed to give rise he used "virtue" (that is continence) as
a mere synonym for chastity and he was as incapable of
imagining that a continent woman might be unchaste as he
was of conceiving the possibility that chastity might be the
attribute of a woman neither virginal nor married. Since
Pamela resisted the seduction of her master she was inevitably both "pure" and "innocent" just as a man who
gave alms was inevitably "benevolent." Thus goodness became mechanically determinable and the idea of righteousness shrank into the idea of respectability.

The character of Pamela is one so devoid of any delicacy
of feeling as to be inevitably indecent. She seems to have
no sense of either her own or any possible human dignity
and she can be admired only if a dogged determination to
resist violation is considered to be, by itself, enough to make
her admirable. Despite the language of pious cant which
she speaks with such fluency there is no evidence that she
has the faintest conception of that disinterestedness which
alone can give piety a meaning.

Yet none of the objections which are so patent to any
critical reader of Richardson appeared as defects to his
enthusiastic admirers since his moral feeling was distinguished from that of his middle class fellows only because
it was more perfectly typical than that of most. It was the
bourgeois respectability of his century purified of all individual eccentricity, uncorrupted by any trace of either
mystical enthusiasm or sceptical worldly wisdom. He
thought what others thought in their most commonplace
moments; he was not Bobus but Bobissimus; and his readers relaxed with comfortable security in an atmosphere

so much like that of their daily lives. Among writers of robuster intellect, Eighteenth Century materialism took other forms. An ironic scepticism developed in minds which had divested themselves of all concern with the transcendental and made them disturbingly critical. But the literal, unimaginative mind of Richardson stripped every idea of the aura which surrounded it and then rested complacently content with the bare formulae of a dry convention.

A little later on he could dare attempt to draw a picture of the Perfect Gentleman because Gentlemanliness — like Purity and Virtue — was not to him an illusive quality, not something evanescent and indefinable which emerges as the result of a delicate balance or a spontaneous harmony in the soul, but a simple, mechanical obedience to easily establishable canons of rectitude and decorum. Right thinking (aided a little by the precepts of a revealed but simple religion) could, he believed, determine what a man ought to do — just how generous, how forgiving, how prudent and, of course, how condescending to his inferiors he ought to be. Hence to create a model gentleman it was necessary only to invent an automaton perfectly obedient to all the rules. For him the flavour, the perfume, and that nameless grace which makes an individual charming counted for nothing, and he would have been almost as much puzzled by the suggestion that his creation lacked the personality necessary to make him appealing as he would have been shocked by the suggestion that a trace of some human failing may contribute, when nicely placed, to the charm of a character.

And yet " Pamela," considered purely as a novel, did have one great intrinsic excellence. The central character is delineated with a dramatic realism quite independent of the moral judgment which either the creator or the reader passes upon her. She is a creature solid enough to be completely dissociated from the personality of the man who described her and to be subjected to analysis again and again as standards change. Richardson was completely helpless when he was compelled, as in the case of Mr. B. he was, to attempt the portrait of a man whose traditions, motives, and passions were outside the range of either his experience or his imaginative sympathy. His rake is ridiculous except when we see him, not directly, but as he appears in the terrified imagination of his intended victim and when we consider him therefore, as a distorted image rather than as a real person. But Pamela herself is a masterly objectification of unconscious vulgarity, to the completeness of which her vision of Mr. B. contributes. Richardson seems to have achieved an imaginative identification with her which is admirably complete and he knew so exactly how such a person would talk, act, and feel that he drew of her a portrait seldom equalled so far as sheer realism is concerned.

It is this fact alone which makes it possible to regard the book as more than a historical curiosity. Its only absolute merit lies in the fidelity with which it represents a certain type of character and if we were to judge it as an *interpretation* of even that small section of human life with which it deals, we should be compelled to relegate it to some sub-literary limbo. Yet it is hardly to be supposed that either the enthusiastic encomiums which were heaped upon it or the international influence which it exerted is to be accounted for by the solitary and purely technical excellence which we have granted it.

Great popularity is seldom if ever the reward of mere fidelity to fact. To win it, the writer, passing beyond mere imitation, must achieve some sort of pattern in which fact is balanced against fact, emotion against emotion, and end result against end result, in such a way as to constitute an interpretation of life and its laws satisfactory to his readers. This interpretation may be profound or shallow, and it may be essentially noble or essentially vulgar; but it is the pattern (often felt rather than intellectually comprehended) which takes hold of the imagination of readers and the pattern which is taken over by subsequent writers belonging to the same school.

Now Richardson did achieve such a pattern. It was, moreover, one which had been imperfectly sketched out again and again — particularly by the second-rate playwrights — during the half century preceding the publication of " Pamela" and he had, therefore, over and above both the merit of his skill in portraiture of a certain kind and the accidental advantage of his conventional respectability, a great charm for his contemporaries — the charm, that is to say, of a new pattern which had long been struggling into existence but which had never been so nearly achieved before. This pattern is the one which is commonly distinguished by the adjective " sentimental," and though the word is so frequently and so carelessly used, the truly sentimental pattern results from an attitude very nearly as definite and inclusive as (though a great deal less exalted than) those which inspire the patterns called the Tragic and the Comic.

In the most impressive of his novels Richardson was later to achieve a work which, despite all his permanent limitations, was not only morally and technically superior to "Pamela" but characterized by a more complete mastery of a more intricate sentimental pattern. Hence we shall postpone until we come to consider this later work the attempt to understand what the pattern is, but we should note even now the fact that it is not to be confused with anything so simple as Richardson personally and his entirely commonplace acquiescence in conventional superficialities concerning the whole duty of man (which is to be respectably prosperous) and the whole duty of woman (which is to be technically virtuous). The sentimental pattern was taken over by many writers whose specific convictions, both ethical and social, would have shocked him profoundly and at least some of whom were immeasurably his superiors in intellect and taste. But the elements common to all of them are the elements necessary to compose the pattern which was destined to dominate fiction for a long time and to survive very conspicuously into the literature of today.

IV

After "Pamela" had been published and praised Richardson, like the sober man that he was, made some attempt to return to the humble occupations which had formerly been his. The pen which had depicted the apotheosis of the serving-maid consented to employ itself in editing a new edition of Defoe's "Tour Through Great Britain" and the brain which had conceived so generally acceptable a reward for virtue busied itself with making analytical summaries for a volume of the diplomatic correspondence of Sir Thomas Roe. But destiny, aided by an inordinate love of praise, and an imagination doubly restless because it had been so severely curbed, again drew him irresistibly towards independent authorship.

He was now living, not far from London, in a comfortable house to which his admirers resorted to pay tribute to his genius and to contemplate with an almost religious awe the domestic life of a man whose example was universally admitted to be no less valuable than the precepts which he gave under the guise of agreeable fictions. Here he could make "ten beds" for such fortunate intimates as were permitted to spend the night under his roof and here in the garden was a summer house to which these intimates might repair to hear the latest pages of manuscript read aloud by the author himself.

The time was to come when Richardson, even though at the height of his fame, could fish shamelessly for compliments and he was ultimately to die, as Dr. Johnson bitterly remarked "for want of change among his flatterers" — to

perish "for want of *more,* like a man obliged to breathe
the same air until it is exhausted." But now at the period of
his greatest creative activity he was living not only in a state
of perfect domestic bliss but under conditions which assured
him a plentiful supply of the life-giving element.

It is true that his wife was generally supposed to be of a
rather unusually self-effacing disposition and true also that
one of his intimates even brought herself to observe that the
daughters behaved in a manner which suggested that
they might be less at ease than would have been anticipated
with so perfect a father. But Richardson hastened to assure
them that even this was also well. "A mixture of fear with
love" was, he said, necessary to make an obliging wife and
as for the "stiffness" of the daughters he could only reply
that "too much reverence is not the vice of the age." "Con-
descension," to be sure, "becomes the character of the par-
ent." He has done all he could to encourage them in proper
freedoms. If they continue to treat him with more than
daughterly reverence it can only be because of what they
must inevitably feel for one who is, however undeserving,
treated with so much respect by his friends.

Nor did any of these friends fail to accept as more than
adequate such explanations. "Most of the ladies that resided
much at his home, acquired," it was remarked, "a certain
degree of fastidiousness and delicate refinement which,
though amiable in itself, rather disqualified them from appearing in general society." And if this was the result of
a formal association, it was not surprising that the wife
who shared his bed and the daughters who had had, from
earliest infancy, the benefit of his corrections, exhibited to

an even greater degree this amiable inability to feel at home among more frivolous companions. But surely the constant presence of the author of "Pamela" was more than enough to compensate for the absence of less improving associates. Give "my love to Mrs. Richardson and to all who have the happiness to be under your roof," wrote Miss Fielding, sister of the author of "Tom Jones." "Methinks, in such a house, each word that is uttered must sink into the hearer's mind, as the kindly falling showers in April sink into the teeming earth, and enlarge and ripen every idea, as the friendly drops do the new-sown grass, or the water-wanting plant."

Mr. Richardson now began, however, to extend somewhat the range of his acquaintance and sometimes consented to absent himself from domestic bliss for the sake of a short exploratory tour into that world of fashion of which he felt himself more ignorant than was wise for one who hoped ultimately to instruct it with tales of virtue in a higher place than that from which Pamela had been so deservedly lifted. Into his circle he admitted the rakish laureat, Colly Cibber, because of Cibber it could at least be said that he professed an admiration for the virtues which he admitted his inability to practise. More surprisingly still, the laureat was allowed to remain even after he had scandalized his friend by finding the latter's admiration for male virginity irresistibly risible. And upon at least one occasion Richardson paid a visit to Tunbridge Wells where he strolled with a timorous delight in the midst of a gay company and did not remember (until near the end of the letter in which the visit was described) his duty to remark that "modesty, humility, graciousness, are now all banished from the behaviour of these public-place frequenters of the sex." "Women," he concluded, " are not what they were" and he seems to have been so struck with the observation that he made it the subject of a paper which he contributed, some three years later, to Dr. Johnson's " Rambler."

It has been shrewdly suspected that Cibber supplied some of the traits for the portrait of the fashionable rake who was to play a prominent part in the new novel and so much superior is this portrait to the previous one that the mere critic is impelled to wish that Richardson had abandoned himself more freely than he did to the society of people less ready than the members of his inner circle to agree with everything he said and to adjust their manners as nearly as possible to what he considered the ideal. But his love of a sort of flattery which only inferiors could give, his need to be immersed constantly in an atmosphere which could only be generated by the soft, almost sensual adoration of ardently inexperienced females, drew him always back to the charmed and isolated group of his most intimate wor-shippers.

From the outside world he could get recognition as a writer, and the approval of the rich and fashionable must have been sweet to one who never ceased to be acutely aware of all class distinction. Yet what he enjoyed most and needed most was not recognition of the sort appropriate to a man of letters but the assurance that his excellence was primarily the result, not of merely literary talents, but of the perfection of that character which he had no doubt begun to console himself by cultivating while still playing the role of industrious apprentice. Avid for flattery of any sort, he liked best the compliments which implied that the conspicuous virtue of his heroine was drawn from some inexhaustible reservoir of goodness within his own heart and the inhabitants of his own private little world were experts in this sort of thing. Thus the indispensable Hill had struck the right note when he wrote " I confess there is one person in the world of whom I think with greater respect than of Pamela and that is the wonderful *author* of " Pamela," and another correspondent (this time of the female sex) struck it again with an even surer hand when she protested that he had only given to this incomparable maiden " the virtues of his own worthy heart."

Nor is it, under the circumstances, very surprising that he sometimes turned from precept to practice when his benevolence was repaid as amply as it was, for example, in the case of one Letitia Pilkington, a literary adventuress who came to no good end but who could repay a charity with words like these: " How was I astonished to find you, like silent-working Heaven surprising oft the lonely heart with good and bounty unexpected, unmerited, unsought. What can I pay thee for this noble usage, but grateful praise; so Heaven itself is paid; and you, truly made in the image of God, will, I hope, accept of the low, but sincere oblation, of a thankful spirit. . . . The sin of ingratitude would lie heavy on me did I not, with the most perfect thankfulness, acknowledge your goodness. Every favor you confer receives a ten fold value from your manner of conveying it. . . .

> Angels enthroned in bliss with rapture see
> Their own divine perfections live in thee."

Richardson felt no need to deprecate the compliments paid to either his character or his work because he considered himself the champion as well as the representative of moral purity. To feign a belief that they were excessive would be to assume that Virtue could be praised more highly than she deserved and Richardson would never be guilty of such an error.

At the distance of one and three quarters centuries it may seem that the company of his adorers was more numerous than distinguished, for though his genius was generally admitted, the intimate circle never came to include a single one of the men and women who made the Eighteenth Century glorious and to us it may appear that the absence of Fielding, Hume, Johnson, Stern, and the rest is not entirely compensated for by the presence of any or all of those second-rate *littérateurs* and now forgotten blue-stockings who clustered about him. Surely a more intelligent man would have questioned at times just how much the flattery of persons like Hill and Mrs. Pilkington was worth; or, to choose other examples, just how much one had a right to be pleased by that of either the obscure poetaster Thomas Edwards or a certain Miss Collier who complained with a pathetic humourlessness that Fielding's "Voyage to Lisbon" was attributed to her pen for no reason except "that it was so very bad a performance and fell so far short of his other works, it must needs be the person *with him* who wrote it."

But Richardson was pleased with all these sops just as he was pleased by the assurance given him by a mother that her son had been, at the age of twelve, inspired to compose a sermon on the text (appropriately quoted in "Pamela")

" The liberal soul shall be made fat." He was fortunate in possessing a temperament which made it unnecessary for him to consider the source of a compliment and which enabled him to judge it entirely by its magnitude. Since he readily assumed that the intelligence and the virtue of any man or woman was exactly proportioned to the admiration which that person felt for him, the value of any fragment of adulation was precisely as great as it was extravagant.

No one was ever turned away merely because he was patently silly or not entirely disinterested. " Believe me, Madam," he wrote to one correspondent, " I am incapable of flattering," and when one considers both the low opinion which he entertained of his rivals and the very moderate returns which he gave to those who flattered him, it must be admitted that the boast involves no more than a permissible minimum of exaggeration. But Richardson never kept any friend who suffered from a similar inhibition. And though he was compelled to forego intimate intercourse with equals or superiors he spent most of the time not actually employed upon his novels in either conversation or correspondence with sycophants.

Only one person seems to have seriously disturbed his complacency and that person was Henry Fielding, who was generally credited with the authorship of a burlesque which mercilessly exposed the weaknesses of " Pamela " and who later returned to the attack by beginning his own first novel as a parody of the same edifying work. Richardson never forgave a slight or an insult but so perfect was the mechanism which protected his vanity that he could indulge his rancour without any impairment of his Christian spirit for the simple reason that he never failed to discover in anyone who offended him follies or vices which deserved chastisement on their own account. Hence he never lost an opportunity to denounce both the moral and literary sins of Fielding's "Tom Jones" because its author had dared to satirize him and he never, indeed, seemed to suspect how little this nervous depreciation of his greatest rival became one who had been elevated to a height which demanded of him some suggestion of dignity.

Yet it is not, for all this, by any means certain that Richardson did not learn something from Fielding. He was not incapable of realizing from experience that the lewd were given unnecessary pretexts for laughter and he was determined that these pretexts should be wanting when he came to compose a second mirror for virtuous minds. Clarissa — for such was to be the name of his new heroine — should be placed a good deal higher in the social scale than Pamela had been, but this was not all. She should exhibit a delicacy which would have been out of place in a serving-maid and she should be inspired by the hope of a reward more appropriate to her station in life.

Richardson, no less than Dr. Johnson, considered that the "great scheme of subordination" constituted the groundwork of God's plan. He saw no reason, therefore, why anybody should aspire to anything higher than the rank and privileges belonging to the station just above his own. But while Pamela had appropriately set her heart upon rising in this world through the instrumentality of her would-be betrayer, Clarissa — whom Providence had, so to speak, been pleased to start where her humble sister had left off -- might legitimately aim at higher things and be rewarded, not with marriage to a gentleman, but with Eternal Bliss.

Unfortunately there is no evidence to show exactly when Richardson first began to sketch out in his own mind the plan of the new work, but by 1745 he was far enough along with it to submit a portion of it for the approval of Hill. This latter was so rash at one time as to provoke something very near a breach in their relationship by offering a criticism of one of the heroine's actions and on another occasion he was foolish enough to take seriously the author's suggestion that he undertake the task of compressing somewhat some of the letters of which the novel was again to be composed. But from the outraged tone of the offended genius he soon realized what was wanted, and he redeemed himself twice over. " It is impossible," he said, " after the wonders you have shown in ' Pamela ' to question your infallible success in this new, natural attempt." And though the second masterpiece of moral fiction was, despite the simplicity of the plot, ultimately to appear in no less than seven substantial volumes " You have," he wrote, " formed a style . . . where verbosity becomes a virtue; because, in pictures which you draw with such skilful negligence, redundance but conveys resemblance; and to contract the strokes would be to spoil the likeness."

The last volumes of the new novel were not to appear until 1748 and since Hill had begun to speak of the work in 1745 it must have been much longer than its predecessor in the writing, but the most remarkable of the circumstances which surround it is the fact that the writing and the print-

ing became public events. Richardson, no longer compelled
to remain content with the encouragement of "my worthy
hearted wife" and her female companions, could now call
upon the members of a numerous circle for admiration, encouragement, and the assurance that nothing in all he had
written could possibly be changed for the better. He was
later to form the habit of having his admirers resort upon
stated occasions to his house and to listen while he read
aloud to them the newest chapters of the work in progress,
but even now he wrote with the praises of his plan, his style,
and his intentions ringing always in his ears. Nor was this
all, since between the publication of the first four and the
last three volumes he was still further delighted by various
correspondents (to whom of course he replied at length)
who not only described the ecstasy with which they were
reading but either engaged in long discussions of the morality involved or implored him to arrange an outcome agreeable to the affection which they had conceived for this
character or that.

While the ultimate fate of Clarissa still hung in the balance, while it was still impossible to know whether her
creator intended to save her for some suitable reward as he
had formerly saved Pamela, or to allow her, as the most
inexorable supposed, to die at last, there were many who
hardly dared to draw breath and those who enjoyed the
privilege of Mr. Richardson's acquaintance hung about his
study as though it were the death chamber of a queen.

Lady Bradshaigh, an aristocratic admirer, could not bear
the thought of reading the final and distressing part when
she learned that it was destined to describe the end of

Clarissa. "Good Sir," she wrote, "do not send it, do not compel me to be ungrateful. You would not wonder at my inflexibleness, if you knew the joy I had promised myself from a happy catastrophe. I cannot see my amiable Clarissa die; it will hurt my heart, and *durably,* I know your manner, and I know my weakness — I cannot bear it." A little later when the blow had fallen she cried out again in what is either agony or a very good sentimental imitation of it: "Talk not of tragedies, I can now bear any; the deepest pain they give is momentary and trifling, compared with your long-dwelt upon, and well told story. . . . I expected to suffer, but not to the degree I have suffered. . . . When alone, in agony would I lay down the book, take it up again, walk about the room, let fall a flood of tears, wipe my eyes, read again, perhaps not three lines, throw away the book, crying out, excuse me good Mr. Richardson, I cannot go on."

From Hill no less was to be expected than that description which he gave of his family circle when he wrote "At this moment I have three girls around me — each a separate volume in her hand, and all their eyes like a wet flower in April." But even Cibber, now seventy-seven years old and, as he set off in pursuit of a reigning beauty, still incapable of practising the virtue which he had begun to "recommend" in his plays a little more than half a century before, was no less touched by a mere foreboding of catastrophe as is witnessed by an account fortunately left by Mrs. Pilkington:

"I passed two hours this morning with Mr. Cibber, who I found in such real anxiety for Clarissa, as none but so

perfect a master of nature could have excited. . . . When
he heard what a dreadful lot was to be hers, he lost all
patience, threw down the book, and vowed he would not
read another line. To express one part of his passion, would
require such masterly hands as yours or his own; he shud-
dered; nay, the tears stood in his eyes; 'What!' said he,
'shall I, who have loved and revered the virtuous, the beautiful Clarissa, from the same motives I loved Mr. Richardson,
bear to stand a patient spectator to her ruin, her final destruction? No! — my heart suffers as strongly for her as if
a word was brought me that his house was on fire, and himself, his wife, and little ones, likely to perish in the flame.'
I never saw passion higher wrought than his. When I told
him she must die, he said, 'God d——m him, if she should';
and that he no longer believed Providence or eternal Wisdom, or Goodness governed the world, if merit, innocence,
and beauty were to be so destroyed: 'nay,' added he, 'my
mind is so hurt with the thought of her being violated,
that were I to see her in Heaven, sitting on the knees of the
blessed Virgin, and crowned with glory, her sufferings
would still make me feel horror, horror distilled.'"

"These," adds Mrs. Pilkington, in a phrase which suggests
anti-climax, "were his strongly emphatic words," and she
continues in order to add her mite of persuasion. "I can
scarcely, Sir, express the pleasure I received from the dear
gentleman's warmth, nay heat, on this occasion; as it showed
me at once the virtue of his own heart, and the power of the
writer who could so melt, engage and fire it. But now, Sir,
I must fairly own with Mr. Cibber, I cannot bear the thought
of the lady's person being contaminated. If she must die; if

her heart must break for being so deceived, let her make a triumphant exit arrayed in white-robed purity. . . . Spare her virgin purity, dear Sir, spare it! Consider, if this wounds both Mr. Cibber and me (who neither of us set up for immaculate chastity) what must it do with those who possess that inestimable treasure? And if the bare imagination of it is so terrible, what must it be when arrayed in the full pomp of such words as on this occasion must flow from such a heart, and such a pen as yours."

It is true that some few who had, unlike the aged poet laureat, abandoned virtuous sentiments as well as virtuous conduct, professed to feel that a tremendous pother was being made about nothing. It is true also that certain fashionable persons like Horace Walpole and Lord Chesterfield were less unqualified in their praises than simpler souls and that these judges, offended by the inordinate length of the work, failed to agree with Hill in finding the redundancy of Richardson's style a virtue. But " Clarissa " had become, even more conspicuously than " Pamela," a public event and its heroine a personage to be discussed more fully and more ardently than any living person.

V

Richardson's spirit had been always undernourished. He had been confined to the printshop during the years when more fortunate youths were undergoing experiences far richer in their emotional content and the effect of the dull routine had been to increase the preternatural sobriety already remarked in the child. He once guardedly hinted at two or three embryonic romances which might possibly have brought some little colour into an otherwise drab existence but "a bashfulness, next to sheepishness" kept him down and there is every reason to believe that both of his marriages were the result rather of prudence than of passion. Moreover, since he read little and frequented only the tamest of all possible societies even the nourishment which he offered himself in the form of vicarious experience was of the most watery sort. The composition of "Pamela," written when he was already fifty years old, had been his first spree — the first act of his life performed because *he wanted* to do something for its own sake, rather than because it was obviously dictated by his methodical prudence. No doubt this emotional starvation accounts for both the eager copiousness of his correspondence and the unwillingness which he exhibited to bring "Clarissa" to a conclusion. He clung pathetically to whatever contacts he managed to establish and he was in no hurry to conclude the imaginary adventures which were enabling him to live more richly than he had ever lived before. But if his verbosity was that of a man who prolongs any conversation rather than return to the undisguised emptiness of his own existence, this keen though unacknowledged hunger for some sort of emotional life was responsible for the fact that the book took on a vividness and colour not only unintended but unwanted.

Richardson still professed to believe that the art of fiction was, in itself, morally unjustifiable. " Instruction," he said, " is the pill; amusement the gilding," and he was genuinely concerned lest his characters should become so interesting as human beings that the reader would attend rather to them than to the lesson which he was intent upon preaching. Hence he provided the book with a title designed to call attention to its moral; he sprinkled the text with footnotes explanatory of the same; and he added at the end a disquisition nearly as long as the present essay. But these efforts were in vain. He could not prevent himself from becoming interested in the story he had to tell or from making it glow with a life of its own.

His personal letters reveal only the dryness, the narrowness, and the pomposity of the man. One will look in vain anywhere except in his books for any sign of his genius; but like not a few writers both before and since, he was carried further by his sympathetic imagination than his intellect could ever carry him and at least this one of his novels is richer, fuller, and deeper than the code which he professed. The moral was deduced as the result of a conscious activity; the emotions were depicted by an imagination uncontrollably eager for experiences richer than any which had been granted to the man who possessed it.

" Clarissa " is no longer much read because its inordinate length repels no less than the priggish formalism of its author's frequently obtruded judgments. But an astonishing power to captivate the occasional person who will surrender himself to it even yet remains in the seldom-turned pages. Richardson, it is true, is still concerned with persons who are unable to transcend his own limitations. He never dissociates the idea of virtue from the idea of conformity and the most admirable person is always the one who most nearly succeeds, not only in adjusting every detail of his conduct to the accepted canons of propriety, but in subduing his heart to them as well. Hence he attributes to his heroes and heroines an almost imbecilically complete submission to all the conventions. Yet they are, nevertheless, real and vivid. So completely does he enter into their emotions, so lively is his imaginative sympathy with everyone who comes within its narrow range, that his favourite characters cannot fail to engage the interest of the reader, who soon finds himself forgetting his impatience with their limitations in his concern with their experiences.

Clarissa Harlow is the model and idolized daughter of a genteel family living in the country. Addresses are paid to her by a dashing rake named Lovelace but her father, fearful lest she should become involved with him, insists upon her marrying a dull, mean-spirited man of his choice. But Clarissa, steadily maintaining her right of refusal but never asserting any right of choice, rejects him and when the duty of obedience is urged upon her in vain a family persecution develops.

At this point Lovelace reappears to beg a secret interview. Clarissa consents and he urges that, since there seems no other way in which she can escape the hated marriage, she throw herself upon his protection. At last she consents and departs with him for London where he promises to respect absolutely her freedom. What he actually does do, however, is to place her in lodgings (after informing the landlady that Clarissa is his secret bride) and then begin to put into operation an elaborate plan of seduction. Clarissa perceives it and is thrown into a panic of despair.

Now Lovelace is genuinely and desperately enamoured of Clarissa. Indeed he really intends, despite his rooted contempt for matrimony, ultimately to marry her. But he is the victim of a peculiar psychology which Richardson sometimes depicts with a surprising acuteness though at other times he allows his villain to become, like Mr. B., a purely mythological monster. Lovelace is determined to exhaust all his wiles before consenting to take his adored victim to the altar, either because (as he sometimes thinks) he wants to be sure that she is genuinely enamoured of him rather than of the safety he can assure her or because (as he at other times explains) he wants to apply the ultimate test to that virtue which must be absolutely impregnable if it is to justify the bowing of his neck to the yoke of wedlock.

Meanwhile Clarissa has come to feel a kind of love for the man whom she also despises and fears; but though he does actually ask her to marry him she refuses, partly because she cannot trust his character, and partly because it seems to her delicacy that he does not sue with either the ardour or the humility which a man ought to exhibit before the woman whom he is asking to become, forever after, essentially his subordinate. Thus the two play at cross purposes until Lovelace, maddened by disappointed and humiliated pride, tried violence and the rape (so long imminent in "Pamela") is actually accomplished.

It was at this point that the excitement of Richardson's readers reached its height. They thrilled with horror at the violation of the heroine and they begged that she should be made to triumph at last by bringing the villain to see the error of his ways. But Richardson steadfastly resisted their importunities and he did so for several reasons. In the first place he had come (as several specific utterances show) to doubt the propriety of representing the overnight reformation of a confirmed sinner and he did not propose to have scoffers again remark with scornful glee that he had rewarded virtue by giving it the hand of a rake. In the second place he insisted that Clarissa had committed a fault when she removed herself from the authority of her parents and he did not wish to show that ultimate happiness could be the result of such an initial misstep.

Moreover, in the third place he had, though forever incapable of understanding the spirit of true tragedy, come to realize that the sentimental effect of Virtue Rewarded is less striking than of Virtue carried from one edifying distress to another. The moral would be purer and the emotion would be greater if Clarissa were compelled to die; and hence die she did, perishing of what one of the characters calls in a rather unfortunate phrase "an incurable fracture of the heart," and leaving behind her a testament which supplies the final evidence of her purity, her sweetness, and the Christian humility of her heart.

Such is the plot of the tale which Richardson requires some eight hundred thousand words to tell and which fills, in a modern edition, nearly two thousand closely printed, double column pages. Any man, said Dr. Johnson, who tried to read it " for the story . . . would hang himself." But Dr. Johnson yielded to no one in admiration for the work and it is by no means primarily " for the story " that it exists. The full title reads: " Clarissa: or, The History of A Young Lady; Comprehending the Most Important Concerns of Private Life; and Particularly Showing the Distresses that may Attend the Misconduct both of Parents and Children, in Relation to Marriage." Nor can anyone complain that this title is either insufficiently explicit or insufficiently exact. Such is precisely the scope of the book though all these particulars are " comprehended " by being completely dramatized so that what we get is almost always genuine fiction and very seldom indeed merely a treatise.

Every important event is told two or three times over in the epistles written by the different persons involved who give accounts of it from their own individual points of view. Letters pass back and forth in all directions among the thirty-eight principal characters and the motives and feelings of each chief actor are not only described by himself but analysed and commented upon by others. Every conceivable opinion is canvassed, every transitory feeling dissected. What is the real character of the man whom the parents of Clarissa have chosen for her? How far was she justified in resisting their wishes? Should she or should she not have accepted under any conditions the honourable proposals of Lovelace once he had become her violator? May a respectable girl consort with a man of bad character in the hope of exerting upon him a good influence; to what extent is the heart a dependable guide; how far should a young lady consult her own taste in accepting or rejecting a suitor; and what should she feel upon this occasion or that? Upon these and a hundred other questions the characters all differ. Lovelace speaks for the rake, Clarissa for enlightened propriety, her confidante Ann How for the rebellious younger generation, and her father for all old-fashioned parents who are sound upon the subject of daughterly obedience.

Richardson was thus the first to make the novel an exhaustive commentary upon the minutiae of daily conduct and "Clarissa" marks more clearly than any other work the turn as the result of which the interest in a piece of fiction comes to be focused, not so much upon events, as upon the causes which lead up to and the reverberations which follow them. The older story-tellers hurry on from happening to happening. Richardson is concerned less with adventures than with the discussion of them. He does not let any event take place without examining all the antecedent causes nor does he ever pass to another until the emotional reaction of every party concerned has been fully examined. And since his mind was as conventional as it was active the result is something at once vivid and commonplace.

"Clarissa" trembles on the edge of the ridiculous. Pomposity, smugness, and fatuity are always just around the corner. And yet it would not be fair to dismiss it as merely pompous, smug or fatuous. In it there is a remarkable refinement of observation, and an amazing insight into all the corners of a small but ardent mind. Richardson's sympathies, for all the narrowness of their range, were extraordinarily acute and so completely does he live in and through

the soul of Clarissa that one is compelled to admit that one
at least knows what Dr. Johnson meant when he said that
there was " more knowledge of the human heart " in one
letter of " Clarissa " than in all of the novels of Fielding. In
it readers could recognize themselves to an extent which was
impossible in any previous novel. Experiences such as might
possibly happen to them were here happening to people like
themselves and they could live with Clarissa on the terms of
an intimacy impossible in the case of any other heroine of
fiction. No one could possibly *behave* like Don Quixote or
Robinson Crusoe, but thousands must have asked themselves
what Clarissa (or Lovelace!) would have done under these
circumstances or those.

Thus their creator at once restricted and enlarged the
field of fiction. He eliminated all extraordinary adventures
and all passions more exalted than those within the range
of the more ordinary sort of person but he examined the
emotions appropriate to bourgeois existence with a minute-
ness never known before and he did for the middle class
heart what Defoe had done for the externals of daily life —
he examined, that is to say, all its little hopes, scruples, and
perturbations, with an eye which delighted to note and to
respect them. Hence it was thanks more to his influence than
to that of any other man that the novel could become, as it
has, a dominant influence in moulding the opinions, the
manners, and the modes of feeling cultivated by a very
large section of any literate public.

For the upper middle class of the Eighteenth Century
" Clarissa " became, as a matter of fact, a book of etiquette,
a mirror of manners and morals. It is impossible to say how

much Richardson actually imposed himself upon his contemporaries and how much his system of ethics and sensibility was something merely crystallized from the atmosphere which had been generated in the course of a social
development. But the fact remains that his book seems to
have established, as it were, the norm which came to be accepted by the members of the upper middle class. In
" Clarissa " one saw reflected an ideal; one recognized in
its characters models which instructed by example how
one ought to act, to speak, to think, and to feel in social life.
One realized that one was, not merely virtuous, but elegant,
right-thinking, and sensitive as well exactly to the extent to
which one found oneself reacting after the pattern of the
more refined characters in that romance.

The fact that its author happened to be, in temperament
at least, an absolute bobissimus was not for him a disadvantage but an advantage since his task was to co-ordinate
the various elements which composed the spiritual universe
of his fellows. Had he ever undergone any profound experience this experience would have had to find some place
in his work; had he ever conceived any idea subtler or deeper
than those which were congenial to the more mediocre of
his contemporaries, this idea would have inevitably disrupted
the vulgar harmonies which he composed. But fortunately
for him neither thought nor experience disqualified him. He
could codify conventional manners and he could do something still more difficult. He could give the dignity of art
or pseudo-art to life as it was led by vulgar people. He could
bring to its full development the sentimental pattern.

Tragedy is the form given to existence in the contemplation of great spirits. But the common man has neither the exaltation of character nor the strength of soul necessary to achieve it even if his story should ever happen to be on a scale which would justify any such grandiose interpretation of its meaning. He must see lives like his own under a form which is not that of tragedy but of something exacting less of the actors and more easily comprehended. If he must give up, as Richardson did, the idea that the motif known as Virtue Rewarded is dominant in the universal symphony, he must find in its place some conception of what constitutes success in life compatible with his timidity, his prudence, his materialism, and his ingrained regard for conventional respectability. Richardson found it and the fact that he did so is the greatest single cause of his enormous popularity.

Hence "Clarissa" became, above all else, the model for sentimental fiction, by which term we mean here to denominate that vulgar sort of demi-tragedy produced when goodness is substituted for greatness as the necessary qualification of the hero and when, as a result, the catastrophe reveals him, not going down in rebellious defeat, but tamely acquiescent to the forces which destroy him.

All the supremely great artists have instinctively avoided this pattern and distrusted the sort of satisfaction which it gives to an audience, but the essentially vulgar soul of Richardson felt its way slowly though unerringly toward it. To Clarissa he gave no positive or active virtues, nor even, indeed, any personality. She is no more than a slightly idealized portrait of the conventional "nice" girl of the period and the whole course of her life is determined by negative principles. Her dominant desire is the desire to achieve, despite the difficulties which surround her, a completely conventional existence and the Virtue which her contemporaries so much admired is not something which leads to any action but something which shines forth only when it resists the forces permitted to "test" it. Since her greatness is of the sort which only unusual trials can reveal, almost anyone might be generously presumed to possess it and her contemporaries took a satisfaction in her story greater than in any of the genuine masterpieces of literature for two reasons.

In the first place her excellence is of a sort which can disturb no one; and in the second place her end, brought about by her one violation of the conventional code, in no way challenges the pleasing assumption that all is fundamentally well both in human society and the universe at large. True tragedy shames and frightens. The greatness of its passions makes us blush for our own comfortable littleness and there is something terrifyingly anarchical in the refusal of its hero to admit defeat. But Sentimental Romance produces effects which are exactly the reverse. It flatters us by pretending that timid little virtues like our own are really great and that the submission which draws a pleasant tear from the eye of the beholder is the proper end of a hero.

"The writers of England excel those of all other nations in the pathetic," wrote the Eighteenth Century divine Sherlock, "and Richardson is, I think, superior to all his countrymen. He makes one cry too much. By a very singular talent peculiar to himself alone, he fills our eyes almost as often by elevated sentiments as he does by tender ones. . . . He abounds in strokes of greatness, sometimes in the actions and sometimes in the sentiments of his characters, which raise the reader's soul, and make the tear of generosity spring into his eye he knows not whence. . . . He has volumes which it is impossible to read without crying and sobbing from beginning to end."

Opinions like this make it evident that Richardson's admirers recognize clearly the distinguishing character of his effects. He was credited, as another contemporary critic put it, with having "tamed and humanized hearts that were before not so very sensible." And he deliberately lent his influence to the movement which was beginning to make an ostentatious tenderheartedness fashionable by dwelling upon every scene which gave occasion for pathos. But what these contemporaries did not recognize was the fact that these effects are of a distinctly low order — that his elevated sentiments are delightful because they are commonplace and the tears which he draws sweet because they are complacent.

Delighting to contemplate a purely passive and suffering virtue, he established the vogue of a new kind of heroine whose chief distinction lies in the fact that she is ill-used, and in contradistinction to the tonic sorrow of tragedy he set up an easy pathos by placing all the emphasis, not upon the strength of the hero, but upon his blameless and pitiful helplessness.

Sentiment is merely the feminine equivalent of passion. Through its influence romantic love, mystical religion, and the thirst for righteousness are diluted and tamed. They are subordinated to prudence and respectability and thus they are made comprehensible to lesser spirits. Juliets are no less rare than Othellos but a bourgeois society cannot be other

han glad of the fact. Fathers must like to believe that their
own more manageable daughters are more admirable as well,
and the daughters themselves, uncomfortably aware that
their souls have scarcely achieved Shakespearean proportions,
must like to feel that the domestic virtues are, by their very
blamelessness, superior to heroism. Who could hope to live
up to a Juliet's passion; who could maintain, indeed, that
the shameless and disconcerting example of her vehemence
is exactly edifying? But the conduct of Clarissa is as impec-
cable as her sentiments are comprehensible. In the very
presence of death she forgives everybody. Moreover she
sketches out a design for her monument and pays the under-
taker's bill in advance in order that her friends may not be
incommoded.

Well may her creator boast that the moral of his work
is pure and that " the notion of *poetical justice,* founded upon
the *modern rules* has hardly ever been more strictly observed
in works of this nature, than in the present performance. For,
is not Mr. Lovelace, who could persevere in his villainous
views, against the strongest and most frequent convictions
and remorses that ever were sent to awaken and reclaim a
wicked man — is not this great, this *wilful* transgressor, con-
dignly *punished* and his punishment brought on through the
intelligence of the very Joseph Leman whom he had corrupted? . . . On the other hand, is not Miss Howe, for her
noble friendship to the exalted lady in calamities — is not
Mr. Hickman — for his unexceptionable morals, and integrity of life — is not the repentant and not ungenerous Belford,
is not the worthy Norton — *made signally happy?*

" And who that are earnest in their profession of Christianity, but will rather envy than regret the triumphant death of Clarissa; whose piety, from her *early childhood;* whose diffusive charity; whose steady virtue; whose Christian humility; whose forgiving spirit; whose meekness and resignation, HEAVEN *only* could reward."

VI

Richardson was now fifty-nine years old. A mere artist might have permitted himself to rest, secure in the conviction that he had accomplished all he could ever hope for. But the moralist has an obligation more stern than that of the man whose talents are no more than entertaining. Richardson, convinced that he was living in the midst of " general depravity," had contributed his " mite towards introducing a reformation so much wanted." Though his age was one " given up to diversion and entertainment," though the pulpit had " lost a great part of its weight " he had, as he said, managed " to *steal in* and investigate the great doctrine of Christianity under the fashionable guise of an amusement." Hence he could not lay down his pen until it had done all the good of which it was capable.

In 1749 Lady Bradshaigh wrote to urge upon him the duty of completing the work he had begun by giving to the world a male counterpart of Clarissa — a gentleman who should be the model of masculine virtue as she had been of feminine. And though he expressed some understandable doubt concerning his fitness for the task of describing that fashionable world of which he was almost totally ignorant, he evidently concluded that the goodness of his heart ought to make up for the ignorance of his mind, since he was soon busy with the plan which was to be executed in the seven volumes of " The History of Sir Charles Grandison."

As early as 1751 one of the ladies privileged to hear fragments read aloud as they were composed wrote to a friend: " We have this day had the satisfaction of hearing Miss

Grandison extricate herself from those difficulties you left her involved in. Oh! my dear, Sir Charles will be all we wish him — I am sure he will — and is destined to show the world what the purest love should be, when inspired by an object irresistibly amiable, like Miss Byron." By 1753 the gatherings formed for the purpose of keeping up with the history as it was written had become sufficiently regular for Cibber to write the author in terms which were certainly warm enough but which some have thought to be hardly as delicate in expression as the subject ought to have suggested: " The delicious meal I made of Miss Byron on Sunday last has," he wrote, " given me an appetite for another slice of her, off from the spit, before she is served up to the public table; if about five o'clock tomorrow will not be inconvenient, Mrs. Brown and I will come and piddle up a bit more of her."

At last the enormous work was published in three installments issued between November 1753 and March 1754. Richardson had been, while he wrote, in constant communication with female friends from whose reactions he could judge what was likely to be the effect of every proposed sentiment and though there is undoubtedly something odd in his division of the characters into Men, Women, and Italians the reception given by the public to his new novel was all he could wish. " Mr. Urban," reviewing it in the *Gentleman's Magazine,* expressed the opinion that " Such a knowledge of the polite world, of men and manners, may be acquired from an attentive perusal of this work as may in a great measure supply the place of the tutor and boarding school." Mr. Cibber, again in raptures over the goodness of heart which the author exhibits, declared that he would rather have the fame due Mr. Richardson's "amiable zeal" for virtue than that due Pope as a poet; and Dr. Young (he of the "Night Thoughts") considered the fortunate author "as a peculiar instrument of Providence, adjusted to the peculiar exigence of the times." A debtor confined to prison wrote to say that his principles, unaffected by the rigours of confinement, had been reformed by a perusal of "Grandison"; Lady Brad- shaigh expressed the opinion that the author "ought to have been a bishop"; and — what is, under the circumstances, perhaps the most impressive of all — at least one reader begged for an eighth volume.

Yet despite the enthusiasm which greeted it we shall not devote much space to the last of Richardson's novels for the simple reason that it marks no advance over "Clarissa" and that it has been, on the contrary, for a long time almost uni- versally admitted to be in every respect less interesting than its predecessor. In the first place Sir Charles is a complete prig, deserving only, as Taine put it, "to be canonized and stuffed." In the second place the didactic purpose almost al- ways prevails over the interest aroused in the characters and their sentiments.

That complicated balance of elements which is necessary for good fiction seems usually to have been achieved by the imagination of a writer whose mind was to some extent divided against itself. It was manifest in the work of both Boccaccio and Cervantes during a particular epoch when each was struggling against a conviction fatal to the spirit in which the work in progress was conceived, and it revealed itself under similar circumstances in the case of Richardson, for though the latter never confessed to himself any purpose beyond the didactic, the eagerness of his hunger for emotional experience gave to " Clarissa " unintended virtues. It even enabled him to represent the point of view of Lovelace with such persuasiveness that Lovelace becomes that second eye necessary for three dimensional fiction and it supplies that ironic awareness of the moral ambiguity of all situations which Richardson could never have permitted himself to acknowledge. But the balance was lost when the conscious purpose achieved a complete ascendency over the unconscious one. In " Sir Charles Grandison " Richardson very nearly succeeded in becoming the mere moralist which he had always wanted to be and like Boccaccio in " De Claribus Mulieribus " or Cervantes in " Persiles and Sigismunda " won a lugubrious triumph over his own art.

Richardson was sixty-five years old when " Grandison " was published and though he had some seven more years to live his chief subsequent work was to be a compilation entitled " A Collection of the Moral and Instructive Sentiments, Maxims, Cautions and Reflections, contained in the Histories of Pamela, Clarissa Harlow, and Sir Charles Grandison, Digested under Proper Heads." Friends, to be sure, continued to importune him. It was suggested by a person who must have had a very improper idea of the nature of his genius that he might draw the portrait of a *bad* woman to serve as a foil for the two *good* ones; and Lady Echlin dropped a much more acceptable hint when she expressed her " wish to see an exemplary widow drop from your pen." But Richardson was not to be persuaded to embark upon any further vast projects. He complained of an increase of the nervous disorders which had long served as an excuse for not reading and which now, so he said, prevented him from writing as well. All obligations had been fulfilled; he no doubt felt that he had, in the words which Dr. Johnson used of himself, done enough for his contemporaries; and he gradually permitted himself to relax into an all but undisturbed enjoyment of his fame.

"Twenty years ago," he said complacently, "I was the most obscure man in Great Britain, and now I am admitted to the company of the first characters in the Kingdom." The statement was an exaggeration since it appears that Richardson was never on very intimate terms with any of the first-rate persons of his time but he was courted with sufficient ardour by a sufficiently large number of third-class celebrities to give him the illusion of being the acknowledged genius of his age. Mrs. Klopstock—wife of the poet who achieved fame with his "Messiah" and afterwards rose to an "Ode to God Almighty"—wrote him to comment on "-Clarissa" ("Oh! the heavenly book") and another German, Erasmus Reich by name, journeyed all the way from Leipzig to kiss the ink-well from which the incomparable romances had flowed. Indeed his innumerable correspondents came to occupy the major part of his time and he seemed to find an inexhaustible delight in phrasing and rephrasing commonplaces.

"Time (as you observe) is the pauper of even woe" he wrote to Lady Echlin and when every letter had been answered it was his favourite occupation to select and arrange those copies of his epistles which it had been, throughout the years, the duty of his daughters to make. Richardson had begun to compose novels when the need for self-expression rose to the point where it could not be satisfied by correspondence; he ceased to write them when this need had so declined that the post was once more adequate.

But while the author of "Clarissa" was busy with the prolixities of "Grandison" and while, a little later, he was equally busy with the harmless occupations of his declining years, the influence of his masterpiece was spreading throughout Europe. It was translated into French, German, and Dutch. Rousseau read it and wrote "The New Heloise"; Goethe read both Richardson and Rousseau and wrote "The Sorrows of Werthe." Thus "Clarissa" became, in part at least, responsible for an international school of fiction and helped turn the whole course of literature.

The world began to languish and to gaze with a kind of narcistic admiration at the spectacle afforded by its own sensibilities. A tender if not always very deep or practically effective regard for Virtue became *à la mode,* replacing cynicism as a fashionable attitude. Everywhere the refined were looking for virtue distressed; everywhere they were luxuriating in a pleasing melancholy. Each person endeavoured to outdo the other in sensibility and it was not so much any of Richardson's specific teachings as it was the overtones of his work — the mood generated by his ardent yet languishing contemplation of minor domestic emotions — which had the widest influence.

On the occasion of our author's death, Diderot sat down and in twenty-four hours composed in a burst of enthusiasm the famous "Éloge" in which, by reflection, we can perceive far better than we can by any effort at direct comprehension, what "Clarissa" meant to the Eighteenth Century. "This author never deluges the pavement with blood; he does not transport you into distant lands. . . . The world where we live is the scene of his action . . . the passions that he paints are such as I myself have felt. . . . The misfortunes and afflictions of his heroes are of the same kind as continually threaten me." Yet it is not so much this apparent actuality of persons and passions which ravishes the soul of Diderot as it is the fluent and relaxed sentiment which suffuses the whole.

He bequeathed to me a lasting and pleasing melancholy; sometimes my friends perceive it and ask me, What is the matter with you? They question me about my health, my fortune, my relations, my friends. O my friends, " Pamela," " Clarissa," and " Grandison," are the three great dramas! Torn from reading them by important business, I felt an overmastering distaste for it; I neglected my work and returned to Richardson. Beware of opening these enchanting books when you have any important duties to perform. . . .

O Richardson, Richardson, first of men in my eyes, you shall be my reading at all times! Pursued by pressing needs; if my friend should fall into poverty; if the limitations of my fortune should prevent me from giving fit attention to the education of my children, I will sell my books; but you shall remain on the same shelf as Moses, Euripides and Sophocles, and I will read you by turns.

Whole volumes have been written in the effort to define this Sentimental attitude which Richardson thus helped to crystallize. In the course of time the adjective itself, once used only in complimentary senses, has come to have only a derogatory significance. But the strangest thing in all the history of both the word and the thing is the fact that the ideological content of sentimental fiction came rapidly to be wholly different from that which its creator had striven to body forth.

Through the influence of Diderot, Rousseau, and Goethe, Sentiment became the handmaiden of democratic idealism and natural theology, in spite of the fact that its popularizer, intent upon "promoting the cause of Religion" and snob to the core, was horrified by both. He had permitted Pamela to marry a gentleman, not because he wanted to suggest that rank was of no importance but because a social elevation was the only adequate reward for transcendant virtue; and he had never dreamed of making the "dictates of the human heart" superior to the conventional code of morality. He distrusted romantic love so profoundly that he had never permitted it to play a dominant role in dictating the actions of any one of his heroes or heroines and so far was he from agreeing with Rousseau concerning the nature of Virtue that upon the margin of "The New Heloise" he inscribed the devastating opinion that its author had "taught the passions to move at the command of vice."

But Richardson, in all innocence, had looked into this "human heart." By the very act of noting with a morbid concern each throb and flutter, he had implicitly suggested that the organ thus meticulously examined was of supreme importance. *He* never intended any apology for romantic ideas; *he* never meant to hint either that love is the greatest of goods or that the dictates of feeling should be put above those of law. But the cult which he founded quite naturally drew its own conclusions. If the heart of the peasant or the serving-maid is as sensitive as that of the lord, then rank is a sham. If love is the tenderest of emotions, then it is, of all possible human experiences, the one most eagerly to be sought; and if the innocent soul is the most nearly heavenly of all earthly things, then it is in the impulses of such a soul rather than in the conventions of a corrupt society that true Goodness is to be found.

Ultimately these convictions disrupted the Sentimental pattern. They are incompatible with that concern with a fixed idea of the nature of Virtue with which Richardson starts and around which, as a centre, he constructs his design. Hence romanticism gradually emerges because the romantic pattern is one formed by making the intensity of an individual experience (rather than its conformity to a standard) the measure of its worth, and because this view of things is the one naturally to be deduced once the supreme importance of the feelings is accepted as a premise. Thus the disciples of Richardson bridge the gulf between his conventionally moral fables and the anarchy of a Stendhal. He had intended to do no more than " recommend virtue " as virtue was conceived by the respectable citizen. But he stumbled upon " the human heart " and first taught men that technique for examining it which was destined to result in a complete contempt for those standards of rectitude which he had wished above all else to support.

Fortunately for his own peace of mind Richardson did not, however, suspect that he was to be the encouragement of anything so pernicious. He did not live to see romanticism flower and he hardly realized the extent to which he was responsible for the more alarming of the developments which

took place within his own time. England was still concerned
with sentiment considered purely as the ornament of virtue,
and the beneficence of his influence was everywhere acknowledged. It disturbed him to think that the coarseness of Fielding had its admirers and he stirred uneasily when he heard
the applause which greeted the appearance of " Tristram
Shandy." But it was rather the wounded vanity of a man
made nervously fretful by another's fame than any fear
for the soundness of his own achievement which troubled
him, and of his new rivals' work he could exclaim with
characteristic ungenerosity " Mark my prophecy . . . by another season, this performance will be as much decried, as
it is now extolled; for it has not the intrinsic merit to prevent its sinking when no longer upheld by the short-lived
breath of fashion."

Richardson died of apoplexy on the fourth of July, 1761,
and before that event age seems to have rendered him
rather more difficult to get along with than he had been in
the days when deference, if sufficiently marked, was certain
to keep him amiable. We have it on the testimony of an intimate admirer that the progress of the disorder of which he
complained revealed itself in " the querulousness of temper . . . which you and I have lately lamented, as making
his family at times not so comfortable as his principles, his
study, and his delight to diffuse happiness wherever he could,
would otherwise have done." But if Richardson was aware
of the fact he must have comforted himself with the assurance that he had at least never failed to give amiability (along
with all the other virtues) that " recommendation " which
he considered so important. And it is only fitting that an

analysis like the present should conclude with some reference to his influence upon the moral tone of fiction.

The result of romantic ethics was to make the continental novel doubtful reading for respectable people but in England at least the force of Richardson's example was to prevail for well over a century and in the list of the characteristics which the fiction of his countrymen owe to him, an eminent suitability to the family circle should not be omitted. He was only a respectable printer but it was his conception of both propriety and morals which triumphed over that of the Gibbons, the Walpoles, and the Chesterfields. After the opening of the Nineteenth Century, no important English novel ever described a scene or drew an inference likely to be offensive to middle-class propriety until books from France and Russia once more reminded startled readers of fiction that there does exist a world of passions which are undeniably human even though not usually discoverable in the well regulated household of a prosperous tradesman.

STENDHAL

I

MARIE–HENRI BEYLE, or, as he preferred to call himself, Stendhal, was fond of saying that he would be read " about 1880." Fifty-eight years before the date thus set for the beginning of his fame he published a treatise " On Love" which sold but seventeen copies in eleven years and there was, accordingly, nothing to distinguish him from the countless other unsuccessful authors who have comforted themselves with a similar faith in the good taste of posterity. But the remarkable thing about the prophecy of Stendhal was the fact that it happened to be right. Not all of his later books found a contemporary public as entirely indifferent as that " On Love" had done, but it was just " about 1880 " that the vogue which has made him one of the most frequently discussed of modern French writers began, and since posterity troubles itself far less frequently about the neglected writers of the past than is commonly supposed, the phenomenon requires some explanation. Stendhal was indeed one of those rare men really " ahead of their time " — not, perhaps, ahead of it in knowledge or wisdom but ahead of it in the sense that he was habituated to certain modes of feeling destined to be more generally shared by the generation which succeeded him than by his own. Hence he was lonely as only an alien can be.

His youth was cast in an age when a certain form of sensibility had expanded in full flower. Rousseau had given to it the classic expression and Rousseau had indeed done much to determine certain of the ways in which Stendhal was to feel. Half of him, that is to say, fitted into the conventional romantic mould, for his heart, proud of its own sensitiveness, expanded in the vague enthusiasm for the beauties of nature and the ineffable ecstasies of love so much insisted upon by the choice spirits of the time. But there was something else in his nature which checked the flow of his enthusiasm. Those of his contemporaries who chanced to read him felt the chilling presence of something dry, and cold, and ruthless, according but ill with the soft emotionalism of Rousseau and his followers. In the very midst of soaring sentiment, a cool detachment and a cautious common sense intruded themselves. The superficial but all-embracing benevolence of the earlier romantic was replaced by a frank cult of self and there were signs, too, of a cynicism all the more shocking *because* it was so matter-of-fact. Stendhal, in a word, was not of a piece and there was something alarming about all his deviations from the familiar norm of feeling.

His contemporaries could not perceive that in him the Eighteenth Century mind was painfully evolving into that of the Nineteenth, that the very aspects of his intelligence which pleased them least were those which would be most eagerly seized upon by a new generation whose perplexities and perversities he had anticipated; and yet such was actually the case. Later novelists were to attribute to him the beginnings of certain new methods in fiction but Stendhal the man, even more than Stendhal the novelist, captured the imagination of succeeding generations and did so because these generations recognized in him modes of feeling near to their own which are absent in the work of any of his contemporaries. Whatever judgment we may pass upon the Stendhalian hero we cannot but realize that at least we are more capable of understanding him than was the world into which he was thrust and that though he is an apparition often reappearing in later fiction he appeared here for the first time.

Fortunately for his biographers, Stendhal was absorbed in the study of his own personality and few if any novelists have struggled harder or more continuously to explain themselves. Not only is he the subject of his own best novels but many volumes of journals, memoirs, and letters testify to the continuous impulse which he felt to set himself, his thoughts, and his doings down upon paper. These documents would make it perfectly clear, even if the novels did not, that he was what we should call a neurotic and it may be that his "modernity" consists in part in the fact that he displayed the evidences of his complex maladjustment more freely than most authors before his time had done. But be that as it may, the fact remains that he and his heroes are merged into one and that the study of his personality, for which he left such ample material, is the most fruitful to be made in connection with him. His life problem was set for him by the events of his childhood and it is to that childhood that we must turn if we are to understand the writings of the man.

II

" My first memory," he said, " is of having bit the cheek or the forehead of Madam Pison-Dugalland, my cousin. . . . I see her yet, a woman of twenty-five, fat and much be-rouged. Apparently it was the rouge which piqued me. Seated in the midst of the meadow called the Bonn Gate field it so happened that her cheek was exactly on my level.

" 'Kiss me, Henry,' " she said. I did not want to, she grew angry, and I bit her firmly. I can see the scene, but that is doubtless because a crime was immediately charged against me and because they did not cease to talk to me about it. My aunt Séraphie, who had all the sharpness of a pious woman who had never been able to get herself married, declared that I was a monster and that I had an atrocious character."

Now perhaps this incident is not as significant as Stendhal thought it. But the fact that at the age of fifty-two he recorded it with meticulous satisfaction is significant indeed. Doubtless Aunt Séraphie was wrong. Doubtless the infant Beyle was not a monster. But the man, well past middle age, who cherished the memory of this childish ferocity, along with innumerable other passionate recollections of childhood, was a man abnormally absorbed in the very remote past and one who was still revenging himself for wrongs which he ought to have forgot long ago. The memory of that bitten cheek was the centre of a complex maze of resentful satisfactions. All of a bitter childhood was attached to it by means of widely ramified threads; most specifically it reminded him of the aunt whom he had so much hated, and besides it pleased him by recalling the fact, real or fancied, that even at that tender age he was already a rebel who dared bite back at the stupid people who annoyed him.

With no less of boastful pleasure he records how he revolted at the age of four against the formal piety of his family and conceived at that age his enduring horror of religion; how, a little later, he terrified his cautiously conservative father by a forged letter inviting him to enlist his son in the radical Bataillon D'Espérance; and how, while the members of his family spoke with hushed horror of the trial of Louis XVI, he felt, when he heard of the execution, " one of the most vivid moments of joy which I have ever felt in my life." Yet there was one member of his family — his mother — whose memory he cherished with a love which all his hate served only to emphasize and whom he idealized with a passion matched only by that which he exhibited in blackening the others.

Of that woman, whose shadow never left him, we know little except what her son has told us. She was the oldest daughter of a Doctor Gagnon; she married, at the age of twenty-three years, one Cherubin Beyle, and of that union Marie-Henri was born on the 23rd of January, 1783, in the town of Grenoble the memory of which, so Beyle said, affected him like the memory of a horrible indigestion — of something in which there is no danger but a frightful disgust. She was, it appears, better educated that one might expect a young provincial woman of the time to be and, if we may believe the memory of her son, more than usually beautiful. But in any case he loved her with the frantic tenderness of a sensitive child and she returned his affection with passion.

Stendhal never heard the term " mother-fixation " and he was familiar with no discussions of the sexual life of the child, but introspection was the chief business of his life; he had, besides, no little of the mania of the wounded but defiant mind for shocking le bourgeois; and accordingly he has left no doubt as to the manner in which he liked to regard his infantile passion. It was, he says, " as criminal as possible." " My mother was a charming woman and I was in love with my mother. . . . I wanted to cover her with kisses and I preferred that she be naked. She loved me with passion and kissed me frequently but I returned her kisses with such fervor that she was often obliged to avoid them. . . .

" In loving her at, let us say, the age of six I had absolutely the same character as when I was furiously in love with Alberte de Rubempré. My manner of seeking happiness had not at the latter time undergone the slightest fundamental change with this single exception: formerly I had been, in regard to that which constitutes the physical operations of love, in the position in which Caesar would have found himself in regard to the use of cannon and small arms if he had returned to the world. I should have learned it very quickly and it would not have made any fundamental change in my tactics."

Stendhal hastens to add that his mother did nothing to encourage this " criminal " love but her failure to participate in it did not in any way change its nature or prevent in him the process of what, in the fantastic terminology of his treatise " On Love," he was later to call " crystallization." We take, he says there, a joy in attributing a thousand perfections to a woman of whose love we are sure; for we see her adorned with a thousand perfections which others do not see. And so it was with his mother. Not only did she fix forever his admirations and his repugnances but, in the opinion of Paul Arbelet, most learned and indefatigable of the students of Stendhal, her image was the phantom he pursued through the course of his checkered career of love.

It is hardly worth while to speculate concerning what would have happened if this mother had lived. Perhaps Stendhal's love, not highly abnormal in itself, would have been gradually detached and transferred to some more suitable object; but death removed her when he had reached the age of seven years and left in her place one of those memories which are so much more potent than any physical presence because, being projections of ourselves, they cannot disappoint or disillusion us and must go on readjusting themselves to fit every growth or whim. At first he did not comprehend what her death could mean and the unfortunate Aunt Séraphie dared reproach him for the scantiness of his tears, but the mother's room was closed and in the midst of a grim household, every member of which he now hated, be began his bitter existence. The others shared his grief but not in any fashion comprehensible or comforting to him. Breaking all relations with society, they lived henceforward in a melancholy isolation which was for them an expression of their sorrow but for the boy only a cold and mournful insensibility, chilling his spirits without giving him any sense that his own passionate regrets were shared by those among whom he was compelled to live.

Unfortunately we have no unprejudiced source of informa-

tion upon which to base any judgment of the character of
the elder Beyle. In later life Stendhal, habitually referring to
him as "the bastard," regarded him only as a rather unsatisfactory source of income and that fact alone is doubtless sufficient to indicate that we cannot wholly trust the testimony
of the son in regard to the father. Moreover, Stendhal, by his
own confession, suffered from a lover's jealousy of his mistress's husband and he gave proof of the depth of that jealousy
by recording in his autobiography the delight with which
he learned that his mother had never loved her husband but
had married him only out of deference to the wishes of her
family. But even if we make all due allowance for the cranki-
ness of Stendhal's character and the violence of his prejudice,
there can remain no doubt that Cherubin Beyle was a man
incapable of any sympathy with the sensitive child who had
the misfortune to be born his son. He was cold, cautious, and
exclusively practical. Proud of his material success and of the
importance which he had attained in the bourgeois society
of a provincial town, he was stern in all his ideas concerning
the education of children, purely conventional in all his
judgments, sourly piestic and utterly incapable of any of that
romantic tenderness upon which the infant Stendhal had
come to depend during the lifetime of his mother. Rightly or
wrongly Stendhal was convinced that such love as his father
might have for him was not in the slightest degree personal
but exclusively the concern of a man with a strong sense of
family for the person destined to carry on his name, and
there was no show of affection between them. "It would have
been indeed difficult for him to have loved me," says Stendhal, "since he saw clearly that I did not love him"; and he

records besides how when his father was boring him one day with a discourse concerning parental love and the affection which children owed in return he replied: "If you love me so much, give me five sous a day and let me live as I like. Besides, you may rest entirely sure of one thing, and that is that when I come of age I shall take employment elsewhere."

There were, to be sure, three persons whom he regarded with affection. There was a maternal grandfather, a gravely liberal admirer of Voltaire, from whom he caught something of the spirit of Eighteenth Century enlightenment; an uncle, whose gay libertinism he came early to admire; and a sister of the terrible Séraphie from whom he learned a passionate romanticism which he was accustomed to call " Spanishism." But unfortunately he saw comparatively little of any of these three. The grandfather never came to the house after the death of his daughter, the uncle was only an occasional visitor, and some of the influence of the last was completely nullified by " that devil of a woman " her sister. Thus the young Stendhal was compelled to spend most of his time with the two people whom he hated most in all the world, and to them was soon added a third — his tutor — whom he would have hated still more if such a thing had been possible.

Perhaps this tutor, a certain Abbé Raillanne, would not have seemed to others as contemptible and vicious as he did to Stendhal. He does not appear to have been what his pupil thought him, a mere hypocrite in the image of Tartuffe, for his stern and formal piety was probably sincere, but we must say of him as of Cherubin Beyle that he was one of the last

men in the world either to understand or be understood by
the young Stendhal. There was neither tenderness nor enthusiasm in his cold religiosity but in its place only an iron
formalism and for him education consisted in an unyielding
disciplining intended to produce an unquestioning submission to all constituted authority. Scrupulous and intolerant,
he did nothing except awake in his pupil an undying repugnance for every virtue he endeavoured to inculcate and
succeed in appearing as a man " enemy of all that is honest "
and " completely detached from every human sentiment."
When he praised the beauties of Virgil whom Stendhal was
resentfully reading under the direction of the hated master
those praises affected him " like the praises of Russian kindness which the poor Poles of today are compelled to accept in
their subsidized newspapers " and, worst of all, the Abbé
insisted upon teaching him the Ptolemaic system of astronomy because, though it is false, " it explains everything,
and is approved of by the Church." Stendhal never forgot this
last crowning insult to his intelligence; years later he wrote
to his sister Pauline, still boiling with anger over the outrage;
and it served to fix forever his undying hatred of priests and
religion. The Abbé Raillanne, in a word, completed the development of that negativism which is one of the most fundamental traits of Stendhal's character and the latter sums up
the effect of his education when he says: " I hated the Abbé,
I hated my father, source of the Abbé's power, and I hated
still more Religion, in whose name they tyrannized over me."

Unfortunately this hate-poisoned youth was not relieved
by any hours of freedom spent with companions of his own
age. Cherubin Beyle, upper middle class citizen of a small

community who liked to think of himself as nearer to the nobility than to the common herd, was afraid of any contacts which his son might have with a world beneath him. He feared nothing more than to allow the boy to associate with the other children of the community and hence the young Stendhal, with a heart full of envy, watched from a window while those who should have been his companions passed in companies which he was never a single time allowed to join. Aunt Séraphie encouraged his father in his attitude of perpetual surveillance; it was only upon rare occasions that he obtained with great difficulty permission even to visit friends of the family; and by way of compensation he was permitted no more than a ride in the carriage with the hated Aunt Séraphie or a walk with his father who enraged him by referring to these melancholy expeditions as "our pleasures." Stendhal never forgave his family for his isolation and never himself recovered from it. Years later he was amazed when he heard someone speak of the city in which he had passed his melancholy youth as an agreeable place and it was always with a sense of some unutterable wrong that he looked back upon his boyhood.

"When I hear people speak of the innocent joys of youth, of the follies of that age, of the happiness of first youth, the only real happiness of life, my heart contracts. I knew nothing of it; more than that, that age was for me a period of perpetual unhappiness, hate, and of a desire, always impotent, for revenge. All my unhappiness might be summed up in two words: I was never permitted to speak to a child of my own age. And my relatives, much bored because of their separation from all society, honoured me with a continuous attention. From these two causes I was, at that period of life which is so gay for other children, bad, sombre, unreasonable, in a word a *slave* in the worst sense of that word, and little by little I took on the sentiments belonging to that state. What little happiness I could snatch was preserved by lying. In another respect, I was exactly like the contemporary peoples of Europe, my tyrants spoke to me always with soft words of the most tender solicitude, and their firmest ally was religion."

Thrown back, then, upon himself — upon his imagination and such books as came his way — he lived in resentful isolation. A translation of Ariosto, recommended to him beforehand by the fact that his mother had known and admired Italian literature, first absorbed him and, taking the demiburlesque extravagance of the Orlando with complete seriousness, he was able to say in after years that this romanticism deliberately pushed to the point of absurdity had "formed his character." Already, too, he was reading both Rousseau and Molière but reading the latter with that mixture of admiration and distaste which followed him all his life, because the flat common sense of the dramatist carried always with it a suggestion of his father's bourgeois spirit. Even in childhood it was evident that it was his hates which played the largest part, by reaction, in determining the direction of his mind. A chance word of his father in dispraise of Shakespeare prepared him for a lifelong admiration of the English poet whom he was later to set up in opposition to Racine, and at very early age he came to repose a complete confidence in the Encyclopedia of D'Alembert and Diderot for no other reason than that he knew the priests hated it.

Since the Abbé Raillanne feared liberty in any form and since his father was a conservative he became, as a matter of course, a violent Jacobin, listening with delight to the accounts of the revolution read aloud from the newspapers and rejoicing to learn that the king had at last been executed.

But Stendhal would not have been Stendhal if there had been nothing to differentiate him from the devoted radical of the revolution on the one hand, and the romantic lover *à la* Rousseau on the other. The very thing which most disturbed his contemporaries was the admixture of conscious libertinism which seemed to accord so ill with his idealization of love but which is so important a part of his character. And this too was fixed in youth. In the midst of graver reading he had managed to come across one of the more famous of Eighteenth Century erotic books — "Félicia, ou Mes Fredaines" — and the delightfully scabrous images which it evoked mingled themselves in his mind with his fancies concerning the life of the gay and worldly uncle who has already been mentioned.

That uncle had been carelessly kind to the boy. He seemed to bring with him something of the gay world from which he came and once he had been permitted to take the young Stendhal to a spectacle, "The Caravan of Cairo." The camels, defiling across the stage, turned the child's head. "I said to myself, very obscurely no doubt, and not so clearly as I write here: 'All the moments in the life of my uncle are as delicious as those which I share at the show. The finest thing in the world therefore is to be an amiable man like my uncle.' " It did not occur to him that this uncle was not as pleased as he by the sight of the camels, but when later he came to read in "Félicia" of the delight of promiscuous love, the images which rose in his mind mingled themselves with the memory of the pleasure he had taken at the spectacle and both attached themselves to the figure of the fascinating uncle. It is true, to be sure, that young Beyle was no more able than the mature Stendhal later proved himself to be of achieving the libertine's state of mind. Even as a child he could not help being passionate when he wanted to be only gallant, but henceforward he dreamed of conquests as well as of romantic devotion. Saint Preux, the admirable hero of Rousseau's "La Nouvelle Héloise," was always getting confused in his mind with Don Juan and from childhood he was resolved to love, not only greatly, but widely as well.

What Stendhal was when he had reached adolescence that he remained all the rest of his life. His experience was far from narrow, for his young manhood was cast in the period of the Napoleonic wars and of those stirring times he might with truth have said that much of it he saw and that part of it he was. Yet as the world expanded it did not cease to be essentially the world of his childhood. He had learned then to think of himself as one set apart from a hostile environment and so he continued always to do. More important still the problems of his youth were the ones which he set himself to work out on the larger scale and the principles he adopted were the principles of a rebellious child. It is no accident that, in the passage quoted above, he compares his relation to his parents to the relation of the oppressed peoples of Europe, for it was upon the sense of community established by that comparison that his paradoxical republicanism was founded and when he endowed his heroes with a Machiavellian morality he justified a childish deception by demanding if lying be not " the only resource of slaves."

At the age of seven he had already formulated his determination to become a writer of comedies; not long after, the possession of a mistress was added to his plans; and around these two ambitions his efforts never ceased to revolve. After convincing himself that the drama was beyond him, he allowed the play to be replaced by the novel and there was even a period during which he imagined himself great as a man of action, somewhat after the manner of Napoleon, but he never ceased to thirst after some sort of greatness which should compensate him for the indignities of his childhood and he never ceased to dream of some breast upon which he could find again the responsive warmth of his mother's bosom.

His childhood had furnished him with the motives of his ambition and its loneliness had cultivated in him the introspection which was to stand him in such good stead but it had, unfortunately, established his limitations as well. The man could never outgrow his childish resentments and could not help referring all things to the earlier experiences from which he could not escape. Even in fiction, autobiography obsesses him and when he sat down in middle age to write frankly an account of himself, thirty-six of the forty-seven chapters deal with his life at home, for he abandoned the effort as soon as he reached the period when his manhood began. He was part of the army of Napoleon at the time of the retreat from Moscow but Napoleon could never be for him as important as Abbé Raillanne who had poisoned his youth with bad astronomy or as that devil of a Séraphie who had forbid him to play with the other boys in Grenoble.

III

At the age of fifteen Stendhal, having escaped from the terrible Abbé, was sent to the École Central at Grenoble. It required but slight acquaintance with the other youths there to dispel the rosy hopes he had conceived of founding a romantic friendship but he was soon seized with an unexpected and at first inexplicable passion for the study of mathematics. Doubtless the suggestion of occult power which surrounds that science appealed to him, but he was further encouraged by an idea which occurred to him and which he ascribed to nothing less than genius: " Mathematics could enable me to escape from Grenoble." He could, that is to say, point to his proficiency as proof of a talent for engineering and his father would send him to study at the École Polytechnique in Paris.

The ruse, if ruse it was, was successful. In November, 1799, the young Stendhal set out and as he took his departure he saw tears in his father's eyes. Thirty-seven years later the man was still proud of the fact that the boy had not been betrayed into any corresponding emotion. "The only impression which these tears made upon me was that I found them decidedly ugly."

No sooner, however, had he arrived than the inevitable reaction set in. He missed the mountains of his native province and as he gazed at the friendless streets his disappointment expressed itself in the recurrent question, " Is this all ? " Face to face with the reality he had so much dreamed of, with the freedom and opportunity which had previously seemed all that was lacking, he realized, like many another provincial newly arrived in the metropolis, that there was nowhere to begin. In Grenoble he had fancied himself in the double capacity of genius and man of the world; in Paris he began to perceive that he was only what later he described as a youth "with the experience of a nine year old child and, probably, the pride of the Devil." The only one of his desires which was completely specific was the desire to be loved. "I arrived in Paris," he says, "with the idea of becoming a seducer of women." But even that modest ambition seemed less easy to realize than it had in the days when he had luxuriated in the pages of "Félicia" and lived in imagination the gay life of his uncle.

He had arrived in Paris armed with a letter of introduction to the family Daru to which he was related, and the Darus took him in. A good many years later he could write "I admire today, *but only* today, the kindness of all that family." At the moment the good offices of these correct and established personages did nothing but disconcert him. The father, an old and dignified man, froze his heart by the frigid formality with which he spoke of his regard for Cherubin Beyle and with which he addressed the young Stendhal as "Monsieur"; nor did the eldest son, Pierre, head of a bureau in the Department of War, embarrass him less. The society into which they introduced him was at once too formidable for his experience and not sufficiently brilliant to satisfy his naïve dreams of the Parisian salon. However accomplished a man of the world he might be in his own fancies, the call which he made to deliver his letters to the Darus was exactly the first visit he had ever made in his life, and when he appeared in the drawing-room it was simply as a raw

rustic of not very prepossessing appearance and no manners
at all.

He, however, who had formed his image of society " solely
and absolutely from the secret memoirs of Duclos, the three
or seven volumes of Saint-Simon already published, and
novels "; he, who imagined himself as a remarkable combination of " a Saint Preux and a Valmont " (hero of the scabrous
" Liaisons Dangereuses ") could not believe that the fault
was entirely his if he found himself inferior and awkward
in a society which he judged sadly second-rate. Feeling in
himself an infinite disposition to love and be loved, he
fancied that nothing except the opportunity was lacking and
he could not but suppose that there existed somewhere a society clever enough to recognize his capacities and thus to put
him at his ease. Meanwhile it was a great bore not only to live
at the Daru house but to be compelled to dine there as well.

Somehow or other his entry into the École Polytechnique
was put off from day to day. His interest in mathematics,
now that it had served his purpose, disappeared suddenly and
the chief business of his life was now recognized to be the
discovery of the still no more than " not impossible " she,
though of course, and incidentally, there were the comedies,
as great but less bourgeois than those of Molière, to be
written. Gradually, however, even the considerate Darus
began to grow impatient. The head of the family suggested
tactfully that it was not yet too late, that so exceptional a
mathematician as Henri Beyle had been certified to be might
still enter and find no difficulty in catching up with his class.
And when this suggestion was not taken, the inactive young
man was bundled off one morning to the Department of

STENDHAL

War along with Pierre. There he was given a desk, soon signallized himself by his tendency to spell *cela* with two *l*'s (an infirmity which impressed him sufficiently to cause him to lend it to the hero of his best novel) and failed so signally to display any administrative sense that the question once more arose in the Daru family as to what might be done with so unpromising a country relation.

Fortunately, however, Napoleon had decided just about this time to make a personal visit to Italy and to dispute there with the Austrians. Pierre, through his connections at the War Department, had positions which he could fill and one was found in the quartermasters department of the Army of the Reserve at Milan. The secret ambition which attached Stendhal to Paris was not of a sort which he could well confess, neither was it one which would appeal to either his father or the elder Daru as a sufficient reason for his remaining without employment and so, though not unwillingly, he set out at the age of seventeen for Italy.

Now ever since the days when he had taken the mock chivalry of Ariosto with intense seriousness the heroic ideal had had a place in Stendhal's mind alongside of the sentimental. Like a great many shut-in personalities he had an admiration for violence in the abstract and his ancient Jacobinism had transformed itself into an enthusiasm for Napoleon, freer of oppressed people and founder of liberty. Theoretically there was no reason why martial glory should not serve his purpose as well as literary distinction or why his amorous conquests should not be made in brass buttons; and yet, before he reached his destination, there occurred a significant incident. At Geneva he paused in his journey to make a sentimental pilgrimage to the birth-place of Rousseau, author of that most unmartial novel " La Nouvelle Heloïse," and an observer might have seen in that action an ominous indication of the exclusively literary habit of mind from which Stendhal never recovered.

Moreover, it did not take him long to realize that the soldiers of Napoleon's army were not at all like the heroes of Ariosto nor, indeed, very much like the image he had formed of the noble followers of their noble leader. There is something about the condition of the soldier's profession which makes it difficult for him to live up to the ideals which are cherished behind the lines. In the rough and tumble of camp life he develops a realistic attitude — a cynicism even — a little shocking to those at home who like to think of him in the robes of a crusader. In the lull between battles he manages to take time from his regular occupation of hating the distant enemy in order to indulge in a warmer, more intimate, hate for some members of his battalion and, while no doubt devoted in the large to the common good, he often, in certain small particulars, most unchivalrously looks out for his own. So, at least, it was in the army of Napoleon, and Stendhal observed the fact with a distress somewhat compensated for by the literary satisfaction attendant upon making an observation. " In place of the sentiments of heroic friendship which I had attributed after eight years of heroic reveries based upon the characters of Ferragus and of Rinaldo I saw sharp and evil egotists; often, in anger at seeing us mounted while they were on foot, they cursed us. A little later they stole our horses."

Soon, however, a momentary exposure to fire, which he

savoured with an entirely literary gusto, revived somewhat his thirst for adventure, but as he approached Italy, with his portmanteau stuffed with books, he approached it rather as the land of art and love than as the field of battle. He was still trailing after him the burden of his virginity but Italy, land of soft night and amiable women, would surely, so he thought, permit him somewhere to lay it down.

Once more he paused in his journey and underwent the most significant emotional experience connected with his military activities. He heard sung the sufficiently mediocre opera " The Secret Marriage " of Cimarosa, whose amorous strains raised him to a seventh heaven of delight, and immediately he began to bewail the hard fate which had destined him to the " coarse trade " of the soldier when he might have devoted his life to music. When he came later, in his autobiography, to describe the experience he said: " In an instant my two great actions: first having passed St. Bernard, second having been under fire, disappeared. All that seemed coarse and low. I felt something like my enthusiasm for the church above Rome, but something decidedly more pure and more vivid. . . . In Cimarosa all was divine." And with that inconstancy which is one of the surest signs that in Stendhal the artistic impulse was not the result of a mind characterized by the tendency to express its perceptions in some particular form but rather of disturbed sensibilities and obscure needs which sought relief in fantasy, he formulated once more a new ambition: " I must live, I must see the world, I must become a brave soldier, and then, after one or two years, I shall return to music, *my only love.*" " To live in Italy and hear this music became," he adds, " the object of my plans."

The incident will serve to define the nature of Stendhal's interest in music which, like his interest in painting, never led him to any appreciation of it as an art form but consisted solely in a sensitivity to emotional values directly translatable into his own experience. "Music pleases me," he wrote later, "as an expression of love" and he always valued a composition or a picture just in proportion as it performed for him the function which novels came later to perform, in so far, that is to say, as it satisfied emotions rising out of his personal predicament. But however unimportant his enthusiasm for "The Secret Marriage" may be as the expression of an aesthetic judgment, his visit to the opera was of great importance in the history of his own inward life, for it seemed to define for him the exact nature of his romantic longings and it remained for him so long the exact equivalent of the emotions he was seeking that at fifty-two he could write: "I do not know how many leagues I would go on foot, or how many days of prison I would endure to hear 'Don Giovanni' or the 'Secret Marriage,' and I do not know for what other thing I would make this effort."

When he had arrived in Milan enough of his enthusiasm for war or enough of the resolution which he had recently made to become a brave soldier by way of preliminary to his musical career remained to cause him to seek a transfer from his somewhat inglorious position in the army and to get himself appointed second lieutenant in the sixth dragoons. Fate, however, decided that it was not as a soldier that he should distinguish himself and though twice he was, for brief periods, with his regiment, by far the greater part of his life in Italy was spent in amusing himself. He learned Italian, looked at pictures, attended the theatre and even took lessons upon the clarinet while still dreaming, of course, of a great love.

And yet Italy, land of opportunities, had none for him. All his companions were happy in the company of mistresses but Stendhal, convinced that no one would better appreciate the kindness of a woman or return her love with more ardent transports, could find none, since the very intensity of his longing made him shy. In the presence of his companions he blushed at the idea of not being considered an accomplished roué, and yet, though he strutted before them, he had later the naïveté to reproach them for not having seduced someone for him. "No one had pity upon me or aided me with charitable advice. . . . If only I had had a friend he would have put me into the arms of a woman." At last, like many another young romantic at once sensual and timid, he betook himself to a prostitute but though she relieved him of the burden of his virginity he could not take much satisfaction in this mere technicality.

Somewhat less than two years after he had embarked upon a military career Stendhal, disgusted with the barrenness of his life as a mere headquarters soldier and disappointed no doubt at his failure to make even a beginning in the career of gallantry, secured his dismissal and set out on his return to France. In one of the several obituaries which he later wrote for himself he said of this period: "It was the finest time in his life, he adored music and literary glory, and he placed a high estimation upon the art of giving a good blow with the sabre," but this is the mere bombast of a man so avid of glory that he was able to take pleasure in writing romantic death notices of himself. Actually the months spent in Italy had apparently carried him not a step nearer toward any of the accomplishments which he fancied were necessary for the peace of his soul. He had certainly won no military laurels upon which he could rest and though he had at last fixed upon a mistress whom he could worship in discreet silence he had made so little impression upon her that when he returned ten years later prepared to overwhelm her with a decade of absent devotion she was barely able to recall him as the possessor of a face which melted into the group which had surrounded her actual life.

But if Italy had not satisfied any of his desires it had, on the other hand, made each more vivid. Every one of his romantic sensibilities had been accentuated, and frustration had perpetuated in heightened form all the romantic longings which a few triumphs might have served to dissipate. Existing as he had done upon the fringe of a great martial adventure, his imagination was stimulated by the news of victories while he had but little experience to disillusion him with military grandeur, and in the midst of a whole army making love in Milan he was compelled to take what solace he could in music which was, for him at least, not so much the food of love as something which stimulated his appetite. Bewailing his fate in later years he lamented that he " had passed without women the two or three years when my temperament was the most vivid." " Certainly," he said, " if I had been loved at Milan, my character would have been very different. . . . The two years of sighs, of tears, of flights of love and of melancholy, which I passed in Italy without women, in that climate, at that epoch of life and without prejudices, probably gave me that inexhaustible spring of sensibility which today, at twenty-eight, makes me feel everything up to the smallest details."

Stendhal, then, returned to Paris more ardent than he had left it but no nearer to the satisfaction of any ambition. The comedies " like those of Molière " were still to be written and the ecstasies of love still to be tasted.

IV

In 1801, before leaving Italy, Stendhal began a journal with the words: " I undertake to write the history of my life day by day. I do not know if I shall have the strength to complete this project, already begun at Paris." The previous attempt here referred to has been lost but after the beginning of the new journal Stendhal's life during many of his most significant years may be read as it was lived and in the intimate record we have, not memories coloured as even a man who tried as hard as Stendhal to be honest must colour them in an autobiography, but the unrevised record of thoughts and happenings. In it we can not only read of his action but, what is far more interesting, we can follow the development of a mind in which the keenness born of inveterate introspection is fascinatingly mingled with that naïveté inseparable from a man whose timidity made it necessary that his knowledge of the world should be almost exclusively theoretical. During these years " Beylism " or the philosophy of his novels was developed in all its complex and passionate inconsistency.

Not unnaturally he found, in the course of his self-examinations at the end of the day, occasions to take stock of himself and to formulate his plans of conduct. He confessed that his noble and republican principles, the energy of his character and a natural impatience which made it sometimes impossible for him to hide the irritation provoked by contact with mediocrity, made him disliked and feared by many, but the inconveniences arising from this fact were, he was sure, not to be avoided by " a *large and virtuous* soul formed in solitude." Near the very beginning of the journal he had indeed gone so far as to confess that "it would be too cruel if one man should possess all the kinds of superiority" and he had, moreover, comforted himself with the reflection that such a man, should he exist, would probably be bored with success while he, Stendhal, would be able to savour his superiorities the better for the very reason that they were not quite universal. He believed that the ideas which he had for several plays, both comic and tragic, were sufficient to justify his confidence that he would some day do something in the theatre and certainly some of his more discerning acquaintances had recognized in him what he loved to call (in English) an "understanding soul." All his life, to be sure, he had been oppressed by a neurotic melancholy, by a sadness "thoughtful, dry, without tears and without consolation"; but a doctor had diagnosed it for him and he recognized in reading the work of the learned Cabanis a description of his temperament which did not wholly displease him.

From his program he had dropped all that referred to military distinction but otherwise it was much the same as it had been in Italy: "I have known myself, I have realized that it is at the temple of Memory that I must knock in order to find happiness and that with me love will be the only passion not driven away by the love of glory, but that it will be subordinated to this last or only at moments usurp its place." From experience (in worshipping from a distance) he concluded that the love of woman, however great its pleasure might be, did not last so well in the memory as Glory did and from this highly characteristic calculation of pleasures he concluded that Glory was the mistress he was least disposed to quit. He did not, however, find it necessary to remark that he had never yet been intimate with either.

Somewhere back in his childhood Stendhal had heard from the lips of his beloved grandfather the phrase " knowledge of the human heart " and it remained with him always. It was not until he had reached middle age that he formulated in a letter the first principles of his philosophy by remarking that there are only two sciences: the science of knowing the motives for the actions of men, and logic or the art of not deceiving ourselves in marching towards happiness. But already this philosophy, at once so complete and so vague, was the one by which he was attempting to guide himself, for he was, like a good epicurean, resolved to be happy and he fancied that he could carve out that happiness if only he could achieve "knowledge of the human heart." Perhaps he never came really to understand any heart except his own and perhaps he understood that imperfectly, but the effort to become what we should call a psychologist filled all that part of his mental life which was not mere dreaming and gave to the novels their value.

Shy as he was and deprived by his timidity of any of that spontaneous and all but unconscious tact which makes many less sensitive people seem unpremeditatively winning, he was thrown back upon principles and plans appearing admirable upon paper but destined either never to be put into practice or to prove somehow incapable of producing the desired effect. Yet maxims, resolutions and principles of conduct intended to guide him in the pursuit of his double ambition continued to stud the pages of his journal. At one time he notes his intention to " acquire a reputation as the greatest

French poet, not by intrigues, like Voltaire, but by really meriting it" and he calmly adds, "for this learn: Greek, Latin, Italian, and English." But when he discovered, some time later, that Shakespeare was uneducated he renounced the project of becoming learned in concluding that "one must feel, not know," and his plans for becoming a successful lover were hardly less elaborate or less fixed. Before going into the company of ladies he would decide upon the tone he should take and even what he should say; upon one occasion he even wrote down what he should reply when, having thrown himself at the feet of a certain lady, she should ask him "What are you?" and he felt confident that in his soul "soiled perhaps by some faults, she will see the most noble passions at their maximum and a love for her which shares its empire with the love of glory and which frequently overrules it." "I dare believe," he added, "that, being at her feet, I shall show her my love in a manner worthy of her and of it, in terms of an immortal beauty." But the difficulty was actually to get himself at the feet of this lady (who did not after all remain queen of his heart very long) or at those of anybody else and no matter how carefully he planned his conduct beforehand it needed but the interruption of other young men, less advanced than he in "knowledge of the human heart" but for that very reason, perhaps, more easy of address, to put him completely out. And yet ill success did not cause him to lose confidence in his method, and out of the super-abundance of his *savoir faire* he could spare some epigrammatically phrased precepts sent to his sister for the guidance of her conduct.

Doubtless he was growing in self-knowledge. Somewhat

later, when he had come to realize that the very ardour of more romantic souls puts them at a disadvantage in the game of gallantry alongside of those who do not have to feign their debonair confidence and that "great souls" are likely to appear somewhat monstrous in a boudoir, he could write with a pomposity which does not disguise the justice of his reflections: "My genius for the grandly pathetic, founded on great philosophy in the genre of Pascal, Helvétius, and Rousseau . . . has possessed me up until now. It has never expanded in naïve gay discourse or in amiable follies. . . . Let us quit therefore the serious which is the necessary result of thoughts continually fixed on all that is Grand. It is the coin with which one buys immortality but not amiable smiles and tender pressures of the hand. Let us, when alone, dream of glory but when in society of how to be found amiable." It is one thing, however, for a shy and sensitive man to resolve in private to be gay and another for him to carry out his resolution in the face of more dazzling companions and the woman who seems so infinitely desirable. Stendhal lacked the touch of humour which — if anything could have done so — would have made such self-examinations as that just recorded of any practical value and he continued to be more conspicuously a lover of glory than glorious and, in love, more ardent than victorious.

Many years before, during his boyhood at Grenoble, he had been violently taken with a pathetic little actress-singer who was a member of a local company presenting plays and comic operas. The famous process of "crystallization" (perhaps merely Stendhal's term for the process, now called transference, by which he habitually invested the women who caught his fancy with all the qualities belonging to the idealized memory of his mother) took place, and he attributed to her every beauty, every nobility and every grandeur. One day he had the courage to ask someone where she lived and he called this act probably the bravest of his life. But when he approached the place he was overcome with fear and when he saw her down the street he took flight as though the devil were after him. " The happiness of seeing her closely, at a distance of five or six steps, was too great, it burned me," he said, and beyond this type of adolescent adoration it was all but impossible for him to go.

Returning from Italy he was taken first of all, but very briefly, with a certain Victorine and it was then a cousin, Adèle Rebuffel (aged fourteen) who enraptured him. In his journal he set down how she gave him a lock of her hair, how she pressed his hand, and how upon one occasion when he quitted her " at a quarter to four " she permitted him a kiss. But soon Adèle was forgotten. Stendhal, convincing himself that it was necessary for his career as a dramatist, began to take lessons in declamation and at his teacher's he met the woman (Melanie) who was, after a time, to give him his first opportunity to learn what love could do for him.

His principles had always been of the worst. He believed he had no scruples against seducing Adèle in her parents' house but gradually he was being compelled to realize that even the most depraved theories of conduct are not sufficient to make a libertine and that somehow it not infrequently happens that while those most horrified at the idea of sin are swept into adultery, the most emancipated cannot manage to find the pitfall they so ardently long for. But his day was approaching.

Melanie Guilbert (or, as she preferred to call herself professionally, Louason) was not a particularly remarkable woman. She was mildly pretty, she was amiable, she was possessed of a very mediocre talent and she had enormous eyes which Stendhal took to be the sign of that beautiful soul which he counted the first requisite of a mistress. When first he saw her he judged that she was " easy " and he cultivated her with the intention of adding her, in passing, to that collection which, as it was painful to think, had not been begun though he was already in his twenties. But soon the, for him, inevitable happened; he was head over heels in love of the most extravagant sort. He could never begin to play the chosen role of Don Juan without finding himself, thanks to that very fixation upon his mother which was the origin of his mania to love, transformed into a Saint Preux and humbly at the feet of the woman whom he had planned to despoil with cavalier insouciance. He wanted to be an egotist, he steeled himself to practise a ruthlessness of which his philosophy approved, but he always ended by being the abject one to whom pity was due.

Moreover, a new complication was soon added. One of his companions hinted a knowledge that Melanie was afflicted with one of those maladies which make the "favours" of a woman properly so called only in an ironic sense, and thus Stendhal was faced with a new perplexity. Such difficulties ought not to arise in a romance. The heroes of even the more irresponsible sort of gallant histories do not meet them and certainly they cannot be set to the music of Cimarosa. Yet

Stendhal in his curious double capacity of romantic realist accepted them without any apparent sense of the disharmony which, for another type of mind, would certainly have profoundly affected in some direction or other the character of his feelings. He considered the question specifically, gravely, and with that *lo-gique* (pronounced in two syllables) upon which he insisted with what seemed to his friends a comic pertinacity. And when he came a little later to be convinced that the chance remark which had alarmed him had not been based upon any specific information he recorded his relief in terms not marked by any tone which would distinguish them from those in which he would have described any other favourable turn in the affairs of his heart.

Yet however absurd these disharmonies may seem, they are not only highly characteristic of the man but they are, in addition, analogous to the dissonances which constitute the chief moral problems of his work. On the one hand the regularity with which the plans of the cynical seducer are checkmated, not by any forces outside of himself but by the half involuntary resurgence of romantic emotions which transform the nature of his feelings, is the source of a comedy of which Stendhal, with his neurotic intensity, was never aware; on the other hand the manner in which he set out with a coldly reasonable detachment to prepare the conditions of an ecstatic happiness is the central phenomenon resulting from his peculiar philosophy of life. His methods, that is to say, were the methods of a utilitarian but his values were the values of a romantic and indeed it might be said that the distinguishing mark both of Stendhal and his heroes is the fact that they pursue with realistic

means a happiness which has illusion as the condition of
its existence.

Subjected as he was to the influence of the contemporary
" ideologistic " philosophers of France whose psychologizing
appealed to his introspective temperament and whose rationalism fitted in with his schemes for conquering life through
a " knowledge of the human heart," he strove valiantly to fit
his actions and desires to a logical scheme. He spoke of his
treatise " On Love " as being concerned with the " physi-
ology " of that passion and in the preface to the second
edition he described it as " simply an accurate and scientific
treatise on a type of madness, which is very rare in France."
He loved, moreover, to adopt a tone of cynical gallantry
imitated from " Félicia," where he had read: " Perfect love is
a chimera. . . . Defend yourself against these violent sentiments which are sure to make you unhappy. . . . Never
involve yourself up to the point where you will experience more pain than pleasure." He imitated it, too, in a
" Catechism of a Roué," which, at the age of twenty, he
drew up for his own guidance but, try as he would, he could
not successfully cultivate in himself anything resembling
such paganism. Nor would he, indeed, have been content
had he been able to do so since the love for which he felt
the need was something quite different and since this need
persisted in revealing its strength by continually transforming the woman to be victimized into the image of the divine
creature for whom in the deepest recesses of his soul he
longed.

One characteristic of love *à la Félicia* he did indeed realize.
He managed to achieve the inconstancy which belongs to the

gallant mode of experience and which he defended in his book on love by saying: " A passionate man sees nothing but perfection in the woman he loves; and yet his affections may still wander, for the spirit wearies of monotony, even in the case of the most perfect happiness." But in reality the fickleness of Stendhal was the fickleness rather of the man made recurrently the dupe of his romantic emotions than of the conscious libertine, and his carefully laid plans would always fail because that which he thought he wanted was not that for which, in reality, he was seeking.

Let us return, however, to the specific adventure in hand and to the young Stendhal whom we left at the moment when that " crystallization " which turned the seducer into a victim had just taken place. Melanie Guilbert was not " easy " in the sense that he had at first supposed; she was not, that is to say, a libertine; but she was, on the other hand, an amiable woman with a rather weak and dependent character who was by nature disposed to an affectionate if not passionate attachment, and she was ready enough to love any attractive young man who should single her out for his attentions. Yet so great was the shyness of Stendhal that he was once more compelled to confine his boldest love-making to the pages of his journal. She permitted, more than she encouraged, his attempts to make love; and yet, as always, he seemed too absorbed in his theories to be capable of any very effective practice.

In the journal he records with delight how he has spoken to her of love with an art learned from a book and he justifies his insincerity with the reflection that his love " like that of Othello before his jealousy " is " of a nature too large and too beautiful not to be ridiculous in society." Therefore, he finds it wiser to express himself after the manner of lesser souls. "When I have enjoyed six thousand livres income for six months I shall be sufficiently strong to be myself in love." He notes too, on several different occasions, that at a certain instant he could, if he had wished, have possessed her but something (in part general timidity, in part the typical psychological reaction of the man for whom the amorous impulses are always fixed upon a phantom of the past and who therefore draws back from any person of flesh and blood because the identification made between the two is not quite convincing) held him back; and instead of taking her he went back to his lodgings and there analysed the proceedings of the evening. "During the first half hour she softened and she dreamed as she listened to me, after this the interest fell and I believe that for an instant I bored her. I ought to take advantage of the first moment of tenderness to possess her." But then a certain incident had made him fear that her soul was not yet quite all that it ought to be. "Tomorrow I had better take her Shakespeare."

A little later he was writing, apropos another conversation which he had had with her: "I am very well contented with myself" and he was excusing the slowness of his progress with the reflection that he, after all, had but little experience: "In six years I shall not require a month and a half to arrive at this point with a woman who pleases me; probably I shall possess her at the end of a month." But characteristically he was immediately seized with a doubt as to whether or not such proficiency was entirely desirable. "Will I be as happy at the end of four weeks? It is only happiness which counts.

. . . Shall I have the heart which I have at the present hour." Even Stendhal, then, was beginning to realize that the expertness of the professional seducer is incompatible with the full ecstasy of the romantic and that one cannot hope to repeat indefinitely the happy transports of first love by means of a long series of adroitly planned conquests. And yet it still seemed to him that, after all, there was not for the present any danger of his being too nonchalant for his own good, for a little later still he was making this note: " It will be time for me to deliver myself over to my too tender nature after the victory; let me attempt to see her as an ordinary woman, to analyse her heart and to play upon her passions. . . . That which has spoiled me up until now is the false opinion I have had [of women]."

It would be difficult to say how long this comedy of the too adroit lover and the mistress who was doubtless already beginning to wish for " less art and more matter " might have continued had chance not intervened; but a circumstance arose which precipitated the dénouement. Stendhal had been planning with one of his friends a wild scheme for achieving an astounding financial success as a banker but the scheme called for a period of apprenticeship in the South and he was loath to leave Paris and Melanie. One day, however, the latter announced to him a change in her plans. There seemed no immediate prospect that the *Comédie Française* to which she had been aspiring would open its doors to her and she decided to accept an offer from a provincial theatre in Marseilles. Stendhal said nothing of what he had had in his own mind but instead he declared his intention of sacrificing everything to follow her wherever she might go and of this bit of deception he was inordinately proud, not because its value in winning a woman already won was very apparent, but because he had at last been able to achieve one of those strokes of Machiavellian policy which he so much admired.

He had begun to prepare himself for his career in finance by reading some books on the subject in the *Bibliothèque Nationale*. He had also confided to his journal a new self-examination and a new set of resolutions which were, this time, to rid himself of his tendency to build romantic castles in Spain. But he was not capable either of abandoning his old delusions or even of perceiving that his plan of becoming a power in finance was another chimera and when, in May, 1805, he set out with Melanie in a public diligence he was still the same doubly duped victim of his romantic feelings and of his Machiavellian delusions. He had attempted to force his own hand by writing: " If I have not M on the way, I shall never be unhappy with her. In the contrary event, I shall be the happiest of men at Marseilles." He had even (and this is a delightful touch) armed himself with a copy of " Félicia " to take on the journey in the hope that this book which had helped to form the ambitions of his childhood would sharpen his resolutions now. And yet, though for six days they journeyed together and though each night they had been set down both at the same inn, this ardent lover who had almost the right to regard himself as a bridegroom could not be brought to consummate the union. Before leaving he had been able in imagination to leap over the action in hand and to form the resolution to acquire practice by making an amorous assault upon every woman he met; but in actuality he could never bring his courage to the sticking point. "I see very well that it is necessary to finish with Louason, but . . . either she or the occasion must aid me."

Stendhal had quitted his mistress at Lyon in order to make a short visit elsewhere. Her *début* was, however, approaching and her lover, naturally wishing to be present, came on to Marseilles (though not in time for the *début*) armed with certain letters of introduction. She made her first appearance — acceptably but with the absence of any grand éclat which was prophetic of her mediocre career — and a little later Stendhal began his business career in Marseilles as a grocer. He was not, to be sure, standing behind a counter or weighing out sugar. It was a commission house into which his letters of introduction had given him an entrée; he preferred to consider this *début,* even less dazzling than that of Melanie, was only the beginning of his preparation for a career in finance; and he could signalize it in his journal by the entry: "I have made a beginning with banking." But even if he did not actually wear an apron, those ironies who presided always over the fate of Stendhal and whose pranks are all the more striking from the fact that their serious-minded victim never recognized them as his gods, saw to it that at the moment when he was attempting to reach a state of exaltation befitting his first triumph in love he should be engaged in the trade which has always stood as the type of all that is most bourgeois and most unromantic.

We do not know just when or under what circumstances he found himself at last in Melanie's arms. From Marseilles he had written to his sister Pauline a letter describing his delight when he felt sure that he was loved; he had also extracted from a Parisian friend an assurance that, in the opin-

ion of the latter, he was not wrong in concluding that
Melanie — who, be it remembered, had not only listened
with pleasure to his declarations for months, but had encouraged him to travel with her and who, finally, had written
him letters urging him to hasten on to Marseilles — cared
for him; and so at last even he could hesitate no longer.
Under the date of 10th Thermidor (Stendhal was patrioti-
cally using the Napoleonic calendar) there is in the journal
an obscure entry, couched in the very bad English which
Stendhal often affected when recording very intimate things,
and which reads: "The evening till the midnight forever."
Probably this signalizes the bridal night but in any event it
is certain that about this time he achieved what he had looked
forward to as his ultimate felicity.

For a time he experienced or thought that he was experiencing all that he had dreamed of and the ambitions of the
Don Juan were lost sight of in the ecstasy of a Saint Preux.
"I am perfectly happy," he declared and it was of the soul
of his mistress that he thought most. "I did not believe,"
he wrote to his sister, "that so beautiful a character existed
in nature. . . . She has a beautiful soul, beautiful is not the
word, it is sublime." Moreover, though he did not speak of
marriage, he was now assuming that the exalted relationship
which he had established would last forever. "I shall love
you until death, and I will never survive you." Decidedly,
then, Stendhal was delivering himself over to that "too
tender nature" which he had recognized as a dangerous element in his character and the only stroke of Machiavellian
policy which he permitted himself was the benevolent but
pointless one of passing off his mistress's daughter as his own

both to Pauline and to his grandfather. If the copy of "Félicia" had not been pitched from the diligence window, it was not, we may be sure, much read during that period.

Persons not affected by that "species of madness" which Stendhal assiduously cultivated found it, however, difficult to discover in the not very vivid personality of Melanie those extraordinary qualities perceived by her lover. To Pauline he had written that, as an actress, she possessed "two or three times more genius than she needs" but the local critics spoke of her with more indulgence than enthusiasm and it is significant that references to her art quickly disappear from Stendhal's journal. The fact is ominous since it was particularly of an actress-mistress that the child Stendhal had dreamed and since, in the early days of his honeymoon, he had written in a fashion which made it evident that he was distinctly affected by the glamour which surrounds those who tread the stage. Perhaps the resolution which he made to teach her philosophy was also ominous since it certainly indicated either that the process of "crystallization" had been arrested before it had resulted in the attribution of *all* perfections to the woman he loved or that the opposite process which, by analogy, we may dub "solution" had begun to take place. But in any event the passion of Stendhal ebbed away with the slow inevitability of the tide.

In no sense was it the fault of poor Melanie. Even if the fates had made her less gently, ineffectually pathetic and much nearer the image which Stendhal had made of her, the event would not have been very greatly different. Those who, like him, are in pursuit of a phantom must always discover that any actual person is not in reality the one they seek. No woman he possessed as completely and knew as intimately as he came to know Melanie could have been the source of anything but a disillusion, for such men as he, falling in love when they make a mistaken identification and falling out of it when they inevitably discover their mistake, cannot love with fidelity anything except either a memory or someone who, by escaping them, can remain an illusion. And Stendhal, in those flashes of self-knowledge which were always ineffectual because, perhaps, he did not fully understand the reason behind the phenomena he could so acutely observe, was aware of the fact. Sometime later he wrote to Pauline: "What I need is a woman who has a great soul, and they are all like novels: interesting up to the dénouement, and, two days afterwards, one is astonished to have been interested in such commonplace things."

At first he had been blissful and exaltedly happy to walk with her in the fields on Sunday and to dream of perfect felicity *à la* Rousseau. But in the pages of the journal one may read under the date of the second of February, 1806, an account of the end of one of these excursions over which the shadow of boredom hangs ominously. "I was dying of cold, she was not too gay . . . not lending herself to any conversation which could give us a little satisfaction. Wind-blown to the very bone, cold, with aching head, arid heart, and not desiring anything . . . I went to take a demi-tasse at the café." In the beginning the melancholy lassitude of Melanie had seemed one of the signs of a superior soul but gradually it came to irritate him and he even, in his puzzled fretfulness, began to grow jealous though his mistress does not seem to have had either the venality, the lightness or the sensuality which would have been likely to give the slightest occasion for any suspicion as to her fidelity. Then, too, as his own passion subsided, he was inclined to accuse her of being incapable of rising to his height of passionate love. " I could have wished in her a little more transport, or, more exactly a little transport. One could not be more happy so far as beauty is concerned, I have that beyond my expectations . . . but I could have wished a little of that transport which I imagine that Angela [the Italian woman adored only from a respectful distance] had." Moreover Melanie did not make the progress she should have made in ideologistic philosophy; she did not seize quickly nor properly appreciate the principles of Beylism and the end was already in sight when he wrote in his journal: " I begin to find M stupid. I recall thousands of traits which prove a lack of *esprit.*"

Meanwhile the practical affairs of the pair were prospering not better than those of the heart, for the English blockade was having a bad effect upon both the grocery business and the theatrical enterprise at Marseilles. When Stendhal had entered upon business he had done so full of hope. It would lead him eventually to fortune and, so he reflected, its commonplace discipline would be good for his too romantic disposition. Now, however, he was disillusioned and he could see no good whatever in the whole affair. Love had proved a disappointment and he began to remember that, according to his plans, love of woman was only occasionally and briefly to take precedent over love of glory. Ambition, therefore, flared up. "Saturday evening . . . I had had perhaps the strongest access of passion that I have ever experienced. . . . The passion brought into play was ambition. . . . I was imagining the happiness I would experience if I were auditor at the Council of State or if I were something else. . . . Dining . . . with Melanie, I ought to have been the happiest of men through love; it seemed entirely extinct, and little by little I became powerfully and almost furiously ambitious. . . . I am ashamed to say it . . . (but) I felt capable of the greatest crimes and the greatest infamies. . . . My passion devoured me, it whipped me forward, I was dying with rage because I was not even at that hour doing anything for my advancement, I would have taken pleasure in beating Melanie with whom I was." And so when Melanie was forced by the disaster which overtook the theatre at Marseilles to seek an engagement elsewhere, Stendhal who, for all his Machiavel-lianism had not the courage to make a clean break, allowed her to depart alone with nothing settled. He conducted her a little way out of the city into which, seven months before, he had entered in high hopes of a perfect felicity.

His first reaction was a joy at finding himself once more a free man. A little later he wrote " After her departure, an immediate joy over my liberty . . . at present, I believe, a just appreciation: there is much feeling of friendship, of love even if she did not wish to tyrannize over me and if she would not always complain." Ten days after they had parted he was acknowledging that " Solitude often makes me sad, the faults of M begin to be effaced." But as was so often the case, the psychologist entered to note a warning fact: " It is difficult not to exaggerate the happiness which one is not enjoying " and Stendhal attempted to find release in the pur-suit of other women concerning whom he had no great illu-sions. Letters, rather sad and resigned than bitter or recriminating, came from Melanie who asked only that her position be defined; but Stendhal could not define it. After a little he returned to Paris and their acquaintance was renewed; they even passed some lovers' nights together again, but for Stendhal at least all the glamour was past and it was not until the whole affair had become a memory again that it could be recaptured in the imagination.

Even in reverie it was not she, however, who filled most often the largest place. In the course of a life devoted to love as much as to anything else, Stendhal never found anyone to give herself so unreservedly as Melanie had done, but for that very reason his affair with her was the most definitely closed of all and she was the one whose image it was most difficult to remake into the image of his non-existent ideal. Yet even Melanie, when she had gone from him forever, received some of the homage which he was accustomed to pay to those who eluded him. Knowing that she had gone to Moscow, he once searched for her among the ruins of that city and in 1808 he wrote to Pauline from Germany: " Here I am a personage . . . the Germans say Monseigneur to me; the important French personages call me Monsieur L'Intendant . . . but I was happier at Paris. If one could put life where one wished, like a piece upon a checker-board, I would go again to learn declamation from Dugazon, see Melanie with whom I was in love. . . . When she did not wish to receive me, I should read in a library, and finally, I should take a walk in the Tuilleries or, from time to time, I should envy those who are happy."

It may be noted, however, that this period to which he wished to return was the one during which he had longed for

Melanie, not the one during which she had been his, yet even she, as she receded into the past and as the lineaments of her face and character began to grow dim in the shadows, could be once more half mistaken for someone she was not. Her only fault had been to love him too well, for in so doing she had allowed herself to be known.

V

The next eight years were externally the fullest of Stendhal's life and yet they were, for him, singularly unimportant. His longing for action had lead him to solicit once again the aid of the Darus, and in 1806 he secured an appointment as *Adjoint aux Commissaires des Guerres* with a post at Brunswick. In 1810 he rose for a time to be *Auditeur au Conseil D'État* and he led in Paris the life of a dandy, with champagne and partridges for his table and an actress for his bed. Then, leaving Paris again, he saw the destruction of Moscow — "the most beautiful fire in the world" — and finally, in his own words, he "fell in 1814." Yet these stirring, eventful years were essentially barren; all but unreal; merely an interlude in the life of a man whose inward, purely personal existence was the only real one.

It was not that he was incapable of practical affairs. He was more than competent in the charge of important duties; his services were even distinguished; but he could not consider them either interesting or important since action, for which he had so much theoretical admiration, seemed always disappointingly flat. Arriving once in Dresden in the course of his duties, his first thought was not of war but of the fact that "The Secret Marriage" was to be sung at the opera, and such of the records of his life during this epoch as remain to us reveal a surprising lack of interest in the great events of which he was part. Writing to an acquaintance in 1812 he exclaims: "How man changes! . . . That thirst for seeing which formerly I had is entirely extinguished; since I saw Milan and Italy, all that I see repels me by its grossness. Will you believe that, in the absence of anything which touches me personally, I am sometimes on the point of tears? In this ocean of barbarism, not a sound responds to my soul! Everything is coarse, dirty, rotten, physically and morally. I have not even a little pleasure except in having music made for me on a little piano by a fellow who feels music as I feel the mass. Ambition is nothing to me any more; the most beautiful *cordon* would not seem to me a recompense for the mud in which I am mired." Even the burning of Moscow was spoiled for him by the character of the other spectators. "One ought to have been either alone or surrounded by people of spirit in order to enjoy it. That which has spoiled for me the Russian campaign is to have made it with people who would have shrunk the Coliseum and the bay of Naples."

And though he had been unhappy on his past visit to Italy, Italy seemed now the promised land. His moments of leisure were given over to reading books about Italy or books with an Italian setting and finally in August, 1811, while he was *Auditeur au Conseil D'État,* he could endure the longing no more. He requested a leave of absence and he set out with the delusion that the soil of Italy would ease the dissatisfaction which he could not explain. The entry in the journal for September 8 reads: "I experienced yesterday evening and today sentiments full of delight. I am on the point of weeping. . . . Shall I say what moved me most in arriving at Milan? One may well see that this is written for no one but myself. It was an odour of manure peculiar to these streets. That more than all the rest proved to me clearly that I was in Milan."

No sooner had he arrived there than he bethought him of

Angela Pietragrua, the woman whom he had adored from a distance during his earlier stay. His plan was to throw ten years of devotion at her feet and in the conduct of this affair we may see how little five years as an active, competent official had changed the nature of his desires or improved his methods of obtaining them. Angela, as it turned out, was a frivolous, sensual woman who made no great fuss over taking a new lover, and indeed when he had explained his sufferings of the previous decade she asked him simply why he had not told her then. But even she was not a little nonplussed when he presented himself. She did not at first remember him but when she did she was amiable enough.

"There came to me some idea of having Madam P in passing; she had said to me that she had many things to say to me." He bought a cane to make himself look younger and soon he was projecting a declaration. Immediately, how-ever, all the old romantic timidity returned. "I counted the minutes. I wished to go to her house at one o'clock. At last noon arrives. I dress. I was tender and disposed to make a beautiful declaration . . . but it is exactly in that state that chance goes against me. I ask the porter if she is in. I am told ' yes.' I mount full of impatience; a pretty little *femme de chambre,* lively and gay, tells me with a mischievous air: 'Your servant; Madam has gone out.' I go to Brera and, while looking at the pictures, I try . . . to render my soul dry and to take things gaily. . . . At two o'clock they drive us from the Brera; I go with M. Rafaelli to see him work at a copy of the Last Supper, at a Christ of Guido Reni. I wish to kill time until three o'clock. . . . I mount to her apart-ment; but no more soft emotions, no more tenderness. I should have seen her two hours before that." Only the suggestion of romance was needed to transform the veteran of a great campaign into the youth who could not find courage to take Melanie Guilbert or even to make him once more the boy who had fled headlong from the danger of meeting face to face the poor little singer of the Grenoble theatre.

Fortunately, however, Angela was willing and far more skilful than he. She led him on, she feigned coyness, and once, when he attempted to kiss her, she gave him a piece of advice which did credit to her understanding of his character. "Receive," she said, "and never take." Stendhal found this maxim " very suitable to his character " and he followed it with happy results. Once Angela sent him away under the pretext that, if they did not part then, they could never part and Stendhal, who was, for all his " knowledge of the human heart," incapable of perceiving that this was no more than a veiled invitation "felt the presence of a superior reason." " I felt myself penetrated with an admiration for her which led me on to tenderness. . . . It is in her arms that I wish to die. This mixture of grandeur of soul and of attachment to me would make me swallow nobly that pill. . . . It would be so sweet for me to weep with Angela."

Then finally, on the 21st of September, "At a quarter to ten I went on to the little church at the corner of the street. . . . I passed again at 10.20; she made me a sign. After a mortal contest . . . in which I played unhappiness and almost despair, she was mine, at 11.30." Next day Stendhal left Milan; a month later he was back; and the comedy was continued with further complications introduced by the presence of a supposedly jealous husband. But though, in after years, Angela deceived him with great *sang froid,* he never could see the affair in any but the most romantic light and when, at last, he was compelled to return to his duties in Paris he wrote to Pauline: "Imagine a man at a charming ball where all the women are gracefully dressed; the fire of pleasure sparkles in their eyes, one may distinguish the glances which they let fall upon their lovers. This beautiful place is decorated with a taste full of voluptuousness and grandeur; a thousand candles spread a celestial light; a suave odour puts one beside oneself. The sensitive soul who finds himself in this place of delights, the nervous man, is obliged to leave the ball-room; he discovers thick mist, a night of rain and mud; he stumbles three or four times and at last falls into a manure hole. There is a short history of my return from Italy."

After Milan and Angela not even the burning of Moscow could seem other than a little flat and every day of a campaign does not furnish a spectacle like that. He was growing more and more weary of the soldier's profession. Potentially it was, he thought, one of the noblest, but in practice it was completely spoiled by the failure of soldiers to act like the heroes of Ariosto. He was completely disgusted with the Napoleonic aim and he managed to be in Italy at the time when his erstwhile hero was thrown down. He did not so much "fall" with Napoleon as wither when Napoleon was cut off and a little later he found his patriotism so reduced that he was able to apply (in vain) to the government of the Bourbons for a place.

Already Stendhal was thirty-one years old but he was still drifting, for not even contact with reality at its grimmest

had weaned him away from the dreams of a prolonged adolescence. Wherever one turns in diaries or letters one finds
still the romantic longings of youth and that same effort to
dramatize himself and his emotions which had made the
earlier pages of his life at once pathetic and absurd. Years
later he was to confess "I see now . . . that my greatest
pleasure is to dream " and that had, indeed, always been so.
He had dreamed as a child, he had dreamed as a youth, and,
even in the midst of his most romantic experiences, his desire to love, to discover some actuality corresponding to a
dream, had been more evident than any passion operating in
its own right. Yet even now he could not resign himself to
the fact that for such as he the only possible salvation lies in
the dream to which art gives its illusion of reality. From
childhood he had thought of himself as a writer yet not even
one play had ever been completed because he was always
breaking off in the middle of a scene to play out the drama
in his own person and always finding that life struck a
false note.

One might have supposed that the Napoleonic debacle,
casting him again upon his own resources, would have driven
him at once into some realization of his predicament, but
he was still unwilling to believe that life could not be made
to conform itself to an adolescent dream. He was sure that
somewhere he could find a woman whose passion would
make him forget the something which he could not quite
remember and that somehow he could achieve a pose which
would startle the world as he had startled the little circle at
home when he had bit the cheek of Madam Pison-Dugalland
or expressed his scorn of his father's bourgeois tyranny.

Somewhere there were men whose "understanding hearts" placed them among "the happy few"; and it was to that company which he must belong.

But when one sets out to practise life as an art one needs money, and one day Stendhal sat down to consider his finances. There was a pension from the government of nine hundred francs, there was an income of eighteen hundred francs from the dowery of his mother, and there was the very indefinite sum which the "bastard" — growing more miserly as he grew older — might be expected to send him. It was too little for Paris but it was enough for Italy and Italy was after all his spiritual home. He could live there "in freedom"; he could have a box at the opera to hear "The Secret Marriage"; and he could develop his soul.

Not long thereafter a heavy but somewhat dandiacal Frenchman began to be a familiar figure in the cafés, the theatres, and the art galleries of Milan. To others he was a *flâneur* with a taste for philosophical speculation and somewhat dangerous political ideas but to himself he was one engaged in a great experiment — that of seeking happiness by rational principles. "*Enfin,*" he wrote, "Italy pleases me. I pass each day from seven to midnight hearing music and seeing two ballets; the climate does the rest. . . . I shall live a year or two at Milan, then at Venice and then . . . I shall tempt fortune in Paris. . . . You find me mad; but what do you wish? All that is worth the trouble, in this world, *is the self.* The good side of this character is to take a retreat from Russia like a glass of lemonade. Blame yourself, my amiable friend, if I have spoken so long of the *me.*" More than anyone alive, he thought, he knew just how the head and the heart were best to be correlated, how philosophy and art could be made to enrich existence and, after the manner of those whom the world has hurt too much, he loved to fancy how his own ruthlessness could pay it back in its own coin. He might seem a harmless person to others but others could hardly realize how completely he regarded the world as no more than his oyster. " I am not," he boasted, " one of those who, when they see a rain storm on a summer's day, think of the ravished crops and the peasants ruined and so make themselves melancholy. I am one of those who think: so much the better; the weather will be fresher and it will be good to breathe; I love the air when it has been swept by rain. I do not consider anything but my pleasure; I accept my own being; I am the Egotist; I am Me."

Life did not, however, yield itself so easily as it should have done to one who thus proclaimed himself its master. Angela would not resume the game and no longer took much pains to conceal from him the fact that there were others whom she preferred. He transferred his passion to another lady, wife of a Polish officer and Mathilde Viscontini by name; but Stendhal, for all his knowledge of the human heart, had no longer even youth to recommend him. He overwhelmed her with passionate declarations, he followed her upon a journey, but she only thought him a little mad. The more perfectly he became master of the rules of success the less events bent themselves to his will, and if he boasted it was only to keep up his courage. Then one day the authorities had the effront-ery to suggest that his pension would no longer be paid un-less he came himself to France to collect it. He had half a mind to tell them what he thought of this outrage, but the

Austrian rulers in Italy had taken it into their heads that he was a dangerous radical and he concluded that it would be best to go home. Paris was not Italy but one could take ones *self* with one.

It was in 1821 that he came again to Paris. He was thirty-eight years old and to the world he was nobody. *He* knew that he was a master of life, that he understood the principles of human conduct from the bottom up and that he knew, too, how happiness was to be won, but he had done nothing to make the world see him as he saw himself. Years before, he had amused his leisure by dashing off and publishing under an assumed name some account of the lives of Haydn and Mozart but that effort had resulted in nothing except an outburst of almost incredulous protest on the part of the man from whom he had stolen his material and then, with an effrontery born of a vast egotism, he had published in 1817 a " History of Painting in Italy " in which all except certain romantic theories was stolen from various standard works. But Beylism was not appreciated nor its author known. Why should he not begin by telling the world what he knew about love? Accordingly the treatise " On Love " was published in 1822 and though, so he said, it " explains simply, rationally, mathematically, as it were, the different emotions which follow one after the other and which taken together are called the passion of love " it fell still-born from the press and though, still further, he tried to console himself by the assurance that he wrote only " for about a hundred readers " he was nevertheless disappointed to know that he had found only seventeen. He was still sure, however, of his methods. " If I could make an analysis of the comic as clear and as complete as (modesty aside and according to myself) that which I have made of *love,* it would be no more than a trifle for me to work in the comic *genre.* I should make bold strokes with the brush as I would do if I had to paint (exactly and not to produce a certain effect) the heart of a young woman who loves, whether the love be of vanity or of passion." Meanwhile, however, not even the comedies begun so long ago had been completed.

Stendhal was now frequenting the salons of certain *littérateurs.* Inspired no doubt by an impulse to imitation he undertook to write a romance and the result was " Armance, ou Quelques Scènes de Paris en 1827 " which was published during the same year in which the scene was laid but which failed even to ripple the surface of the life it described. At last, however, his moment was approaching. Not long after " Armance " was completed he sat down to write another novel and in 1830 "The Red and the Black " was off the press. Before the end of the same year he had completed " The Charter House of Parma " and it is chiefly upon these two books, written in rapid succession, that his fame as a romancer rests.

Now Stendhal was one who had theories about the writing of novels as he had theories about everything else. He was a romanticist but a romanticist with a difference, and in the extensive repertory of his hates few took precedence over his hatred for the inflated eloquence of such reigning romanticists as Chateaubriand and Hugo. He professed to regard Napoleon's Civil Code as a model of style; he had supreme faith in the adequacy of his schematized psychology; and his artistic credo was not unlike that of the " scientific naturalist " who appeared a generation or two later. Fortunately, however, " The Red and the Black " was not written chiefly out of his theories. When he sat down to his desk something deeper than his system of rationalizations took possession of him and in spite of himself he tapped, not his theories, but the source from which those theories had themselves sprung, creating by a fiat of the imagination that world — long sought in vain — where he would find the complex needs of his strange being satisfied and where people would actually behave as he was convinced they should.

From this moment forward Stendhal's life belongs rather to the critic than to the biographer because it was more and more with pen and paper that he came to express himself, and because, even for him, the life of his characters became gradually more vivid and absorbing than any life of his. Yet this bifurcation is one which affects only the form of the ex- pression and hardly at all the things expressed. Stendhal did not take on new interests but instead projected himself for- ward into a new medium — that of art — and concerned himself with the effort to understand and to solve in fiction the problems which he had inherited from childhood and found unsolvable in life. He had failed to achieve his desire, failed even to understand what it was and hence, realizing that, with the passing of youth, the possibilty of doing so had passed also, he launched children of his brain who might start out anew under varied conditions, in order that he might share their experiences and see how they would fare. For him Beylism had not worked; it had brought him neither hap- piness and success nor even the splendid, spectacular failure which he would have been glad to accept. But other Beylists (born of his brain) should be more fortunate than he.

VI

Always the desire to be great in some respect had been with Stendhal more definite and more constant than the desire for greatness of any particular kind. He had abandoned one career after another and he had put off until his youth was past even those literary efforts which, since childhood, he had planned to make. He had been a soldier, business man, diplomat and lover without finding satisfaction in any capacity. His whole life had been a search for a role which he could play whole-heartedly. And now when he came to write novels he began to multiply his personalities — to give himself a multiplicity of lives with which to experiment — not only because the pleasure of watching himself live was the only one he had ever had, but also because in novels he could set according to his own will the conditions of the game. In life, unfortunately, these conditions had been set for him.

Just before "The Red and the Black" was published a turn for the better took place in his material fortunes. The election of Louis-Philippe made him once more acceptable to the government; he was appointed consul at Trieste, and soon after removed to Città Vecchia, thirty-five miles from Rome, where he remained most of the time until his death some twelve years later in 1842. But even physical residence in Italy was no longer so important as it once had been. From his home came voluminous letters bewailing the boredom of his situation, and he could no longer throw himself passionately into any real adventures. But as Henri Beyle faded away "Julien Sorel" and "Fabrice del Dougo" became more real and soon their creator was beginning to re-embody them as " Lucien Leuwen " in the romance never to be completed but known by the name of the hero. To an old friend he might write that he was " sad from having no one to love " but the truth was that he had, in the heroines of his novels, personages far more satisfactory than Melanie Guilbert or Angela Pietragrua had ever been.

Of these *alter egos* who lived for him, Julien Sorel, hero of " The Red and the Black," may be taken as typical and in him may be discovered Stendhal's dream of himself. Julien is of humble birth, son of a coarse-grained father whom he hates and, because of humiliations, fired with a double ambition — to succeed and to be loved. The external circumstances of his life are quite different from those of his creator but his character and his methods are the same. Like Stendhal he formulates a Machiavellian plan (in which conscious hypocrisy plays a large part) for the cultivation of his personality, and like Stendhal he is not wholly aware of the incompatibility between the ideals of the Saint Preux and the Don Juan. His character is purged of all that Stendhal recognized as potentially ridiculous in himself and his schemes are made more successful than Stendhal was ever able to make his own, but he remains essentially an *alter ego,* merely more perfectly Stendhalian than Stendhal himself.

And what may be said of Julien Sorel may, in general, be said also of the heroes of " The Charter House of Parma " and " Lucien Leuwen." Both the settings and all the circumstances under which the characters make their *débuts* are varied, but the central figure is in each case the same romantic egotist seeking the same satisfactions through the same means. Stendhal did not care how completely the accident of birth varied the details of the problem to be solved — probably indeed he preferred to set it each time anew — and he even consented to give Lucien Leuwen an admirable father, but the problem must be always the same — how a young man, at once romantic and clear-sighted, may go about to win a knowledge of the human heart and through that knowledge achieve the kind of success which consists in the realization of self.

Moreover, his heroes are, again like himself, victims of a not wholly comprehended bitterness. They feel themselves invested with a certain right to move in a moral universe beyond good and evil, because something — unusual sensibilities and unusual, hardly defined, wrongs — sets them apart. The world is their oyster and they will open it ruthlessly, yet the pearl which they are always hoping to find is a delicate jewel — some great love or the opportunity for some dazzling ultimate heroism. And so it is that they too go about dishonourably in search of honour, and attempt to attain an ideal love by seducing and abandoning the wives or daughters of those who befriend them. Aristocratically disdainful of the vulgar, they are nevertheless champions of the people against their oppressor and this paradox is related to all the others. For at bottom their perversities are masquerading as the protests of a man who finds the world not good enough for him. Just as Stendhal himself felt relieved of any loyalty to the aims of Napoleon because the soldiers of Napoleon did not fulfil his idea of what military chivalry demanded, so his heroes abandon their mistresses because the latter are not quite worthy, and act the hypocrite because the world is too low to deserve honest treatment.

Thus whether "Beylism" be studied in the person of its creator or in that of one of his characters, it is not, as he supposed, a logical philosophy of life, but rather a complex of ideas, desires and quasi-ethical principles which attain such unity as they have, not because of any necessary relation of one to another, but because they found themselves together in the personality of Stendhal and were by him transferred to his characters. To be a Beylist one must believe (1) in romantic love, (2) in the cult of the ego, (3) in the morality of the superman, (4) in military glory and (5) in political liberalism. One need not act always in the direction which all of these beliefs would seem to recommend. The egotist may momentarily be lost in the lover; the cult of self and the morality of the superman may interfere with the lover of political justice. But one must at different times be aware of all these impulses and one must think of them not as essentially contradictory but as somehow fusible into a philosophy never quite grasped.

Believing, as Stendhal himself professed to believe, that "the most perfect form of civilization would be a combination of all the dainty pleasures of the Nineteenth Century with the constant presence of danger," one must long for the good old days of Louis XIV when "a man might at any time be called upon to leave the drawing-rooms of Marley at three days notice to repair to the battle-fields of Senef or of Ramillies," and yet one must, on a different occasion, be intellectually superior to "that really rather absurd prejudice which was called *honour* in the days of Madame de Sévigné, and which consists first and foremost in sacrificing one's life to serve the master whose subject one is by birth." One must also, like Julien Sorel, be capable of dropping a tear over the sorrows of the people while, at the same time, one is scornful of democracies like that of the United States because, though one admits somewhat naïvely that its inhabitants are perfect in integrity and civic virtue, they neither have romantic souls nor support an opera.

Now in the case of Stendhal himself the psychological determinants in this *mélange* of warring elements are clearer than they ever are in the case of the characters to whom he transfers them. His own mental life may be explained in terms of a reaction to his earlier experiences, as an effort to divest himself of the fixations of his childhood and, while purging his hatreds away, to salve his wounds with the triumphal successes imagined during the period of his intensest humiliations. The death of the too well beloved mother had burdened him with a romantic longing which no actual person could satisfy, and the hatred of his father had generated in him that fixed delusion of persecution which seemed to justify an amoral struggle against an inimical world. Sheer negativism had made him a Jacobin in the midst of a conservative family, but he had, nevertheless, all those feelings of aristocratic superiority which are commonly cherished by morbidly sensitive souls who compensate by imagining themselves endowed with some capacity or some fineness of feeling belonging exclusively to those whom Stendhal loved to call " the happy few."

But however clear the psychology of Beylism may be when it is thought of as an attribute of Henri Beyle, it is less so when it is thought of in connection with the characters of his novels considered as persons entirely separate from him, and it is less clear for the simple reason that though Stendhal attributes to them all that he recognized as significant in himself he could not, because he himself did not thoroughly understand, explain their personalities on the basis of the factors which determined his own. Hence they appear as Beylists without having gone through the experiences which, in the case of its creator, generated that philosophy.

When a novelist draws his material, as Stendhal did, from himself, when he creates characters in his own image in order to put them through adventures emotionally satisfying to himself, he must, before his novels attain the full validity of art, detach them from their psychological origins and make them something capable of an existence independent of himself and of the purely individual needs they were created to fulfil. So long as their interest or their significance is understandable only in relation to the author, they are documents (perhaps highly interesting ones) for the study of his personality, but they are not in any complete sense works of art and it must be confessed that the novels of Stendhal are, in this respect, inferior to those of other masters no more renowned than he. Nor is it merely that the virtue of the heroes (exaggerated by way of compensation for Stendhal's own bungling efforts) is often too remarkable for the taste of the reader. The fact is that the novels are too perfectly fitted to gratify the emotional needs of their creator to be wholly satisfying to anybody else and that the secret of the personality of the characters can never be unlocked with any key furnished by the works in which they are found. The key is Stendhal himself.

And yet, though these novels may not be wholly satisfactory as art, they have exercised a fascination over many minds and an influence upon novel writing which may be attributed in part to the interest of the man who half reveals himself in them and in part to the fact that, whether through accident or not, they furnish a sort of bridge between the romantic literature of his epoch and the psychological realism that was to follow. Perhaps a nature as unstable and chaotic as his, is not likely to produce perfect art, but its restless, rebellious eccentricity is very likely, on the other hand, to throw off hints and to discover new modes of sensibility. It is in minds like his that intellectual or emotional " sports " destined to play important roles take their rise, and so it was in his case. In the very heart of romanticism something anti-romantic was born.

As to the romantic elements they are so obvious that it is hardly worth while to insist upon them. Not only is his tendency to revolve around the ideas of Love and Glory typically romantic but so too is that whole conception of the " storminess " of the superior character. And yet the ideal of analysis tends to replace that of ecstasy so that Beylism differs from, let us say, the philosophy of Rousseau by the presence of a certain cynical dryness, by the abstraction of all that is genuinely transcendental and the introduction of utilitarian principles which lead him to consider even the pleasures of romantic love as the result of an agreeable delusion — which a rational man may permit himself to use as he uses alcohol — rather than as a mysterious gift of God.

Writing to a friend from Moscow in 1812 he said: " I have been reading the ' Confessions ' of Rousseau for the last eight days. It is solely from the lack of two or three principles of

Beylism that he was so unhappy. This mania to see duties and virtues everywhere put pedantry in his style and unhappiness in his life. He allies himself with a young man during three weeks; bang, the *duties* of friendship, etc. . . . This man forgets him after two years; he tries to find some black explanation. *Beylism* would have said to him: 'Two bodies approach one another, a heat and a fermentation is born; but all states of this sort are transitory. It is a flower which one must voluptuously enjoy, etc.' Do you get my idea?"

And however inharmonious or unstable the particular combination of discordant elements which Stendhal called Beylism may be, his variations from the romantic were variations in the direction in which the temper of Europe was moving. Not only is there present in him that conflict between rationalism and romantic sensibility which was to destroy the latter but there is also clearly foreshadowed that moral nihilism into which the nineteenth century was unwillingly driven. His heroes were very imperfect supermen struggling desperately against their romantic impulse in the effort to achieve a Nietzschean morality and coming near enough to it to make Nietzsche one of the most enthusiastic of Stendhal's admirers. The experiences of the latter's infancy plus the literature upon which he nourished his morbid sensibilities fixed certain romantic conceptions indelibly upon him, but if one can imagine him with certain of the delusions to which he recurrently fell victim stripped away, he would be very nearly a contemporary man looking at the contemporary man's bleak world and wondering what may be found to take the place of all that we have outgrown.

In the course of some very brief remarks upon the novels

of Stendhal, Croce let fall the phrase "unconscious irony," and it is, perhaps, the most pregnant one ever applied in an effort to describe these works. No writer since Stendhal has ever succeeded in completely resolving the conflicts which form the moral substance of his fiction. Romantic love persists in spite of all possible disillusion with it and the typical contemporary hero is one who, like Julien Sorel, gropes his way toward new standards and new ethics while he is still emotionally controlled by the world in which he half believes. But man, more and more convinced of his littleness, is more and more inclined to regard his predicament with bitter irony. The last delusion of grandeur gone, he is haunted by the suspicion that the play in which he is the protagonist is not tragedy but farce and so he finds in the heroes of Stendhal who still trail the remnants of the romantic robes an unconscious irony which the author never makes explicit because he never, except in flashes, perceived it.

And yet, significantly enough, the idea of the comic as of something which he ought to but could not quite grasp haunted him uneasily. It was of comedies that he dreamed as a child, it was to comedy that he devoted his first unsuccessful efforts to write, and one may trace through his life a recurrent but baffled search for some comic spirit which would resolve the discords of his sensibilities. Thus, in 1805, he was recording in his journal his belief that a feeling for the comic represents a stage beyond the feeling for the tragic, and noting the fact that the laugh is the final weapon which one man can wield over another. But a little before he had noted: " I commence to perceive that there are many things which a too passionate heart does not perceive: the comic, the naïve, the fine sensations of style " and more than thirty years later he was offering (in " Henri Brulard ") a similar excuse based upon self-criticism. " This Spanishism prevents me from having comic genius: First I turn my regard and my memory from all that is base: Second I sympathize, as I did at the age of ten when I read Ariosto, with everything that is recounted concerning love, forests (the woods and their vast silences) and generosity." Stendhal, then, not only knew that he was incapable of the comic spirit but knew also, to a certain extent, why this was so. The little boy who had loved his dead mother so tenderly and who had taken Ariosto with perfect seriousness could not perceive the hard outlines of anything for very long. Sooner or later the mist of sentiment interposed itself.

We are not permitted to wish for any writer that his temperament or experience had been different. Had Stendhal's mother lived and had his father been a different man he might, perhaps, have been himself a very different writer, but it is at least equally possible that without his wounds he would never have been a writer at all. And so we may not wish away what he called his Spanishism. Yet the fact remains that though it was probably the element which his contemporaries could best appreciate, it was the thing which, as he himself realized, stood in the way of an achievement toward which he made certain ineffectual struggles. Doubtless it would be asking too much to expect that, even if he had had less of it, he would have been able to perceive the wry comedy of his own existence, but granted that little less he might conceivably have written fictional comedies anticipating by a century those which many of our contemporaries are still struggling to write. As it is his novels are imperfect in the sense that to appreciate them fully the reader must bring to his reading something which Stendhal himself did not put in them. He must, as it were, regard them from an oblique angle in such a fashion that their unconscious irony, invisible when they are seen from the author's own point of view, furnishes the key to the pattern.

VII

In 1835, when Stendhal (aged fifty-two years and one month) had two great novels behind him and a third in the process of composition, he brusquely abandoned for the time being the work upon which he had embarked and began to write an autobiography of his youth.

Three years before, so he tells us, he had been standing upon the Monte Janiculum in Rome, absorbed in the magnificence of the view spread out before him, when his thoughts of the grandeur of Rome had suddenly been interrupted by the realization that he would soon be fifty. Half-incredulous, he counted the decades upon his fingers — the sum was correct — but though he tried to comfort himself with the thought that better men than he had died before him he could not shake off a burdening sense of responsibility. It was not, he thought, any concern with his fame. M. Daru, he had been told, had once called him " stupid as a carp." Perhaps it was true and he believed that, if, when he had been translated to another world, he should seek out Montesquieu and Montesquieu should say to him " My poor friend, you never had any talent at all" he should not be surprised.

He was, however, troubled by a sense that after all these years of assiduous egotism he was still a stranger to himself. Among his friends he passed for a cold man, even for a roué, and though he knew he was not that, he was not sure what he was or what he had been. Was he gay or melancholy, intelligent or stupid? " I see clearly that a great many writers who enjoy a great fame are detestable. . . . But is to see the faults of others to have talent oneself? I perceive that the worst painters see very clearly the defects of each other. M. Ingres is right in all he says against M. Gros, and M. Gros in all he says against M. Ingres." "I ought," he concluded, "to write my life. Then when it shall be finished, in two or three years, I shall know perhaps whether I have been gay or sad, man of intelligence or fool, courageous or timid, and, in short, happy or unhappy."

For the moment nothing except a few pages came of the project but the idea would not let him rest. During 1833 and 1834 he had been working on "Lucien Leuwen" and he could not get on with it. It was abandoned, the autobiography known as "The Life of Henri Brulard" was begun, and in less than four months, between eight and nine hundred pages of manuscript (all that we possess) had been completed. "Lucien Leuwen" was tinkered with again after the autobiography had been dashed off but though he had six years yet to live it was never completed, and the contrast between his rapt absorption in the one and his laborious struggle with the other is not without its significance.

For cathartic though they were, neither "The Red and the Black" nor "The Charter House of Parma" had served to purge his soul. They too had been written in a burst of creative energy but their effect had been merely to relieve, not to cure him. In them he had got as far as he was destined ever to get from his purely personal concerns and in them he had done as much as he was ever able to do in the direction of transforming the attitudes developed by the experiences of his childhood into that philosophy of life which he offered to others under the name of Beylism. Now, however, he was circling once more about the childhood from which he could not get free. Most of the new book was concerned with the time before he was really launched upon life, and in it he indulged with frank abandon his interest in the youth from which he never escaped. Cherubin Beyle, Aunt Séraphie, and the Abbé Raillanne come vividly to life, and his childhood hatred flames up with them. The past is not dead but living, and it is, he seems to realize, the remotest figures from whose influence he cannot escape. The lonely and defeated egotist finds little food for thought in his years of service in Napoleon's army, but in imagination he returns to Grenoble and seeks there to find the answer to the riddle of his own soul. Seeks? Perhaps in a measure finds. "My love for her was as criminal as possible." And if he can never quite possess and comprehend himself completely at least the direct discharge of his emotions as he allows himself to relive old resentments and old rebellions is free enough to carry his pen flying across the pages.

To say that "The Life of Henri Brulard" is Stendhal's best book, that the posterity to whom its author looked must find its direct revelations more completely satisfying than any of his imaginative treatments of his ego, is, of course, to say that in a measure he failed as a novelist. Yet the fact is hardly to be doubted. The reality which emerges from the pages of "Brulard" is more continuously fascinating than any fantasies he was able to create, the man more intriguing than any of the roles he allowed himself in imagination to play. He had never quite succeeded in transforming the personal into the universal, and while the amoral heroics of his characters seemed shocking to his contemporaries, they sometimes strike us as a little theatrical and forced. But

"Henri Brulard" takes its place with the great confessions; it is a book as searching and honest as any a troubled man ever succeeded in writing about himself.

When it came to be written, Stendhal had very nearly lived out, or rather dreamed out, his life. In 1840 "The Charter House of Parma" (written it will be remembered a decade before) was published. It drew an enthusiastic review from Balzac and gave to its author the only real taste of fame he had ever received. But though the letter which he wrote in acknowledgment reveals plainly enough how sweet to him was the taste of that contemporary favour he had pretended to despise, it did not enable him to get "Lucien Leuwen" completed in the year and a half which still remained to him. In "Henri Brulard" he had explored his soul as deeply as he was able to do and there was nothing to drive him on.

On the rainy thirtieth of April, 1837, Stendhal had composed several pages which began "I remember that Jules Janin said to me 'Ah! what a beautiful article we should make about you if you were dead!' . . . I have the fancy to write this article myself." A brief account of his life follows and then the epitaph which he had written for himself (in Italian) in 1821:

Here lies
Arrigo Beyle, of Milan.
He lived, he wrote, he loved.
He departed at the age of —
In 18—

To this were added the following notes: "He loved Cimarosa, Shakespeare, Mozart, Correggio. He loved passionately

V., M., A., Ange., M., C., and though he was nothing less than he was beautiful, he was loved much by four or five of these initials. He respected only one man: Napoleon. End of this notice, not *reread* in order not to lie."

The epitaph was carved upon his tombstone in the cemetery of Montmartre. Perhaps a better one would have been a sentence from " Henri Brulard ": " I am going to be fifty, it will be time for me to know myself."

MARCEL PROUST.

MARCEL PROUST

I

BEHIND every great work of art lies the effort to form some conception of the good life. The artist may seek it as Richardson did in the subjection of the will to the conventions of society or he may, like Stendhal, start off in the opposite direction with the full conviction that the ego is the source of all happiness. But experience and observation furnish him with certain materials and he must decide what wisdom would do with them.

Often enough it happens that he is very distinctly the child of his century. Not only is his experience in some sense typical but so too are his thoughts and his enthusiasms. He finds himself, as Boccaccio did, a simple pagan at the time when his countrymen are living a pagan life; or, like so many of the novelists of the nineteenth century, he is absorbed in the same problems as those which are occupying the majority of the philosophers, the moralists, and the sociologists who combine with him to form the intellectual class. His individual problem is, accordingly, essentially the same as the problem of the society in which he lives and he is best understood in terms of that society.

But not infrequently also it happens that, on the contrary, some idiosyncrasy sets him apart. The life which he has been compelled to lead is radically different from the normal life of his contemporaries. He is sceptical of their faiths, cold to their enthusiasms, incapable of taking a part in their labours. Regarding events from an unfamiliar angle he perceives relationships to which the rest are blind; cut off from the satisfactions permitted to most he is compelled to seek others whose very existence is unsuspected. And when his work appears it appears as a kind of revelation. The world which it represents is our familiar world and yet it is not. The elements we recognize without difficulty, but the pattern into which they are arranged amazes us by its completeness no less than by its novelty. Here are standards we never thought of applying, goods we never thought of pursuing. And though this way of looking at life may in time be added to the catalogue of those which have become accepted as possible, it seems at first as bewildering as it is delightful.

Such an artist is obviously not to be interpreted in terms of the spirit of any age. No doubt the very fact that he is able to be understood by it may be taken as proof that at certain points the two touch, but the original source of the effort which results ultimately in a new vision of the world lies somewhere in the idiosyncrasies of the artist. For him, the starting point was the fact that he could not share the aims and opinions of his fellows; that for some reason he must either give a new meaning to life or rest content with finding it forever meaningless. And hence the effort to analyse him must begin with the statement of these idiosyncrasies.

Now it is obvious enough that Marcel Proust is such an artist. To enter the first volume of his great romance is to find oneself plunged immediately into an unfamiliar world whose strangeness is more than a mere strangeness of scene.

For however remote the persons and the places may be, it is not so much their remoteness which is responsible for the sense of novelty as it is the angle from which they are regarded. Seen through Proust's eyes, the most familiar people and the most ordinary events would take on an aspect of unfamiliarity. He notes the things not usually noted and stresses the things not usually stressed. Only the sensations which ordinarily seem too fleeting to be recorded are set down, only the distinctions which seem ordinarily too intangible to be defined are noted, and only the pleasures so tenuous as to be ordinarily not counted are considered real enough to make life worth living. Everything is measured by some sense of values as unusual as it is consistent and by the simple but summary process of redefining the adjective " important" a whole new world is created.

Indeed it would hardly be an exaggeration to say that he writes as though he had never read the works of his predecessors; as though he were not even aware of the preoccupations and the enthusiasms which made up their world. Yet he was, as a matter of fact, rather more widely read than novelists are accustomed to be both in the literature of his own and in that of other countries. He translated Ruskin and he professed for George Eliot an enthusiasm which seems doubly difficult to understand in the case of a man whose seriousness was of a sort so different from hers. But it is obvious that he saw their works as he saw the life of his time — from some oblique angle of his own; that their judgments were not his and their way of " accepting the universe" not only different from his own but essentially meaningless to him. He had a secret of his own — a magic formula which alone could give meaning to life — but that formula was one which it took many years to discover and the results of a merciless discipline to apply.

The last two volumes of his novel are devoted to the attempt to state in explicit form the nature of his secret. They define more clearly than any critic could define what his aim had been throughout all the preceding volumes and they reveal with what amazing skill he had worked, first to create for himself a life of his own and then to set down in the form of an idealized autobiography an apology for that life. Yet though these last volumes form, perhaps, the best possible introduction to his work as a whole, the biographical essayist may be permitted to go back a little further still and to begin, not with the philosophy which had been so clearly formulated before the composition of the romance was begun, but with the conditions which made such a philosophy necessary. For Proust had been from childhood cut off from both ordinary life and ordinary satisfactions. Almost in infancy he had been compelled either to construct values of his own or to find himself in a vacant world; and it was the little boy, discovering in misery and loneliness the consolations of contemplation, who made possible the romancer whose most obvious characteristic is a tireless and yet preternaturally disinterested curiosity.

No work of literature could possibly illustrate more perfectly than does " Remembrance of Things Past " the characteristics of what Nietzsche called Apollonian art. It takes no sides and though it makes many thousand distinctions it pronounces no judgments which are other than purely relative. Curiously aloof and curiously undynamic, it never for a moment seems to consider life as anything which could (or should) be acted upon. In it events have all of the inevitability and something of the intangibility characteristic of a dream. But his detachment is not, like the artificial detachment of a naturalistic school, merely a literary method. It is the result of the attitude inevitable in a man who had learned long ago to stand outside the stream of life, to feel himself no part of it, and to compensate for the absence of active or vital impulses by the cultivation of those contemplative pleasures which for most men are secondary at most.

Nor was this, in the case of Proust, a possibility discovered late in life. It was something of which he had been compelled to begin the cultivation almost as soon as consciousness awoke and something to the perfection of which he had devoted his entire existence, learning to make thought and observation take the place of doing as blind men learn to make touch and hearing take the place of sight. His life was a retirement, step by step, from life; a penetration, step by step, into that particular world of art which was his. It was a substitution of observation for doing, and a substitution so complete that in the end the book which was to record the observation absorbed its author entirely and he ceased to have any life other than that which had come to a focus on the pages before him.

Yet literature was not for him, as it had been for Stendhal, essentially a *faute de mieux*. It was not a gratification through the imagination of active impulses which had failed to find adequate expression. For the peculiar quality of his work arises out of the fact that in his case the transmutation was complete; that the will to power, the desire to function effectively in competition with his fellows, had been replaced by the desire to understand them completely. He no longer rebelled against his unfitness for active life and no longer even regretted that it should have set him apart. In the fact that it had done so he had come to see, not a handicap, but a blessing; something which had enabled him (in this respect more fortunate than most) to realize in time how vain is the effort to seek happiness in the gratification of the will and which had taught him to look for satisfaction in the understanding where alone it can be found. Others were deluded and led on by the promises which passion never more than half fulfils. He, because he had been granted less, was so much the less its dupe.

Even in childhood he had caught glimpses of the joy which comes when an object appears, not as something to be grasped, but as an idea to be understood *sub specie aeternitatis,* and it was the aim of his life to transform those glimpses into a continuous vision, to see everything and to see it always as he had seen certain things for certain instants. He would collect observations and impressions. He would observe nature, study character, and hear tales. But he would consider none of these things as ends in themselves. He would gather them together, take them all into himself, and then, in that moment which justifies life, he would see them as one picture, feel them all as he had sometimes felt in a fleeting moment some scene or some situation. And the sum of all these ephemeral things would be no longer ephemeral. The whole would be rescued from time as the scene set down by a great painter is rescued. It would be fixed, change-

less, and perfect. The vision would be eternal, and that consciousness which was himself would be eternal also. For to
have grasped all of oneself even for an instant is the same as
to have grasped it forever. Time can add nothing to what is
already complete.

II

The combined authority of biographies and tombstones has tended to attribute a particular significance to dates of birth. They are generally set down with a triumphant simplicity and it is true that they have, at least, the advantage of being among the very few things which can be asserted without dispute concerning any human being. But science has not yet decided just how much we bring with us on the occasions which they record and it is not unlikely that we really begin to be what we are destined to remain upon some later occasion far more fateful for us, even though it is not recorded in obedience to any law in the archives of any municipality. Thus Marcel Proust first saw the light of day at Paris on the tenth of July, 1871. But there is no evidence that the creature who was later to bear the same name actually came into being until some nine years later when, on returning from a walk in the Champs Élysées, he was taken with an attack of asthma so severe that his father despaired of his life. Care was lavished upon him and from that moment on he never ceased to claim the privileges as well as to suffer the inconveniences of an invalid. None of his friends seem to remember him before that time and indeed he does not seem to have remembered himself. Not even that "all" which he determined to recover in his book includes the child who had not yet been set apart by his malady. The first memories recorded are the memories of a life already circumscribed and the disease is taken for granted as completely as if it had been some congenital defect.

Doubtless this asthma was a nervous disorder and one is

permitted to suspect that it was a symptom or a device rather than a cause of the peculiarities of his temperament. It enabled him in childhood to claim, from his mother especially, the extravagant affection which he demanded, and in later life it served also as an excuse for fantastic habits which he doubtless did not want to give up. But it was real enough nevertheless and it marked the first step in that progressive retirement from active life which was to constitute the course of his outward existence. The little Marcel — and it was thus that he continued until his dying day to be known — must make a life of his own since he obviously could not share the life of his fellows.

The Prousts were exceedingly prosperous. The father was a distinguished physician, and the life which they led was a life in which no comfort need to be foregone. Every care was lavished upon the child, and no indulgences denied except those (though they were many) which might be thought incompatible with his fragile health. He lived well in a house on the Boulevard Malesherbes, attending school only when his health seemed certainly to permit. Most of the summers were spent at Illiers near Chartres and there was usually besides an autumn vacation at Trouville or Houlgate. But comfort — luxury even — was taken for granted as the mature Proust never ceased to take it and his sorrows were already only of that immaterial sort which some insist upon classifying as a kind of indulgence.

At first, most of them centred about a need for affection which not even the boundless devotion of his mother could satisfy. From a father, indulgent enough in his way but too robust of soul actually to understand the needs of a neurotic child, he turned to the mother (a Jewess) who could respond less out of a sense of duty than out of a profound, comprehending tenderness. And he repaid her by making her the centre of his universe in a sense which is, perhaps, most clearly revealed in that fine passage of his novel in which he describes how he discovered that the charm of Venice had dissolved when he had parted from her in anger — how the town which he saw before him had ceased to be Venice; how its personality, its name, seemed to him lying fictions which he "no longer had the courage to impress upon the stone"; and how "the palaces, the canal, the Rialto became divested of the idea that created their individuality and disintegrated into their common material elements." After he had become a man he burst into tears when he heard the story of a friend's friend who was ashamed of his mother's awkwardness and at fourteen he answered the banal question "What idea makes you miserable" with the simple phrase "To be separated from Mama."

In the household there grew up a ritual intended to symbolize this desperate devotion. The child, sent early to bed, lay wakefully waiting for the moment when the company should have departed and his mother would come to give him the kiss without which he could not sleep. Once, he remembered, he was afraid that she would forget. By his nurse he sent a note to the dinner table and when the nurse returned with the rebuke implied in the statement that "there is no answer" he was driven to a desperation described at length in the volume devoted to the memories of his childhood. But even that was not sufficient to exorcise the horror of the memory and he returned to it again in that last section which describes how, in an ante-chamber of the Guermantes residence, the whole of his life came back to him.

"It was the evening of my mother's abdication which, together with the slow death of my grandmother, marked the decline of my will and of my health. Everything was decided at the moment when, no longer able to endure to wait until the morrow to put my lips upon the face of my mother, I took my resolution, leaped from the bed and went, in my nightgown, to station myself at the window (through which the moonlight entered) until I should hear M. Swann depart. My parents accompanied him, I heard the door open, ring, close itself again. At this moment even, in the house of the Prince de Guermantes, I heard still the sound of the steps of my parents as they showed M. Swann out and the reverberating tintinnabulation — interminable, shrill, and refreshing — of the little bell which told me that at last M. Swann had departed and that Mama would soon mount the stairs; I heard them still and it was they themselves that I heard, situated though they were so far off in the past. It must be that this tintinnabulation had been always there and also, between it and the present moment, all the past indefinitely unrolled that I did not know I carried within me. I grew dizzy to see below me and yet in me — as though I were leagues high — so many years."

But the little boy who could thus attach supreme importance to a ceremony learned also in other ways to make the idea of a thing more real than the thing itself. He loved nature as he saw it in the mild excursions permitted him but he never knew that merely animal participation in the life of the trees and the beasts which Wordsworth described as the first stage of his fellowship with them. Instinctively he realized that it was in some other way that he must know them and he was literary almost from infancy. Once, so he tells us, he was so struck with the beauty of a landscape drenched by a recent rain that he brandished his closed umbrella (a characteristic detail) and exclaimed in his enthusiasm "Zut, zut, zut," realizing at the same time the inadequacy of the expression and overcome with the sense of a need, of a duty even, to grasp the scene by imprisoning it in words to which the mind could return.

To certain temperaments the experiences received through art must always seem experiences received at second hand. To them, imagination is only an attenuated and faded actuality, only an inadequate photograph without depth or colour. But to others reality is merely obscured by the grossness of direct sensation. It lies, not in phenomena, but in that idea behind them which can be grasped only after it has been detached. And so it was with even the childish Proust. Perhaps because activity could be for him only occasional instead of continuous, perhaps for some deeper reason, seeing or doing was merely a preparation for that contemplation which would later make sights and deeds real.

The history embodied in names and places fascinated him because history is essentially the idea left behind by events that have ceased to flow; and art fascinated him because art is the technique by which the idea is made to emerge from the events or the objects which it chooses as its subject. Hence, as he was to write years later, in one of the essays composed before the great work began to appear, " When I was a little child the fate of no person in the sacred history seemed to

me so miserable as that of Noah, because of the deluge which
kept him confined for forty days in the ark. Later, when I
' was often ill and during the long days when I also had to
remain in the ark,' I understood that Noah had never been
able to see the world so well as from the ark, despite the fact
that it was closed and that there was night over the earth."

Keats had his Grecian urn to teach him an important lesson, but Proust — if we may take as literal fact a fine passage
in his novel — learned it at a tender age from the little magic
lantern which solaced his lonely hours in bed. Immortalized
by certain daubs upon glass, and ready, at every instant, to
come alive were the figures of a legendary story. " Riding
at a jerky trot, Golo, his mind filled with an infamous design,
issued from the little three-cornered forest which dyed dark-
green the slope of a convenient hill and advanced by leaps
and bounds towards the castle of poor Geneviève de Brabant. — And nothing could arrest his slow progress. If the
lantern were moved I could still distinguish Golo's horse
advancing across the window curtains, swelling out with
their curves and diving into their folds. The body of Golo
himself, being of the same supernatural substance as his
steeds, overcame all material obstacles — everything which
seemed to bar his way — by taking each as if it might be a
skeleton and embodying it in himself: the doorhandle, for
instance, over which, adapting itself at once, would float in-
vincibly his red cloak or his pale face, never losing its nobility or its melancholy, never showing any sign of trouble
at such a transubstantiation. . . . And as soon as the dinner-
bell rang I would run down to the dining-room, where the
big hanging lamp, ignorant of Golo and Bluebeard but well

acquainted with my family and the dish of stewed beef, shed the same light as on every other evening; and I would fall into the arms of my mother, whom the misfortunes of Geneviève de Brabant had made all the dearer to me, just as the crimes of Golo had driven me to a more than ordinarily scrupulous examination of my own consciousness." — "Forever wilt thou sigh and she be fair."

So tyrannous indeed did this idea of art become that it alone could give reality to an object. To hear it said that a familiar church was "built in the twelfth and thirteenth centuries" filled him with great joy because, thanks to that knowledge, the whole region in which it was found was made suddenly "to take its place in the order of centuries, with a storied consciousness of the Romanesque effort," and when, in the city, he was taken to play in the Champs Élysées he wished only that it had been described in some well-loved book in order that its dullness might have been transformed.

Indeed — fanatical though unconscious Platonist that he was — the idea of art was more important than even art itself. Taken to see a great actress whom he had long worshipped in imagination, he experienced, during her performance, the bitterest of disappointments because the reality was not real and it was only in retrospect that he could realize how fine her performance had been. To be in the actual presence of the work was to be distracted from it. It flowed and it changed; it took place in time; and hence it could not be grasped or realized. But the memory left behind was permanent, was eternal, and was part of him. Thus even art seemed a mere event until the idea behind a specific work was detached from that concrete and hence transitory material in which it was embodied.

Yet even the infant Proust was not content merely to retire into a world of dreams. He felt the necessity which the creative artist, as distinguished from the mere dilettante, always feels — the necessity of transforming his own experience into art. The two worlds were not, he knew, absolutely discontinuous. The secret was the secret of extracting the permanent and the significant from the transitory and the trivial. Hence he was fascinated by the people around him, stirred by the tales they told of other men and other events. Dimly at first, but with increasing clarity as time went on, he realized that the materials of the life which seemed so fragmentary and unsatisfactory were not essentially different from those which had been made into meaningful wholes by the writers whom he admired; and he began, more and more consciously, both to collect observations and to search for that manner of regarding them which would enable him to perceive what significance they had for him.

Among the houses which the Prousts sometimes visited was that of a certain M. Weil, maternal grand-uncle of Marcel. It appears that this M. Weil had contacts with a world rather more fashionable than that which the Prousts inhabited, for the latter were only very substantial bourgeois who held that to "climb" was, if anything, rather more disgraceful than to permit oneself to sink in the social scale. It appears still further that echoes from this superior world very early reached the ears of the young Marcel and that in his mind they mingled with the impressions which he had received from the fabulous tales of the past. Indeed it may very well be that the conversation of M. Weil first gave to his imagination the orientation which it always retained and that it was responsible for the fact that the world of social life was chosen to be, in a very particular fashion, *his* world. But in any event the seeds, if seeds they were, fell upon soil already prepared. The merely phenomenal present was linked to the meaningful past by names and it was in fashionable society that names were to be found. Hence to the young Proust it seemed that the task of transmuting a mere living person into an idea, the task of attributing to him a more than merely passing significance, was already half accomplished if his flesh was the flesh of heroes already part of immortal story.

In later years the members of this class were to furnish him many and very bitter disappointments. The shock which he felt, even as a child, when the fabulous idea which he had formed of some great person was suddenly confronted by a wholly commonplace reality was to be repeated in severer form when his intellect told him that this great aristocrat or that was stupid, vulgar, and ill-bred. He was always to note with pained surprise how unaware the greater number of the great were of the obligation resting upon them and he was always to be amazed that their names meant something so much more profound to him than they meant to them. But he has left us in his novel, wherever the name Guermantes is mentioned, some record of the impression which the idea of the aristocracy had made upon his childish mind.

The world of fashion was, then, the world of great names and it ought, he felt, to be also the world of great memories.

But that was not all. The young Marcel had formed for himself an idea of life as it ought to be led, of life devoted to the cultivation of exquisite sensations and to the practice of perfect manners based upon perfect sympathy. Morbidly sensitive, wounded even by the idea of wounding, he fancied that among people released from every obligation except the obligation to live beautifully, he might observe such a life. Hence he set out, very definitely, to penetrate the secrets of the magic circle of the élite and if he found that the circle did not exist — if, indeed, no inconsiderable part of his work was to consist in describing its non-existence — the idea remained, nevertheless, always with him and continued to determine the field of his observations even though he had ceased to believe that he would discover what he had first sought.

Nor did Proust ever cease to find fascinating a distinction which he had already made as a child and which constitutes one of the many constantly recurring themes of his novel — the distinction between the kind of manners which arises out of a delicate regard for the feeling of others and the kind which is either mere form or an authorized insolence. He tells us that when, in his childhood, the family received a visit from " M. Swann" it was his custom to slip away and order the syrups "as though not going for anything in particular," because his grandmother thought it " nicer " that these syrups should not " seem anything out of the ordinary, which we kept for visitors." But this is not something meant to stand by itself for it is intended as a foil both to the insolence (not described until many hundred pages later) of that perfect gentleman M. de

Charlus and to the ambiguous affability of the Princess de Luxembourg, who was so anxious not to seem an inhabitant of a sphere higher than that of little Marcel and his mother that " by an error in adjustment she made her eyes beam with such benevolence that I could see the moment approaching when she would put out her hand and stroke us, as if we were two nice beasts and had poked our heads out at her through the bars of our cage in the gardens."

After his fame had been established many of his former friends confessed that, though they had found him charming, they had never suspected his genius. They had seen in him essentially a dilettante, rather absurdly concerned with the details of social life, and they had accepted, because of his gentleness, the incongruous spectacle presented by a confirmed valetudinarian who emerged from the sick-room to sit, wrapped always in his fur coat, in some exclusive salon. The man was more or less concealed by what appeared to be his eccentricities and it cannot be denied that this apparently trivial side to his character was the one which seemed to gain the ascendance as the child grew into an adolescent.

With schoolboy companions he discussed ideas and founded the inevitable review, but even these companions noted with disapproval a politeness almost too perfect and a hankering after what seemed to them the frivolous delights of formal society. The delicate child who — even in the days when a nursemaid conducted him to the Champs Élysées — preferred conversation to games, had become now an adolescent who so obviously preferred the mothers of his friends to the friends themselves that these latter laughed at his folly and predicted that he would grow into nothing except a snob and a dilettante. Nor was there about his way of life anything which seemed to contradict the assumption, for though there is reason to believe that he never ceased to be conscious of the purpose of his quest, it was impossible for others even to guess what he was seeking.

He graduated from the lycée and his father wished that he should enter the diplomatic service. There was also at one time the hope that, since diplomacy did not appeal to him, he might consent to become a magistrate. But though he entered the Law School of the Sorbonne he could not fix upon any career, and despite his interest in both philosophy and literature it was the combined rôle of valetudinarian and man-about-town which seemed to please him most.

It was remembered of him that at fifteen he was already frequenting a certain salon where he sat beside the mistress like a little page, upon a huge puff, while the illustrious personages of the government who passed by stopped to pay their respects to the little man; and at twenty he was, with his frail body, his melancholy eyes, and his almost ridiculous gentleness, hardly different from the child whom one of his most intimate friends remembered in the Champs Élysées: " handsome and very shivery, enveloped in woollens, but precipitating himself into the presence of ladies, old or young, and pouring forth a flood of words which somehow managed to touch their hearts whether he entered upon subjects ordinarily reserved for adults, or merely inquired concerning the state of their healths." The only difference was that he was now practising his manners under slightly more formal conditions. Somehow or other he had insinuated himself into the great world. He came to be seen occasionally at the literary salon of Mme. de Loynes, more often in that of Mme. Armand de Caillavet. But literary people were too much like himself to please him entirely. Through a school-friend he got himself introduced into the drawing-room of Mme. Strauss-Bizet, one of the most brilliant of the time, and from there, it is said, he set out to conquer the whole of society.

No one will ever know to what extent these expeditions were consciously and purely exploratory. Perhaps there was a time, perhaps there were at least moments, when he actually participated without *arrière pensée* in the world of social ambitions. But the pertinacity with which he asked questions; the insatiability of his curiosity concerning who was who and exactly how one was to act if one were of such and such rank and found oneself in this or that circumstance — these things seem to indicate that it was at least never for long that he forgot that some use was to be made of his experiences. Nor is it possible, as one reads the recollections which friends have contributed, not to be struck by the fact that his position was so ambiguous as to make it seem, in retrospect, curious that the ambiguity was not more conspicuous then. Something in his mind, also, corresponded to the strange habits of his invalidism. He was only a licensed spectator, not a real participant, and the notes which he sometimes put down upon paper were supplemented by many hundred which were stored away in a memory which forgot nothing of what it needed. For however much he rearranged and combined his materials in the writing of his book, that premise of a "total recall" upon which it is founded was no fiction and a friend discovered in it almost the exact words used many years before in a sketch of which he only had kept a copy. Proust was not enjoying society so much as he was preparing to enjoy it. He was getting ready for that moment when his experience could be made to form part of a whole which should have, for him, the value of a work of art.

III

Theoretically as well as actually Proust was, then, devoting himself to literature; but he alone seems to have believed that the supposed devotion was more than an excuse for idleness. It is true that he published in 1890 a volume of essays entitled "Les Plaisirs et les Jours." It is true also that he contributed certain articles to certain reviews and that, especially, between nineteen hundred and nineteen hundred thirteen, he wrote for *Figaro* various essays which dealt for the most part with fashionable life. But he was regarded rather as a man-about-town who happened to write a little than as a writer who frequented society. He was classified as a *mondain* and it was only with difficulty that many, even after his great work had begun to appear, were persuaded to think of him in any other light.

Yet the indulgence of his parents seems never to have faltered. Become a man, he still inhabited in the family apartment the room which had been his as a child, and he was abundantly supplied with the money which he spent lavishly for dinners given in the most expensive establishments as well as in huge tips whose fantastically unnecessary generosity was already becoming a legend. Convinced that the crises of his asthma were less frequent at night than during the day, he adopted the nocturnal habits which he was never to give up. He rose late and he did not breakfast until after his father had already departed; but even after the coffee had at last been disposed of, hours were yet to be spent in the almost interminable process of dressing and in writing a prodigious number of letters which he seemed to seize every occasion to dispatch. It was not until the approach of evening that he was really ready to devote himself to either his pleasures or his work and when he at last set out it was, as Lucien Daudet, one of his most intimate friends, remembers, rather as a little boy than as a man. His mother, apparently unaware of the incongruity, would solemnly request his friends to take good care of him and with a curiously childish air he would kiss her good-bye.

Again it is impossible not to wonder a little at the extent to which he was not only accepted, but loved, by people who would have found one-half so many eccentricities intolerable in any other. But the testimony of those who knew him is consistent both in regard to these eccentricities and in regard to the charm which caused them to be, not forgotten, but indulgently taken for granted. All insist upon the seduction of his conversation, upon the flow of his humour and upon that generosity in all his relations with others which seized every opportunity to express itself by the equally lavish expenditure of money or thoughtfulness. " His verbal gaiety was," writes the Duchesse de Clermont-Tonnerre, " so astounding that he entertained, without ever tiring. Young people the furthest removed from his literary culture or his artistic tastes loved him as a comrade — so rare that they must protect him."

But it was not only with words that he charmed. Thus Paul Morand tells how, upon one occasion, he had happened to mention the fact that he must consult an expensive specialist. Shortly after, he was astonished to receive through the mail a very considerable sum of money which Proust had sent to pay the doctor and, as Morand remarks, the legend of Proust's generosity ought not to be developed at the expense of the legend of his goodness. The fabulous tips which he persisted in giving, his insistence upon taking his friends to only the most expensive of restaurants — such things as these were merely the material evidences of an extravagant determination to consider the comfort of others down to the last possible detail, not only because he was himself morbidly sensitive but also, perhaps, because he felt the necessity of apologizing in this fashion for the strain which his peculiarities imposed upon friendship.

Critics of his novel have not failed to reproach him with the complete absence of feeling for amelioristic sociology, with something which amounts, almost, to an unawareness of the fact that movements exist for the promotion of the greatest happiness of the greatest number. But he at least suggests the corollary of the familiar paradox that lovers of humanity are often extremely unpleasant people with whom to have intimate relations. He made up for his inability to do anything for people in general by his kindliness towards those whose lives touched his, and it is not impossible that he thought about the duty of man to man as he thought about the duty of the writer to his country when he remarked (in reply to enthusiastic nationalists) that he did not see how the artist could serve his nation better than by being a good artist.

The only reproach which his friends could possibly level against him was the reproach that he carried politeness to extravagant lengths. His school friends had invented a verb " proustifier " to describe the conduct of a person who was pushing good manners too far and the tendency to do so was with him almost irresistible. He scattered broadcast the most elaborate letters thanking various persons profoundly for nothing at all, and in his conversation there was, as one friend remarks, "an enamel of words which one does not usually hear: 'I hope that you are not angry — your goodness to me — their goodness to me — he is so kind to me,' etc." Even the most real and passionate of his friendships were declared in terms which, seeming extravagant even to Latins, seem doubly so to us, and one cannot but suspect that the conscientiousness of his manners must have made him awkward at the very moments when he was most carefully trying to do the right thing — just as his clothes were, for all his meticulousness, notoriously not quite what they should have been. But it was impossible to resist the untiring good will behind even the gesture which was a little grandiloquent and one forgave him the excesses of his excellent intentions whether they led him to say too much, to give too much, or, as happened upon one occasion, to arrive in the country before sundown "exaggeratedly dressed in evening clothes, high-hat, white gloves and all" just at the moment when the company to which he had been bidden was preparing to go fishing in the Seine.

Unquestionably a part — but only a part — of all this was the result of a deliberate program, of a determination to insinuate himself by the only means he knew how to employ into the circles he wished to examine. There can be no doubt of his goodness, no doubt of his passionate devotion to a number of his friends; but there can be no doubt either of his capacity for a profound and sustained irony, made possible by the fact that his realist world was a private one which existed inside of himself. Thanks to this irony and thanks also to an absolute subordination of everything else to the determination to know certain things which he believed it necessary for him to know, he could make what was only curiosity pass for liking when the occasion arose.

Thus, for example, he attached himself to that rather absurd decadent Count Robert de Montesquiou, wrote to the Count the most extravagant letters, and even endured his insolence, all because, apparently, he was learning the things which were to be used in the portrait of M. de Charlus. Montesquiou, who had already served as a model for Huysmanns, was to live long enough to witness the triumph of Proust, to suspect uneasily that rather too much of himself was in the latter's most amazing creation, and to murmur, not without a certain pathos, " I too should have liked a little fame." But the memory of de Charlus will outlive the memory of Montesquiou, despite the latter's books, and Proust must have smiled to re-read the letters in which he had been talked down to. Again it must be repeated that he was capable of the most genuine goodness. But no one will ever know how often he feigned what there was no real occasion to feel or how much is implied in the statement which he made, late in life, when he was asked if he did not fear that his book would make enemies. " Now that my work is finished," he replied, " it is all the same to me." Before it was finished he had had none.

The elder Proust died in 1903 and Marcel, now possessed of abundant money in his own right, could look forward to an indefinite period of preparation for his work. The following year there appeared his translation of Ruskin's

" The Bible of Amiens," the result of an interest which had continued over a number of years. But the time was already approaching when he should retire more and more into himself and when the visits which he still occasionally made to the fashionable world were to become more and more obviously merely exploratory expeditions undertaken for the sake of information which he could gain, rather than for the satisfaction of even a partial participation in the pleasures of a reception or a dinner. In 1900 he had spent some time in Venice and he had always been delighted by travel, but all except the most minor journeys — elaborately prepared for by fumigations intended to prevent asthmatic attacks on the way — were abandoned, and thus by gradual stages he prepared himself for the period when he was only rarely to quit his chamber.

Much has been said of this retirement from the world. Some have spoken of it as though it were the result of a definite decision; others have insisted that it was too gradual a process to permit that it should be used to divide Proust's life into two distinct epochs. But though the retirement grew more complete as time went on, and though he had certainly begun as early as 1890 — when he was only nineteen years old — to take notes to be used in the composition of some work, we may probably trust the statement of his brother that the death of their mother in 1905 was the event which marked a definite turning-point. From then on Proust went less and less into the world and devoted himself more and more closely to his work.

Doubtless the loss was the keenest sorrow he ever had to experience for he had carried over into manhood the desperate attachment which had made his mother the centre of his world, the one presence which could give meaning to daily life. But the loss was also, in all probability, one which it was absolutely necessary that he should endure. The phenomenal present had always been relatively less important to him than that world in which memory, contemplation, history, and art are united by the fact that they are alike permanent, changeless, and immaterial. But before his work could become possible it was necessary that this relative unimportance of the present, this relative indifference to the momentary gratifications which the will is forever promising, should become absolute, and that his whole effort should be devoted to discovering in the mental record of his experiences that particular one of their possible meanings which can only be perceived when they have ceased to be merely the beginnings of something hoped for and become, in their own right, finished wholes.

At the age of twenty-one he had written, in an essay contributed to an amateur review, some prophetic words. " Perhaps the sweetest of those flowers of sentiment which reflection soon withers is that which we may call the mystic hope in the future. — A day comes, alas, when we no longer expect at each instant to receive a passionate letter from a friend until now indifferent, when we realize that characters do not change all at once." And though it is probable that Proust never felt very strongly that "mystic hope in the future" it was necessary that he should no longer feel it at all, necessary that something should write "Finis" to his experience. And it was the death of his mother which did just that. His only hope of happiness now lay in the possibility of so grasping the past that it should no longer be something which had slipped away but something which was now, for the first time, actually possessed.

It is not recorded that he ever confessed even to his most intimate friends the nature of the quest upon which he had embarked. They found him as warm and as thoughtful as ever but more and more disinclined to quit the apartment which had now been transformed into a fantastic sick-room, and they attributed his strange life to nothing except the malady which gave rise to various rituals so complicated that they seemed the chief occupation of his existence. Upon the nature of this malady he discoursed learnedly. To Antoine Bibesco he wrote how he had consulted a doctor " who told me that my asthma had become a nervous habit and that the only way to cure it was to go to an anti-asthmatic establishment which exists in Germany where they would (for no doubt I shall not go) 'break the habit' of my asthma as one demorphinizes the morphine fiends." Another doctor, so he told Lucien Daudet, had said to him that it would be possible to make the asthma disappear but that he did not want to do so because " To the extent to which you are asthmatic . . . your disease is for you an escape and enables you to dispense with other maladies " — a theory of pathology which so impressed Proust that he put it into the mouth of M. de Charlus who uses it as a veiled apology for his homosexuality.

Nor did he seem willing to do anything except placate and coddle the disease which had so completely taken possession of him. He commonly did not arise until six in the evening; fumigations took place at all hours; and the num-

ber of things which he could not endure continued to multiply. Since he could not tolerate air which might carry
irritating matter, the windows were always closed; since
steam-heat distressed him, he sat in a cold room wrapped
in a complicated system of coats and shawls. And though for
a time the difficulties raised by social expeditions were not,
as Daudet says, insurmountable, yet at least they had to be
elaborately prepared for. Friends who called — and he was
still avid of conversation — were likely to be requested to
send outside the handkerchief which was perceived to ex-
hale perfume and told that he had, unfortunately, been compelled upon a previous occasion to air a chair for three days
in the courtyard because it had retained some trace of the
scent employed by a visitor.

Proust was not unaware of the grotesqueness of the spectacle which he presented. At a later time he was to write rue-
fully to Sir Philip Sassoon how a certain English visitor had
been heard to remark that the greatest impression which he
and his wife had brought back from Paris was that of
M. Proust and how he had added, by way of explanation,
" To tell the truth he is the first man we ever saw dining in a
fur coat." But if there were observations which he felt it
necessary to make he made them, indifferent alike to the
absurdity of the spectacle which he presented and to the
suffering which he might be compelled to endure the next
day as a result of the fatigue entailed or the perfume emitted
by some roses decorating the salon he had visited.

Once, to the amazement of everyone, he appeared at a
great reception — to find out whether or not the Prince de
Sagan wore a monocle; on another occasion, now firmly

fixed as part of his legend, he paid a call upon a lady of
fashion — to ask if she would be so kind as to show him
the hat she had worn some twenty years before. The head
waiters at the Ritz and other fashionable restaurants became
confidants from whom he demanded the most detailed information concerning the personality, habits, and histories
of the habitués, but his interest was becoming more and
more frankly the curiosity of a man completely detached
from the life he was documenting.

Persons were important only in so far as they could contribute something to his work by presenting him with a
gesture, an opinion, or a word which could be attributed to
one or another of the characters taking shape in his mind
and destined, each one, to represent a whole class of individuals. For though Proust was to put much of his acquaintances as well as much of himself into his novel, the passion
for concrete detail which seemed to his friends the most
characteristic thing about him was only incidental to his
passion for generalization. He was always looking for the
characteristics and the typical as it is revealed by the sum
of particulars. What he wanted was the archetype or the
idea — the one changeless, immaterial thing which exhibited
itself under varying forms. And thus though the distinctions
between the Duchesse de Guermantes and the Marquise de
Villeparisis are hardly less striking than those between the
Duchesse and Madame Verdurin, yet the former stands less
for one person than for one *kind* of aristocrat just as the latter
stands for one *kind* of bourgeoise. Highly individualized
though each is, they are all, nevertheless, more than mere
individuals.

Evidently the novel — though still never spoken of except in the vaguest terms — was assuming a more concrete form in his mind. As early as 1906 he seems to have definitely begun work upon it and it was, says his brother, about 1910 that the epoch of his most complete retirement began. From that time on until the last years when the work was almost done " he was entirely given to it, saw no existence outside of it and, in some fashion, did not think he had the right to rest before this exhausting labour was finished."

To a friend he once wrote: " The meaning of this book is real, passionate, very different from what you know of me, and, I believe, infinitely less bad, not meriting the epithet ' delicate ' or ' fine,' but living and true (though I do not think that to say that is to say realistic.)" He had not always, however, spoken with so much confidence. To his friends (says one of them) it seemed that he was entangling himself in a multitude of preliminaries and scruples and even to himself it must have seemed sometimes that the task he had set — the task, not only of recovering every significant experience of his life, but of combining, transforming, and symbolizing them all so as to make a consistent whole — was an impossible one. But every sorrow as well as every scruple was to contribute its part to the total and when the work was all but completed he could signalize the fact that each had done so — could remember how his mind had taken unconscious notes, how scores of individuals had posed for every one of his characters, and how the darkest period of his discouragement had been just before the dawn — just before that Great Enlightenment which was to give all of his life back to him and give it back in a form rich with the meanings unperceived at the time when it was being actually lived.

Despite (or because of) his obsessive concern with Time, Proust never knew the hour of the day and never dated his letters. Moreover there is nothing about the form of his novel more obvious than the fact that chronology counts for little in a work which assumes mere simultaneity to be the least significant of all the relationships which can subsist between things. And in view of these facts it is not surprising that there is no way of dating the Great Enlightenment which may, for that matter, never have taken place in any fashion so dramatic as that described. But the enlightenment was real, it supplied Proust with the secret which he had been seeking throughout all of his previous life, and it is to the novel that we must look for the most rational account he could possibly give of its nature.

Readers of even the first section will remember the now famous incident of the *madeleine*. The narrator, cold and unhappy, raised to his lips a spoonful of tea in which he had soaked a morsel of cake. No sooner had the warm liquid and the crumbs touched his palate than a shudder ran through his whole body and he stopped, intent upon nothing except the exquisite pleasure which had invaded his senses. It was individual, detached, and without suggestion of its origin; but it was, nevertheless, complete. " At once the vicissitudes of life had become indifferent to me, its disasters innocuous, its brevity illusory. — I had ceased now to feel mediocre, accidental, mortal. Whence could it have come to me, this all-powerful joy? — What did it signify? How could I seize upon and define it? "

He takes a second spoonful and a third, but the potion loses its magic. " It is plain that the object of my quest, the truth, lies not in the cup but in myself. The tea has called up in me, but does not itself understand, and can only repeat indefinitely, with a gradual loss of strength, the same testimony; which I, too, cannot interpret, though I hope at least to be able to call upon the tea again and to find it there presently, intact at my disposal, for my final enlightenment." — Suddenly the memory returns. — " And once I had recognized the taste of the crumb of *madeleine* soaked in her decoction of lime-flowers which my aunt used to give me (although I did not yet know and must long postpone the discovery of why this memory made me so happy) immediately the old grey house upon the street, where her room was, rose up like the scenery of a theatre to attach itself to the little pavilion, opening on to the garden, which had been built out behind it for my parents; . . . and with the house the town, from morning to night and in all weathers, the square where I was sent before luncheon, the streets along which I used to run errands, the country roads we took when it was fine. And just as the Japanese amuse themselves by filling a porcelain bowl with water and steeping in it little crumbs of paper which until then are without character or form, but, the moment they become wet, stretch themselves and bend, take on colour and distinctive shape, become flowers or houses or people, permanent and recognizable, so in that moment all the flowers in our garden and in M. Swann's park, and the water-lilies on the Vivonne, and the good folk of the village and their little dwellings and the parish church and the whole of Combray and of its surroundings, taking their proper shapes and growing solid, sprang into being, town and gardens alike, from my cup of tea."

This memory was no mere memory. Often before, on long sleepless nights, he had felt the need of recalling his childhood, and indeed had succeeded in recovering isolated fragments without colour or significance. But the effort actually to recapture them had been vain. The fragments had remained fragments and, since they were recalled by conscious effort, destined to show only a past which retained nothing of the past itself. Sometimes, between sleep and waking, the present had seemed almost to merge with his childhood for, called back to consciousness by discomfort, he had found himself saying "Why, I must have gone to sleep after all, and Mama never came to say good night." But the vision evoked by the *madeleine* was something entirely different from even this. It did not so much inspire a memory as establish an absolute identity between the two moments when the same sensation had been experienced. The sense that the past was a shadow and the present only substantial, seemed to have been proved an illusion for the past was as real as ever it had been. It was existing in the here and now, must have always existed in the here and now. Memories such as these were no longer memories at all — they were the past not only come back but come back in a form which no longer evolved and dissolved as events taking place in time must do. — "Forever wilt thou sigh and she be fair."

This incident of the *madeleine* concludes the "Ouverture" of the novel. In "Chapter One" which follows, Proust begins the description of his childhood at Combray; this leads on to the story of Swann's love; and that in turn merges into all the other inter-related stories which follow. Meanwhile, though the reader can hardly have forgotten the incident itself, he may very well have never realized its central importance, because the theme which it introduces is not actually returned to until the very last of the sixteen volumes, when it reappears at its chronological place in the life of the narrator. The latter (here as everywhere only partially distinguishable from Proust himself) has almost reached the end of his active existence. Albertine is dead, his illness has cut him off more and more completely from even an outward participation in the active life of his fellows, and he is sure now that even the hope of achieving a work of literature, the last hope which seemed left him, must be abandoned. Even the cherished memory of certain beauties which he had seen has lost the power to charm, and when he remembers how Bergotte had once said to him, " You are sick but you are not to be pitied because you have the joys of the spirit," it is only to reflect bitterly upon the depths of Bergotte's miscomprehension. For how can the cold data furnished him by his clear eye and his just intelligence be called " joys of the spirit " when they are so sterile and so joyless? " But it is, sometimes, he adds, at the moment when all seems lost that we receive the knowledge which can save us. We have knocked at all the doors which lead nowhere and the only one through which we can enter, the one which we might have searched for a hundred years in vain — we stumble against it and it opens."

On the afternoon of a reception he had descended, full of sad thoughts, before the door of the residence of the Guermantes, and, startled by an approaching carriage, he had raised one foot to the sidewalk while the other remained in the gutter. In an instant, every melancholy evaporated. " All my discouragement vanished before that same felicity which, at various times in my life, had been evoked by the sight of some trees which I thought I had recognized in a carriage excursion near Balbec, by the sight of the belfries of Martinville, by the taste of a *madeleine* soaked in tea, by many other sensations of which I have spoken and which the last works of Vinteuil seemed to me to synthesize. As at the moment when I tasted the *madeleine,* all inquietude concerning the future, all intellectual doubt, was dissipated. The doubts which had just been assailing me concerning the reality of my literary gift and even concerning the reality of literature were lifted as by enchantment. . . . Each time that I performed, in a merely material fashion, the step, it remained useless; but if, forgetting the Guermantes *matinée,* I succeeded in recovering what I had felt when I had thus placed my feet, the dazzling and indistinct vision brushed me again as though it said 'If you have the strength, seize me as I pass and solve the riddle of happiness which I propose to you.' And almost immediately I recognized it. It was a vision of Venice of which my efforts at description and the pretended snap-shots taken by my memory had told me nothing but which the sensation (felt formerly when I had stood on two unequal paving stones of the baptistry of St. Mark) had given back to me, together with all the related sensations of that day which had remained waiting in their place in the series of forgotten days from amidst which a brusque accident had made them come forth. In a similar fashion the taste of the little *madeleine* had recalled Combray for me. But why had the images of Combray and Venice given me at these two moments a joy like a certitude and sufficient — without other demonstrations — to make death a matter of indifference? Asking myself that and resolved to find today the answer I entered into the Guermantes residence."

For a little while he rested in an antechamber to wait until a piece of music should be finished, and there, twice in quick succession, visions visited him again. A servant struck a spoon against a plate and "The same kind of felicity which the unequal stones had given overcame me. Again the sensations were of a great heat but entirely different — a mixture of an odour of smoke softened by the fresh odour of a forest setting; and I recognized that that which seemed to me so agreeable was the same line of trees which I had found it so troublesome to observe and to describe . . . [but] before which I now found myself — so completely had the sound of a spoon against a plate given to me, before I had had time to get hold of myself again, the illusion of the sound of the hammer of an employee who had been arranging something about the wheel of a train while we were stopping before the little wood." A few minutes later a domestic approached with some refreshments. "I wiped my mouth with the napkin which he had given me; but immediately — like the personage in the Arabian Nights who, without knowing it, performs precisely the rite which makes appear, visible to him alone, a docile genius ready to transport him afar — a new vision of blueness passed before my eyes. . . . The napkin which I had taken to wipe my mouth had exactly the same roughness and weight as that with which I had had so much difficulty in drying myself before the window the first day of my arrival at Balbec; and now, before this library in the Guermantes house, was spread out, like the tail of a peacock, the plumage of a green and blue ocean. And it was not these colours alone which I was enjoying but, in its entirety, an instant of my life which they evoked, an instant which had been, no doubt, an aspiration towards them though, perhaps, not enjoyed at Balbec because of some sadness or fatigue. Now, freed from all of the imperfection inherent in the perception of external things, pure and disincarnate, it filled me with gladness. . . .

"So many times in the course of my life reality had deceived me because at the moment when I perceived it my imagination, my sole organ for the enjoyment of beauty, could not apply itself by virtue of that law which requires that only the absent can be imagined. And now here, suddenly, the effect of this hard law was neutralized, was suspended, by a marvellous expedient of nature which had projected a single sensation — sound of the fork and of the hammer, same inequality of paving stones — both into the past where my imagination was permitted to taste it and into the present where . . . was added to the dreams of the imagination that of which they are usually deprived, namely, the idea of existence. And thanks to this subterfuge it had permitted my being to obtain, to isolate, to immobilize — for the duration of a lightning flash — something which it will never apprehend: a little of Time in the pure state. . . .

"That which the being two or three times revived in me had just tasted was indeed, perhaps, fragments of existence withdrawn from time; but this contemplation, although of eternity, was fugitive. Yet I felt that the pleasure which it had given me at rare intervals in my life was the only one which was fecund and real. . . . And I had now decided to devote myself to it and to fix it; but how, by what means? . . . The method which seemed to me the only one, what was it besides that of creating a work of art? And already the consequences forced themselves upon my spirit; for it was a question of reminiscences like the sound of the fork or the taste of the *madeleine*. . . .

"If enough time were left me to finish my work I would not fail to mark it with the seal of that time of which the idea imposed itself upon me with so much force that day; and in it I would describe men — even though to do so would be to make them seem monstrous creatures — as occupying in Time a place more considerable than the so restricted one which is reserved for them in space; a place, on the contrary, prolonged without measure since, like giants, plunged in the years, they touch simultaneously the epochs lived through by them, the epochs so far separated — between which so many days have come to place themselves — in Time."

What shall we say of this Great Enlightenment, of this revelation which so obviously came to Proust with all the force of a religious conversion? Doubtless the psychologist will want to offer his explanation and if he happens to be of the type which feels that the significance of any mental phenomenon has been exhausted when it has been related to some "complex" or "fixation," he will rest content with pointing out that the past to which Proust wished to return was merely the past which contained his mother. But even if this explanation be accepted for whatever it is worth and for however far it will carry us, the fact remains that the content of such an emotional experience is something entirely different from its origin and the psychologist of less limited view will not fail to note that Proust's " conversion " very obviously belongs among the varieties of religious experience.

The form which it took and the terms in which it was expressed were doubtless determined by the philosophy of Bergson, which had interested him profoundly in his college days and which, besides, left a deep impression upon his whole philosophy of art. But completely godless though Proust was, it is impossible not to observe the striking fact that the quality of this experience of his is precisely the quality of the Mystic Vision. For that sense of timelessness, combined with that sense of a peace which lifts the soul above any concern with the mere accidents possible to a temporal existence, is exactly the sense which every great mystic has attempted to communicate when he has undertaken to describe the boundless recompenses of his " way."

Each one of them, quite naturally — and like Proust himself — tends to identify the experience with the technique by means of which it is achieved. The Swami is as sure that his particular discipline is essential as the Christian is sure that the ecstasy which he feels is a blessing reserved by his God for none except those who meditate upon the sufferings of His Son. But the experiences undergone are as similar as the magic formulae for evoking them are different. Even the merely secular vision — like that, for example, which visited Havelock Ellis and which he so eloquently describes in " The Dance of Life " — is essentially the same as the Christian or the Buddhist and the words used to describe it almost equally incapable of communicating something essentially incommunicable. For himself St. Augustine evoked it when he said " In thy will find we peace "; Spinoza when he repeated " Under the eye of eternity " ; and Keats when he could say of those Attic shapes " Forever wilt thou sigh and she be fair." None of the formulae will work except for those who are already upon the threshold and if we think of each as pure expression, then, perhaps, none is in itself much more satisfactory than that which the young Proust achieved when he brandished his closed umbrella and exclaimed, " Zut, zut, zut." Have not the Hindus found a simple " Ah " quite sufficient and the Christians often discovered that nothing is more satisfactory than a mere " Oh. Altitudio " ?

In connection with the more detailed discussion of Proust's novel as a novel it will be necessary to return to his conception of Time and to the predominant importance of that conception in determining its form, but for the present there is no necessity to say anything more except that the formulation of this conception made it possible for him now to get rapidly forward with the work which had hitherto been bafflingly intangible. The asthma grew rather worse than better, but the confinement which it entailed was perhaps not the greatest of hardships to a man to whom nothing except the inward life any longer counted, and it certainly gave him ample time for composition.

Long nights through, often with mounting fever, he lay writing in bed, his papers scattered over the room, and himself in a state of desperation produced by the fruitless attempt to rediscover the pages lost in the confusion. The difficulties before him, even now that the great secret had been discovered, seemed insurmountable and no possible lifetime long enough to finish the task. He had, for example, to read in its entirety a whole volume of Darwin before he could write one of the fine pages in " Cities of the Plain," but such labours as these were not so difficult as those entailed by the constant re-documentation which he felt necessary and which could only be accomplished at the cost of exposing himself to the dangers which arose whenever he left his room.

To a friend whom he was about to meet he wrote the warning: " You must not pay any attention to my face for I have the appearance of being dead " ; and indeed his whole appearance had changed, for he was now pale and wasted. Because of his frailties and his anxieties, every act of his life had become enormously complicated. Every letter that he dispatched was accompanied with a variety of directions designed to meet any contingency, for he had an obsessive fear that letters would go astray and at least one specimen address has been preserved: " Monsieur Faure-Biguet, editor of the Echo of Paris, in care of ' The Echo of Paris,' 3 Place of the Opera, Paris (2nd and 3rd arrondissements). If this letter does not reach the person for whom it is intended, please return it to M. Marcel Proust, man of letters, 102 Boulevard Haussmann, Paris." And as for communication with the outside world it had become a matter of such complexity that only the quotation of the following from a letter to Emmanuel Bibesco can indicate it. " I have some important things to say to you. Unfortunately as I went out last evening (it is just on account of this that I have important things to say to you) I shall be tomorrow, Wednesday (today when you receive this note) in the midst of a crisis and not able to receive. However will you, in any event, telephone me around nine-thirty in the evening. If I am in a state to speak, I can perhaps tell you to come. If you telephone to the concierge tell him to come up and tell me that you are at the telephone if I am not sleeping or smoking [Proust's usual word for his fumigations]. But in any event if your evening is taken it can perfectly well be put off some days. I have no need to tell you that when I say something important I mean something important to *you;* I know, alas, that the things which concern me are no longer important to anyone since I lost my parents."

But the book was nevertheless getting itself written, and Proust was now obsessed with fears concerning its possible reception. At first only two volumes were planned but he was afraid that the first, which would doubtless have to be published by itself, would not be understandable without the remaining part: " It is so complex that it will not reveal itself except after all the *themes* have commenced to combine." Besides it was hardly possible that it could sell very much — at least until the public should have had time to become accustomed to it. And as for the critics, were they not notoriously people who put " good taste " before everything else, despite the fact that " good taste " is always, in art at least, reactionary?

But as early as the end of 1906 the first seven hundred pages

were finished and corrected. Where could he find a publisher? After a time the manuscript was submitted to several,
only to be refused, for as one of them wrote: " I cannot understand why a gentleman should employ thirty pages to
describe how he turns and returns on his bed before going
to sleep." Finally he decided to have it published at his own
expense and requested a friend to take it to Grasset where,
this time, it found a resting place. The first part, " Swann's
Way," appeared in 1913, and though comparatively little
notice was taken of it, preparations for the second volume
were going forward when the war broke and Proust, who
had waited so long, had to wait six years more before the
second section, " Within a Budding Grove," should appear.

Meanwhile the work seems to have gone steadily forward
— coming, as it now was, to fill many thousand pages of
manuscript — and it is doubtful if there were very many men
in all France as little concerned as Proust with the great
catastrophe. Though he had permitted himself to take a side
in the Dreyfus case, he had always been above most of the
battles of his generation and, indeed, so exclusively an inhabitant of his particular world of values that most of the
issues which divided the citizens of his country into camps
failed to engage his passions to the slightest degree. He had
been aware that some were Catholic and some anti-clerical,
that some were republicans and others royalists; but though
the divisions interested him intellectually they were as unimportant to him emotionally as though they had been the
wranglings of Byzantine theologians growing unaccount-
ably warm over the distinction between homoosian and
homousian.

And so, when the war came, he was unable to participate in its passions. He speaks once or twice of feeling a certain thrill which came from a sense of union with his fellow countrymen but for him the war was chiefly an epoch during which even intelligent people became monstrously stupid and vulgar. It hurt him to hear academicians use the word "boche" with self-conscious pride; he was dumbfounded when people spoke as though the invasion of Belgium somehow proved that Wagner's music was second rate; and he longed only for a return to sanity. He was not pro-German, not even an internationalist in any politically significant sense of the word, but stupidity was to him the greatest of the vices and he probably felt as he makes M. de Charlus feel — disgusted with the folly with which even a just cause can be defended. And indeed a high place must be given among his intellectual virtues to that detachment which made him incapable, even in war time, of allowing his judgment to be corrupted by any national sentiment.

Though a Frenchman he was not — *mirabile dictu* — a provincial. His old friend Daniel Halévy signed the manifesto of the "Party of the Intelligence," one of whose projects was: "An intellectual federation of Europe and of the world under the guidance of Victorious France, guardian of all civilization," but Proust wrote to Robert Dreyfus with admirable good sense that he saw no reason for thus "proclaiming a kind of '*Frankreich über alles*,' gendarme of the literature of all people — a rôle which it would be more discreet not to assume before the other people have confided it."

Presently, however, the war was over and a masterpiece was once more worth publishing. The *Nouvelle Revue*

Française, having re-issued " Swann's way," put the next section ("Within a Budding Grove") on sale in 1919 and in
November of the same year Proust received the Goncourt
prize. The other sections were to appear at reasonable intervals. Fame had come late but when it came it came almost
overwhelmingly. The first volume of C. K. Scott-Moncrieff's
remarkable English translation appeared in 1922 and soon,
as Pierre-Quint remarks with some amazement, " even
Americans" were to be found among Proust's devoted
admirers.

IV

The criticism of a novel presents, as Percy Lubbock has pointed out, a difficulty not encountered in the criticism of any other art form. Because of its length it cannot be grasped in its entirety as a lyric is grasped and even the most careful reader has inevitably forgotten much of the beginning before he has reached the end. Its formal virtues — the relationships and proportions of its parts — often pass unobserved for the simple reason that all the parts cannot be appreciated at the same time and what we criticize is not the work itself but that very imperfect memory of it which remains with us. And if this is true of all novels it is doubly true of one so extraordinarily long as Proust's, one which could not possibly be read in less than a week or two and which, as a matter of fact, most of even its passionate admirers know only as it can be known when it is read, volume by volume, at periods separated by weeks, by months, or even by years. Under the circumstances it is not strange that very different opinions have been expressed concerning the most important of its virtues and the best way to approach it is, probably, to consider first the qualities apparent upon even the most casual acquaintanceship, leaving for the last any attempt even to mention its unifying conception.

What, then, are the first impressions received by the reader who begins the " Ouverture " with which the work opens? Let us suppose that he has a little more patience than the literary adviser who " could not understand why a gentleman should take thirty pages to describe how he turns and returns on his bed before going to sleep " and let us suppose, even, that he has sufficient sensitiveness to feel (at the very second page) the poignancy of that passage which describes the despair of the invalid who has mistaken the not-yet-extinguished light in the corridor for the first sign of the dawn destined to put an end to his lonely vigil.

Granted this modicum of patience and this elementary sensibility, the reader will soon find himself in a twilight world of extraordinary fascination. He will be amazed by the precision with which all but incommunicable shades of reverie are communicated and amazed by the novelty of the particular realm of feeling which Proust seems to have chosen. He will recognize in his own experience the same shades and dubieties of emotion, but will realize at the same time that no previous writer, nor even he himself, has ever before focused the attention upon them in so effective a fashion. That which is ordinarily only the dimly perceived background of our minds has become here the foreground or, to change the metaphor, reality has undergone a transformation comparable to that which might be produced in some inconceivably rich piece of music if the part ordinarily subordinate were made predominant and we heard the main melodic line only faintly while the accompaniment — now perceived to be unsuspectedly rich — rolled over it.

But no sooner has the reader had time to formulate this impression, no sooner has he classified Proust as an extraordinary elegist and as a master of twilight psychology, than he becomes aware of the fact that characters and stories, remarkable now for their dramatic concreteness, are emerging. Thus the story of Swann's love, brilliantly objective, forms a novel complete in itself and not yet perceived to be, even in its completeness, part of a larger pattern. Almost forgetting the narrator, one becomes absorbed in Swann, in his passion for the vulgar Odette who happens — without having in her soul anything corresponding to them — to have the body and the attitudes of a renaissance painting; in his enslavement to this woman " who had sorrow in her eyes but none in her heart."

A little further on, the narrator returns again to the experience of his own boyhood; one is introduced to the Guermantes; and one meets the bourgeois group of affected music lovers united under the leadership of the redoubtable Madame Verdurin. Faced with this extraordinary collection of vivid characters one is tempted to change one's opinion and to hold that it is as a creator of character that Proust most conspicuously excels. One remembers his gallery of grotesques — almost Dickens-like in the brilliancy of the gift for caricature exhibited; a gallery which includes a long series of portraits from that of the narrator's great-aunt (whose life was made up of curiosity and the conviction that she never slept) to that of the enraptured amateur of music whose ecstasy could be measured by the amount of saliva which trickled down upon her chin; a gallery in which may, perhaps, be placed even the greatest of his creations — the fascinating but perverted M. de Charlus who is carried through his social triumphs, gradually allowed to disintegrate under his vices, and finally exposed at his horribly comic nadir complaining to the proprietor of the establishment where he had himself whipped by an apprenticed milk-boy: " I did not want to speak before the little fellow who is nice and who does his best. But I do not find him brutal enough.

His face pleases me but he called me ' crapule ' as though he were repeating a lesson."

On the other hand again the greater part of four whole volumes is devoted to the story of the narrator's love affair with Albertine. From these volumes one remembers countless passages of subtle analysis among which, more or less at random, may be chosen that one which opens " The Sweet Cheat Gone." The servant enters with the dramatic announcement, "Mademoiselle Albertine is gone." Then: " A moment ago, as I lay analysing my feelings, I had supposed that this separation without a final meeting was precisely what I had wished and, as I compared the mediocrity of the pleasures that Albertine afforded me with the richness of the desires which she prevented me from realizing, had felt that I was being subtle, had concluded that I did not wish to see her again, that I no longer loved her. But now these words: ' Mademoiselle Albertine has gone ' had expressed themselves in my heart with an anguish so keen that I would not be able to endure it for any length of time. . . .

"Tender toward myself as my mother had been toward my dying grandmother, I said to myself with that anxiety which we feel to prevent a person whom we love from suffering: ' Be patient for just a moment, we shall find something to take the pain away; don't fret, we are not going to allow you to suffer like this.'"

And considering such a passage, one returns again to the idea that Proust is most remarkable in the description of subjective states, in following the involutions of his spirit, and in communicating his egotistical absorption in the poignancy of a cherished pain.

What then, among so many excellences, is the virtue which is peculiarly Proust's? Though there is not in the entire novel a page which is not immediately recognizable as undoubtedly his, he seems (while we are under the spell of his consistency) to possess all the qualities which a novelist should have. One thinks of this fragment or that; one calls to mind a subtle page of reverie followed by a brilliantly dramatic scene. And one is tempted to commit the monstrous error which some have been guilty of, the error of praising " Remembrance of Things Past " as a brilliant miscellany, as a scrap book of purple passages. Indeed, even though we reject this error, it seems hardly possible to escape the necessity of writing a series of essays devoted to this or that aspect of his work.

One such essay would, for instance, be concerned with the contrast just discussed between Proust as a master of the subjective and Proust as the creator of brilliantly observed characters. Another would consider the construction of his interminably evolving sentences which, despite the oddness of the impression at first created, are soon found both to emit a delicious music of their own and to follow with an amazing suppleness all the delicate contours of his thought. A third would attempt to define that moral attitude, or rather that lack of a moral attitude, which results from an all-enveloping aestheticism — an aestheticism which is as far as possible removed from that characteristic of " decadent " literature and which arises out of Proust's remarkable sensitiveness to all phenomena, coupled with his power of accepting *pro tem* the premises of any philosophy of life when it is necessary to do so for the purpose of understanding his characters.

Passing then to his treatment of various themes or subject matters, one would have to consider his treatment of love and jealousy. And in connection with the former one would have to note especially a masterly synthesis of apparently incompatible elements, for Proust achieved a kind of romanticism — succeeded at least in attributing a very high value to love — while coldly dismissing most of the illusions which are commonly called upon to support romanticism.

Thus in the first place he (or, if one prefers, the " I " of the novel) had no illusions concerning the fact that the woman we adore is in herself no more than a mere puppet temporarily invested with qualities which exist in ourselves alone. As a mere youth " I said to myself sadly that this love of ours, in so far as it is love for one particular creature, is not perhaps a very real thing, since if the association of pleasant or unpleasant trains of thought can attach it for a time to a woman so as to make us believe that it has been inspired by her, in a necessary sequence of effect to cause, yet when we detach ourselves deliberately or unconsciously, from these associations, this love will revive . . . to bestow itself upon another woman." And the lesson thus begun was completed when, on being taken to see a mistress for the love of whom his friend was living in torture, he recognized her as the little Jewish girl who had seemed to him of so little worth some years before when she had been thrust upon him in a bawdy house.

In the second place Proust (or the narrator) never fails, even in the midst of his own unhappy passion, to dissociate the ideas of love and of permanence, to compare his attitude towards this or that with what the attitude is destined to be

" when I shall have ceased to love Albertine." Indeed one might say that Proustian love shows no trace of any of the elements which usually accompany and which are, perhaps, usually thought necessary to romantic love. For it is not only the ideas of objective reality and of permanence which are absent; one notes also that his Love has neither reticence nor selflessness since he is as ready to analyse even the most intimate of its sensual aspects as he finds it frankly unnecessary to make any pretence of a primary concern with the happiness of the beloved. And yet not one of the least of the charms of the novel is the fact that in it one discovers once more the possibility of Love as a serious theme in a novel which remains, nevertheless, wholly modern in its freedom from the shabbier of romantic delusions. Proustian love, despite all that is left out of it, has a power to torture and to absorb which cannot belong to sense, simple and unadorned. To the making of it has gone (besides sense) only sentiment, but it has become, nevertheless, something marvellously elaborate and well-nigh unique in literature.

And finally, in this series of imaginary essays, there would have to be one devoted to a consideration of Proust's interest in formal society, to his passionate absorption in the details of etiquette; for that interest is undoubtedly responsible for one of the most striking peculiarities of the book, even though it has not been sufficiently noted that he is hardly more delighted by the traditions which determine the conduct of the Queen of Naples than he is by the fact that the servants in his mother's household have traditions of their own — among which is a sort of poetically real deafness to any bell which may be rung during the sacred period of their repast.

Something has already been said concerning one of the possible reasons for this interest in formal society. It has already been explained that Proust was attracted to it by the glamour of historic names whose possessors seemed, by virtue of the very fact that they bore them, to be lifted above time, and that, besides, he was fascinated by the idea (so imperfectly realized in any actual society) of manners as a technique of gentleness. Yet it would, no doubt, be necessary in such an essay as we are imagining to defend him against the charge (sometimes made) of being a snob — to point out that, on the one hand, his interest in humble people is no less conspicuous than his interest in great ones and that, on the other hand, he certainly did not hesitate to represent most of his aristocrats as stupid, vulgar, and dull, even though, it may be conceded, he never ceased to wonder that they could be so. But since we are only imagining and not actually writing this essay on Proust and the World of Fashion it is not necessary to do more than to quote the passage which immediately follows, a passage whose mounting irony ought by itself to be sufficient to dispose of the suspicion that Proust held to conservative a view of the sacredness of privilege.

He has, in the second volume of " The Guermantes Way," been discussing the attitude behind the condescending affability exhibited by the Princesse de Parme toward inferior creatures like himself. " Her mother," he explains, " . . . had instilled into her from her earliest childhood the arrogantly humble precepts of an evangelical snobbery; and today every line in the daughter's face, the curve of her shoulders, the movements of her arms seemed to repeat the lesson: ' Remember that if God has caused you to be born on the steps of

a throne you ought not to make that a reason for looking
down upon those to whom Divine Providence has willed
(wherefore His Name be praised) that you should be superior by birth and fortune. On the contrary, you must suffer the little ones. Your ancestors were Princes of Trèves and
Juliers from the year 647; God has decreed in his bounty
that you should hold practically all the shares in the Suez
Canal and three times as many *Royal Dutch* as Edmond de
Rothschild; your pedigree in direct line has been established
by genealogists from the year 63 of the Christian Era; you
have as sisters-in-law two empresses. Therefore never seem,
in your speech, to be recalling these great privileges, not that
they are precarious (for nothing can alter the antiquity of
race, while the world will always need petrol) but because
it is useless to point out that you are better born than other
people or that your investments are all gilt-edged, since
everybody knows these facts already. Be helpful to the needy.
Furnish to all those whom the bounty of heaven has done
you the favour of placing beneath you as much as you can
give them without forfeiture of your rank, that is to say help
in the form of money, even your personal service by their
sick-beds, but never (bear well in mind) invite them to
your parties, which would do them no possible good and, by
weakening your own position, would diminish the efficacy
of your benevolent activities.' " Proust was interested in the
idea of *noblesse oblige*. He was also not unaware of what it
usually comes to in practice.

But to turn now from the consideration of such aspects
of his work to the unity which embraces all these details.
What is " Remembrance of Things Past " *about?* One may

say, of course, that it is the autobiography of an imaginary personage whose life and whose character bear many striking resemblances to the life and character of Proust himself — that it describes the development of that person's sensibility, carries him through his strange love affair with the mysterious Albertine, and ends with the Great Enlightenment which made it possible for him to see all his experiences under the form of a work of art. With equal truth it might be maintained that this autobiographical form is no more than a thread, that the real story of which all the separate stories are a part is the story of the rise and fall of certain social groups; that (in a technical sense) the main catastrophe is brought about by the gradual decay of those social standards typified by the traditions of the Guermantes group, and that to it are related various minor catastrophes of a similar sort — the disappearance of " the faithful " from Madame Verdurin's second-rate salon and the dissolution both of M. de Charlus' integrity and of Berma's fame. Indeed one might seize upon the last appearance of the latter (a famous actress) as typifying in little the tragic feeling of the whole, for in no restricted passage is that feeling more poignantly evoked.

Berma, sick and outmoded, sits in her empty drawing-room while all her invited guests are displaying themselves at the reception given in honour of her young rival Rachel. Silently she munches the little (and to her forbidden) sweets " as though performing the rites of a funeral." Then her daughters, for whose sake she has sacrificed her health, can no longer endure to be separated from the brilliant assemblage. Though uninvited they make their way to Rachel's reception; from the ante-room they send in their request to be admitted; and thus they give Rachel the opportunity to reveal to all the world how complete is her triumph. She sends word for them to come in and they come " ruining at one stroke the social position of Berma as they had already ruined her health." . . . " But Rachel was already composing in her head the gracious phrase with which tomorrow she would overwhelm Berma in the corridors of the theater. ' I was distressed, desolated, that your daughter should cool her heels in an ante-chamber. If I had only understood. She sent me card after card.' She was delighted to give this blow to Berma. Perhaps she would have recoiled if she had known that it was to be a mortal blow. We like to make victims without putting ourselves precisely in the wrong and while permitting them still to live. Besides, in what had she done wrong? She would have to say a little later, ' That is really going a little too far, I wanted to be more agreeable towards her daughters than she had ever been towards me, and because of that they accuse me of having assassinated her. I call upon the Duchess as witness.' " Proust had believed in the forms of politeness and, like the forms under which *noblesse oblige* pretends to find expression, they too become most often only a technique of cruelty.

Thus in one sense it might be said that the story of " Remembrance of Things Past " is the story of the narrator's disillusion with certain things upon which he had rested his faith in the possibility of a beautiful life — that he had believed in both politeness (which is the means by which ordinary people express their good will) and in the promptings of that sense of *noblesse oblige* (which leads the great to

even larger gestures of benevolence) — that he had believed in them only to discover how, for the most part, they
exist only as hideous counterfeits.

But quitting temporarily — and in the middle — this effort to extract the meaning of the novel, let us turn for a
moment to the consideration of its form. It has already been
remarked that the order of its events is not the order of time
because to emphasize the relationship which exists between
merely simultaneous events evidently seemed to Proust to
obscure the more significant relationships which unite situations separated by days, by months, or by years. But to say
this is not to explain the form adopted, which is, as a
matter of fact, not likely to be appreciated unless the volumes
of the novel are read consecutively and which, indeed,
can hardly be grasped in all its complicated perfection
until the first volumes are re-read with the last still in
mind.

Proust himself, it will be remembered, spoke of the various
themes whose full significance would not be clear until, in
the later volumes, they had begun to combine; and this
remark of his gives the key to his method, for it is, as a matter
of fact, not unlike the method of an elaborate musical composition. One may, if one likes, study it first in some small
unit like the first volume — much as one might begin to
study the structure of a symphony by considering the first
movement alone. Thus in the first part of that first volume *
one might note how the incident of his mother's failure to
kiss him good night is first referred to on page thirteen, is
dropped like a musical phrase, reappears successively on

---

* Page references here are to the English translation.

pages twenty-six, twenty-eight, thirty-two, and forty-four, but does not receive its full development until just fifteen volumes later when the narrator is standing in the ante-room of the Guermantes residence. Moreover this method is the one consistently followed throughout the book in which the themes play about one another like the themes of a fugue. Each separate scene is related to others by the fact that some general emotion, or thought, or observation recurs in each. The love affair with Gilberte is looking forward to the fuller development of the same themes in the love affair with Albertine and even the process of forgetting the latter, which fills the major part of a whole volume, is antici-pated in the more summary tale of Gilberte by a few pages on that "irregular process of oblivion" which is destined to be later so elaborately developed.

The motifs appear one by one. It would be possible to go through the work and to note, as one would note in a sym-phony, that at this point or that each one of the themes — love, taste, manners, etc. — is introduced for the first time merely in passing before it is returned to again and again for more and more complete development. In "Swann's Way," for example, the slight, apparently purposeless inci-dent centring about the daughter of Vinteuil serves to sug-gest the theme of homosexuality later so elaborately treated and, though probably no reader who did not turn back would realize the fact, the very first pages of the whole work hint at most of the major themes. Thus the escape from Time is alluded to on page three where it is immedi-ately followed by the incident of the magic lantern, which, as the first work of art introduced, serves to suggest the technique by which Time is to be transcended. And one result of this arrangement is to make the novel in another respect like a piece of music, for of it may be said, more truly even than of most great novels, that the second reading is more rewarding than the first. To know what is coming does not detract from the pleasure — is indeed necessary to the full enjoyment of it — since each incident is, like a musical theme, only enriched by a knowledge of the variations to follow.

This original and perfected form has its own self-justifying beauties, but to consider the intention which determined its choice is to be led back again to that obsession with Time whose influence is discoverable in every detail of Proust's work and which gives it its unity. Thanks to the method which disregards chronology he was able to bring together, for purposes of contrast or comparison, widely separated periods or — as he said in a sentence previously quoted in its context — to show men as monstrous creatures straddling between the distant past and the present. Moreover it was necessary for his purpose to do just this because the full horror of Time had to be revealed in order that the miraculous joy which comes through the escape from it might be properly appreciated.

Thus the commonplace fact that faces grow old and characters change becomes, for him, something to be analysed with a fascinated terror. When, for example, he is describing, in the second volume of " Within a Budding Grove," the impression made upon him by a group of beautiful girls he cannot refrain from adding: " Alas! in the freshest flower it is possible to discern those just perceptible signs which to the instructed mind indicate already what will be, by the desiccation or fructification of the flesh which is today in bloom, the ultimate form, immutable and already predestinate, of the autumnal seed. The eye rapturously follows a nose like a wavelet that deliciously curls the water's face at daybreak and seems not to move, to be capturable by the pencil, because the sea is so calm then that one does not notice its tidal flow. Human faces seem not to change while we are looking at them, because the revolution which they perform is too slow for us to perceive it. But we have only to see, by the side of any of those girls, her mother or her aunt, to realize the distance which, obeying the gravitation of a type that is, generally speaking, deplorable, her features will have travelled in less than thirty years, and must continue to travel until the sunset hour, until her face, having vanished altogether below the horizon, catches the light no more."

But this change in faces is only trivially important in comparison with that change which takes place in character — the change which, as he realized at the fateful reception given by the Guermantes, makes men into creatures totally different from what they were. Hence it came at last to seem to him that it was folly to speak of Albertine, of de Charlus, of himself even, as though any one of them were an entity maintaining its identity while time flowed past; and he realized that if his novel was to attain the full significance which he wished, it must manage somehow, not only to attain timelessness itself, but also to suggest the triumph of Time over the persons and the experiences which the novel alone could rescue. For the most essential distinction between art and experience is exactly that the former is changeless while the latter flows.

Antiquities and history were beautiful to him, not because they had been subjected to the ravages of Time, but because of the impression which they gave of having achieved at least a partial triumph over it. Time itself is the enemy of all beauty because Time produces change and it becomes an aid to the discovery of beauty only when, if the expression be permitted, it is pluperfect — only when, that is to say, all the changes which it can produce seem, as in the historical and the antique they do, to be already complete; only when the pattern of which they are a part has been unrolled so that it can be seen as the whole it had not yet come to be while it was still unrolling.

Proust's problem as an artist was, then, the problem of finding the means of rescuing something from the flux, of establishing in the eternity of art the experiences which he had undergone or observed. But how was this to be accomplished? What was the bridge between the two realms? There was memory of course, and memory seems to the uninitiated the only enemy of Time. It alone seems to link what we are to what we were and it gives a false sense of continuity to our lives. Through its aid the days that are passed may be recovered after a fashion. But memory collects rather than joins together, and what it gives us is a bag of detached and dissimilar fragments. The aggregate of them is the thing which we ordinarily call ourselves, but it remains only an aggregate, not a meaningful whole. Hence though merely to remember in the ordinary fashion is generally the last expedient of the man who feels himself dissolving in the eternal flux, this mere memory leaves him aware that it preserves only the detritus of himself out of the common ruin into which the passions and purposes of one moment are thrown by the next.

From the dilemma presented by the fact that memory reveals its impotence at the same time that it seems the only instrument which we possess, Proust was rescued by the Great Enlightenment — by the discovery that for him there was possible a kind of memory not identical with the ordinary sort: a vision of the eternity in which even the most completely forgotten experience had already taken its place. This vision was mystical and hence, by very definition, not to be explained in any terms except its own; but it cannot be repeated too often that in it lies the meaning of the novel, every detail of which it controls. And if we cannot analyse further a thing ultimate in its own nature, we can at least note the quality which it bestows, can at least ask how it determines the impression produced by the work which it dominates.

In the first place it gives to "Remembrance of Things Past" that curiously detached and passionless character which the novel preserves even when passion is being so brilliantly described. Doubtless it had enabled Proust himself to achieve that complete substitution of contemplation for will which he had begun to find necessary just as soon as he realized how little active he could expect to be; and as a result of this fact it enabled him to write a work so cool, so calm, and so pure that its artistic perfection is never disturbed by anything which seems to arise in a mere human being whose impartiality can be disturbed as — occasionally at least —

that of most writers is, by the private passions or desires of a man.

In the second place it furnished him with his particular means of achieving an effect which every really great work of art must in some manner produce: it supplied him with a point of view from which even calamitous events could be seen as no longer actually painful. Always aware of the whole of which any incident is a part, he can, in his novel, calmly accept his own sufferings as well as the sufferings of others because it is the pattern of which they are a part, rather than either the pleasure or the pain of the moment, of which he is most acutely aware; and by thus seeing the passing events of time as part of a static eternity in which the end is simultaneous with the beginning, he achieves that indifference which is not the indifference of the insensitive but the indifference of the gods.

Events become, even as he recounts them, already a part of legend and thus life is magically transmuted into art. He himself, as well as M. Swann and M. de Charlus, are no longer mere human beings but analagous to the figures painted upon the slides of the little magic lantern which had fascinated him so long ago. Their suffering and their wickedness have now ceased to have any significance except as parts of a formal design; the first is no more painful and the second no more terrifying than the distress of Geneviève de Brabant or the wickedness of her implacable enemy Golo when these two, emerging as they were always ready to do from eternity, bodied themselves forth on the window-curtain or the door-knob.

V

In a fashion only half-humorous Proust had referred to the writing of his novel as the preparation of his tomb — in a fashion only half humorous because, as a matter of sober fact, he did not expect to find anything else in life capable of interesting him. Actually only some three years of life were left after the Prix Goncourt was awarded to the second section of his novel, and the six last volumes appeared posthumously (1923–1927).

But as the " tomb " approached completion a change was observed to come over him. Proud of the eight hundred and ten letters of congratulation which were said to have arrived from all parts of the world, he was far from indifferent to the fate of his work and not a little troubled by some almost inevitable misunderstandings which arose concerning its nature — as he was, for example, with that revealed by the critic who spoke of him as working with a microscope when, so he protested, it was actually a telescope which he employed.

Even his health seemed better. Thus in 1920 the Princess Bibesco found him supernatural in his youthfulness. He was, she says, "the young man of the book, the Marcel Proust of Combray, of Balbec, of Doncière, the friend of Swann, of Saint-Loup, of Oriane de Guermantes, of Albertine — he was no longer the blackbearded man of my youth." He began, even, to go out into the world again and in order to show his gratitude to his friends he gave magnificent dinners at the Ritz. But the old sense of insecurity, the old feeling which seemed to be a fear lest he should not be welcome, was still there. His tips were again fantastic and in a few nights he is said to have spent the whole of his prize money. Moreover he had by no means lost his air of being a scientific observer rather than a participant. When in 1920 he was re-presented to the Princess Bibesco whom he had met once before six or seven years earlier, " He looked at me with his great eyes which no longer seemed sad, but animated by an extraordinary life. Making no concession to the conventions, he scrutinized my face with a curious and tranquil gravity. Then, addressing Walter Berry, he began to speak of the design formed by my nostrils, as if I had been an inanimate figure. ' It is that line, he said, ' that I remember. She is the one I was looking for.' "

This lightening was, however, only temporary. The life of the invalid, made prisoner by his malady, was resumed. Fever was now almost continuous and it was only with the aid of drugs that he could sleep. And rich though he was, he had, or pretended to have, some sense that he was financially ruined. Yet, despite his air of innocence, he was not unaware of the fluctuations of the Bourse. " Dear friend," he said sadly, " I have just rediscovered, in a drawer I had not opened for fifteen years, some old securities that I didn't know I had. My fortune has crumbled. Perhaps you can tell me what you think. Despite their Germanic and princely name, they are not at all either German or aristocratic; I think that they are *Royal Dutch*." " Now on that very day," adds Pierre-Quint who recounts the anecdote, "*Royal Dutch* had, in a fantastic bound, risen to sixty thousand francs.

Watchful of the course of the exchange he was trying to find out, despite his air of innocence, if the opportune moment for selling had arrived."

Proust was still writing, but gradually he was being overcome by weakness, and we shall permit ourselves only one more glimpse of him. Antoine Bibesco goes with the Princess and another lady to call upon him, but the faithful servant comes to the door. "Monsieur has just had a terrible crisis. He hardly breathes. It is to be feared that he cannot receive anyone, not even the Prince Antoine." — Presently Proust hears the conversation, and calls to Antoine Bibesco while the others are asked not to pass the threshold of the little salon. "Monsieur," explains the servant, "is very much afraid of the perfume of princesses."

On November 18, 1922 the news passed around among his friends: "Marcel is dead." Long before, he had compared himself to a certain gentleman who had so long postponed a projected trip to Spain that acquaintances greeted him with the exclamation "Oh, so you have returned!" In his own case, he said, friends had become so accustomed to thinking of him as dead that, if they happened to see him, they believed he must be re-incarnated. Now he was gone in earnest.

* * * * * * * * *

Very diverse opinions have been expressed concerning the rank which ought to be accorded to Proust as a novelist, and when such matters are discussed it is as well not to enter into dispute. But perhaps it is, on the contrary, worth while remarking that at least he very perfectly realized the conception of the artist which was formulated by his philosophical master, Bergson.

The latter, it will be remembered, held that artistic vision is distinguished from ordinary vision by the fact that it manages to escape from the effects of habit and to see a thing itself rather than the conventionalization of it with which we happen to be most familiar. The artist, discarding everything except his own sensations and his own mind, is actually far less influenced by other works of art — which is the same thing as to say by the conventions established by others — than even the most inartistic of men; for the latter, without being aware of the fact, is a slave to such conventions as have filtered down to him. Hence the artist, combining sensations afresh with the aid of nothing except his own intelligence, is enabled to conceive of them as forming patterns hitherto unrecognized and to make others see them under forms totally new.

And whatever other qualities Proust may or may not have, one can hardly deny him his freshness of vision which makes his novel very unlike any other. No matter what he looks at, he sees as essential certain aspects which have generally been either unobserved or dismissed as unimportant. Whether narrating a series of events, describing a scene, or cataloguing the contents of the mind of a character at any moment, he is certain to select incidents, to set down particulars, and to list details which most would have omitted in favour of certain others now in their turn passed over by Proust. The result is the creation of a strange new world. Perhaps we recognize its elements even though we have not ever before been consciously aware of their existence; but the whole which they compose is new. We enter the pages of "Remembrance of Things Past" as we might enter a realm totally unfamiliar, and before we are aware of the fact we have closed a door behind us, forgetting the standards and the conventions of familiar life as completely as we forget its personages. For the world which the novel reveals is more than merely strange; it is also so consistent, so self-sustaining, and so logically complete that we are never by any reference led back to the other world of our ordinary concerns.

In contemporary literature we are far more accustomed to literary virtues of another sort. In the novels of a Sinclair Lewis or a Theodore Dreiser it is the closeness of their relation to everyday existence which strikes us most often. These novelists see what we ordinarily see, stress what we ordinarily stress, and judge as we ordinarily judge. One can, indeed, hardly distinguish the point at which reading leaves off and daily experience begins. The pages seem to merge into the stream of contemporary life and it is this fact which gives to them the kind of importance which they have. But it is this fact also which prevents us from doing what it is impossible not to do in the case of Proust — from, that is to say, entering a possible world entirely different from the one we know best and shutting the door behind us.

Moreover, it must be admitted that, quite aside from the delight afforded by the mere freshness involved, the spiritual world of Proust has elements of charm lacking in most contemporary novels because of the fact that the sensibility everywhere exhibited is of an extraordinary sort. Mention has already been made of the fact that he managed somehow to recapture the feeling of romantic love without introducing any of those illusions which the modern finds it all but impossible to enjoy. And perhaps this love of his, this emotion which is so obviously neither the sacrament of the conventional romanticists nor the devaluated amusement of the cynic, might be made the type of his sensibility, for in many other respects also he manages to attain an attitude poised somewhere between the extremes which have so often seemed inevitable alternatives. He was disillusioned enough with many things — with morals for example — and he had neither any code nor any standards beside those which his taste supplied. Yet in the midst of what might seem to be anarchy there were still capacities and faiths which he retained. He still believed, for example, in the sufficiency of the senses — at least as furnishers of the material which contemplation might transform. But, on the other hand, he never, like so many moderns, found himself in a universe limited and debased by the impossibility of escape from psychology, anthropology, and Freudianism. The world was still absorbingly, still amazingly, interesting. Women — most women — were to him magical and mysterious. Conversations were witty, artists incalculably great. In a word, he respected his desires, his tastes, and his amusements and hence, though experience might be predominantly painful, it was neither meaningless nor mean. And that perhaps is the secret of the individual charm of his world. It is one viewed with the critical freedom of modern thought and one in which scepticism rules. Yet it is somehow glamorous as well. Nor is it, perhaps, impertinent to remark that in this respect (though assuredly in this only) Proust was like Boccaccio, since both were faced with the task of creating a world out of the ruin into which an accustomed world had been thrown by the decay of the principles upon which it had rested. Boccaccio had had to do without the aid of the theology which had given shape and meaning to the universe of the Middle Ages; Proust had to do without most of the dogmas which had got themselves established since the Renaissance.

Some have not failed to reproach him with a lack of reticence, of decency even, and they have pointed to certain scenes, like that in which the narrator is represented as eavesdropping upon Jupien the tailor and the perverted de Charlus, as evidence of the fact that he lacked, as well, even the most elementary instincts of a gentleman. But to raise such objections is to forget that Proust, having retired out of active life as completely as though he had been dead, was no longer " playing the game " and accordingly had no concern with the rules. With nothing to gain and nothing to lose, he no longer cared even for the opinion which others might form of him, and he was accordingly as little concerned with the moral judgments which might be passed upon him as with those which might be passed upon his characters.

To make the most exquisitely minute discriminations always, but to judge between the things discriminated never — that is the essence of his method. Had he cared to do so, he could doubtless have written a whole half-volume devoted to the exact nature of his ungentlemanliness in consenting to eavesdrop — he has certainly devoted many pages on more than one occasion to the analysis of much less conspicuous breaches of the code — but he would have been no more judicial in his treatment of it than he is in the treatment of M. de Charlus's erotic devotion to jockeys and train-

men. No man was ever more completely than Proust a slave
to sensations; no man ever lived more entirely by and for
the nerves; but by shutting himself off from all but the
memory of these sensations he not only recovered them with
unexampled fulness but recovered them in a state more
nearly pure than would have been possible for anyone who
had a living future which could occupy him with plans and
desires — recovered them, that is to say, unmixed either with
his own personal concerns or with those moral fervours and
antipathies which, for such at least as he, are in fact no part
of a personal concern.

But the reasons which lead certain critics to hesitate to
grant Proust the supreme place among novelists of the
twentieth century are more often of a sort somewhat subtler
than these just referred to and seem to find their roots in a
feeling that, however excellent his work may be in its kind,
the kind is, nevertheless, not the one demanded of the Great
Novelist whose coming they have been so long awaiting.

Nor can it be denied that Proust's work fails to afford that
" synthesis of modern life " which has been the subject of
so much discussion or that, indeed, it fails even to treat the
themes which the age seems to impose. Thus — to consider
the most obvious aspect of the fact — his work is wholly
without what some would describe as social consciousness,
and from it alone one would never guess that, for at least
seventy-five years, nearly every novelist of first rank has expounded — explicitly or implicitly — some attitude towards
the problems raised by our universal concern with social
justice. Most of the novelists of the nineteenth and twentieth
centuries felt constrained to take life seriously in a sense that

Proust does not, since, and with a clear conscience, he per-
mits himself to live the charmed life of a dilettante, not
troubling himself much about the fate of civilization, acting
as though there were nothing more important than the careful discrimination between shades of feeling, and devoting
himself with the selfishness of the contemplative saint to the
achievement of his own private salvation. He surrenders the
effort so characteristic of our fiction to be in some sense
dynamic, to master the life it treats. He does not hope to
dominate or even to influence the civilization of which he is
part but instead — and again like the most other-worldly of
monks — only to find some way of accepting the evil inevitably woven into the fabric of any life which takes place
in time.

Moreover, even among those who are content that the
novel should detach itself from sociological concerns, there
are some who are chilled by the subtler aspects of Proust's
detachment from the problems which seem the problems of
contemporary existence. " Remembrance of Things Past " is,
they would insist, simply not concerned with the things
which the modern novel has the duty of concerning itself
with, simply shirks that obligation which other contemporary
novelists — James Joyce and Thomas Mann for instance —
have at least accepted. No one who had been told in 1913 that
a very great work of fiction was about to appear could have
imagined that it would be anything like what this one turns
out to be; no one could have dreamed that a novel which
was to be proposed as the most distinguished of our generation could possibly be, not only aloof, but essentially mystical
as well.

But on the other hand, is it not true that these critics themselves have been demanding " form," that they have grown weary of mere document and discussion, and that here in Proust's novel they are presented with one of the most beautiful, one of the most accomplished, and one of the most perfect formal designs ever achieved by a writer of prose fiction? And is it not true, also, that, whereas they have longed for someone who should find a way of achieving order and peace for himself and his readers without removing them from modern life, Proust does just that?

He demands, to be sure, that he be accepted under the conditions which he imposes, that he be permitted to state the problem in his own terms before he can solve it. And it is true, furthermore, that these conditions are very different from those currently accepted; true that he offers the method of mystic renunciation to those who are asking (as a pagan might have asked a Christian Father) how a passionate man can find happiness through an active life in the modern world. For to those who demand how life can be made acceptable he replies simply: " By renouncing it."

But great works are so rare and so precious that it is hardly worth while to reject one of them merely because it is not of the *genre* which we expected. "Remembrance of Things Past " is Proust's *Apologia Pro Vita Sua,* and if the life which it defends seems to us a very odd one, at least the defence is successful and Proust in his novel has achieved certain qualities (like charm, and order, and peace) which seemed to have departed forever from modern literature. His world has definitely taken its place in the not very long list of those possible worlds which art creates; de Charlus, Saint-Loup,

the Duchesse de Guermantes, Françoise, and Madame Verdurin have definitely taken their places in the not very long
list of characters who are more real than reality. Something
— both in the particular sense defined by Proust and in the
more general sense in which the phrase is applicable to all
great literature — has been rescued from Time. It is not often
that that can be said.